Sermonettes for a Sunday Morning

Pastor Novella Harris

authorHOUSE®

AuthorHouse™
1663 Liberty Drive
Bloomington, IN 47403
www.authorhouse.com
Phone: 1 (800) 839-8640

Published by AuthorHouse 11/09/2017

ISBN: 978-1-5462-1064-1(sc)
ISBN: 978-1-5462-1066-5 (hc)
ISBN: 978-1-5462-1065-8 (e)

Library of Congress Control Number: 2017915072

Print information available on the last page.

FOREWORD

"For in Him we live and move and have our being; as also some of your own poets said, For we are also his offspring.

"Therefore, since we are the offspring of God, we ought not to think that the Divine Nature is like gold or silver or stone, something shaped by art and man's devising." (Acts 17: 28-29 NKJV)

I chose this scripture as a tribute to our good friend Pastor Novella Harris. The Apostle Paul was quoting Aratus, an Athenian Poet who lived almost 300 years before he skillfully and apologetically explained to the Athenians who their unknown God really is. Verse 29 utilizes art materials to define further who we are in CHRIST. Pastor Novella Harris is a sculptor and is able to use her creative skills to bring clay to life. As a minister of the gospel, she utilizes the same creative skills to articulate the Gospel of JESUS CHRIST. She is an entrepreneur who founded Sure Foundation Child Care INC., a life long dream of an intellectual oasis for children to learn and grow and matriculate into adulthood. Pastor Novella Harris is an educator who has achieved at every level.

James Metz BA; MBA; M.RE; M.Th.

I have known Pastor Novella Harris for over 30 years. In that time, I can attest that she has been an educator, mentor and spiritual advisor to countless men and women. GOD has blessed Pastor Harris with keen insight into the Scriptures that enable her to extract the heart of a passage and make it relevant to her readers while keeping its hermeneutical value intact. Certainly, as she gave her congregation nuggets of spiritual wisdom each week over several years, it was a heavenly decree that a literary migration of her Biblical revelations gather into one volume where parishioners could feast on its contents again and again.

For the Christian, this work provides conduct and conversation for everyday living. In this challenging world that vacillates with every whim of doctrine, fashion, and trend, her words remain steadfast, inspired and continuously relevant. It is a necessary read for the serious Christian.

David Sweet AAS, BA, BRE, MSED
Minister/Senior Deacon/Trustee/Friend

This book is a unique compilation of biblical truths designed to encourage your spiritual growth. It is a glimpse into the heart and mind of a powerful woman of GOD. Rarely during our human existence do we find a person who will make themselves completely transparent for your betterment. However, this book does exactly that. Her selection of mini sermons will touch every aspect of your life with biblical truths. Realizing the emphasis of this work is spiritual, it contains much that will be of interest to anyone with a desire to know GOD personally and intimately. These messages represent only a small sample of her many inspiring sermons that I have heard preached. I have sat as a spiritual daughter gleaning knowledge of JESUS from her for over twenty plus years. They amply illustrate knowledge from her study and life experiences of walking and depending entirely on GOD. HE is a fountain of living waters which can provide all that we need to survive our earthly existence. I believe that the author, Pastor Novella Harris, my spiritual mother has created a full work of spiritual knowledge concerning, faith, testing, victory over trials and enduring the tribulations of life. Each mini sermon is packed with high-value substances, and you will have an incredible journey as you travel through each page. It is her human intelligence and love of GOD that will help you to discover new depths, but most importantly you will be encouraged to continue your walk with CHRIST.

Linda C. Pyatt Jr. Deaconess, Financial Administrator, and Armour Bearer at Grace Cathedral International.

There comes a time in everyone's life where their faith is tested. Trials and obstacles that arise that will cause us to call on Jesus. Have you ever been backed up against the wall to have no one to turn to? In Pastor Harris' book, Sermonettes For A Sunday Morning, you will learn how to use your faith to get you through those obstacles.

This book will show you step by step how her vision changed her life while changing others'.

While traveling through the collections of Bible stories you will learn and imagine what the great theologians have experienced. This book is written in clear, concise words to grasp your understanding of what it is to have a relationship with God. It will compel you to use your faith. Pastor Harris tries to convey through writing many examples of how faith was used in her life and in the lives of others to make life-changing events. For example, a traumatic event occurred from 2012 through 2015 for Pastor Harris when she became confined with an illness that immobilized her capacity to move from her bed. During that time she prayed and meditated earnestly to the LORD, and HE whispered in her ears to write Sunday messages to the parishioners at Grace Cathedral International.

Finally, these excerpts are blended to increase your desire to stay in the Word. The various components are woven together as an integral aspect of the Bible. They are refreshing, encouraging, and healing. Pastor Harris; faith was tested, and she claimed the victory for healing through her writings.The book will change your life as it did hers.

Gladys Watford, Mother, Teacher,
Mentor at Grace Cathedral International

In the past couple of years Novella Harris, who also serves as Pastor of Grace Cathedral, has been very busy writing her first book. I cannot tell you the countless hours she has spent, both early mornings and late nights putting these Sermonettes and prayers together.

What is unique about this book is that she intersperses prayers with the Sermonettes.

As you read thru this book, you immediately sense that the author is a great prayer warrior.

The Sermonettes are prophetic, and I am reminded of 2nd Chronicles 20:20 KJV, "...Believe His prophets, and you will succeed."

GOD rewards the faithful servant. Novella has been successful in her life. This book is a continuation.

Many have cried out for a life changing collection of Sermonettes and prayers.

I believe this to be that book. If you are hungry for more of GOD, this is the book.

As you read these Sermonettess and prayers, you will be transformed by a feeling of GOD's presence as you allow the words to permeate your spirit. This book encourages you to proactively and aggressively pursue an intimate relationship with your SAVIOR. GOD gave Novella exactly what to write to motivate real and lasting change.

She writes to inspire women and men to realize all that GOD called them to be.

The Body of Christ today is becoming more acutely aware that there is a thirst and deep need for a new dimension of worship. This book brings us closer to fulfilling that desire for greater intimacy with GOD.

If you are ready to experience a greater outpouring of the HOLY SPIRIT, this book is a must read for you.

It was delightful to be able to write this foreword for my wife of 53 years.

Bishop R.W. Harris, AAS, BRE, BA Prelate,
Grace Cathedral International

DEDICATION

I thank GOD for maintaining the purpose in my life.

I want to thank all those who supported me with words of encouragement in making this book a reality.

Bishop R.W. Harris, Prelate, allowed me to publish my Sermonettes in the church bulletin.

Linda Pyatt, and Martha Pinkney, supplied needed corrections.

Lady Caroline Williams gave me the inspiration to complete this book.

Pastor Joyce Clarke showed me by her example that I can do all things through CHRIST, who strengthens me.

Reverend Barbara Metz and Apostle Elise Banks surrounded me with an unbroken circle of prayer.

Darlene Mc Cabe shared the information needed to begin the publishing process.

Jalana Harris and Jermaine Rucker's valuable assistance contributed to finalizing the book.

My cousin Verneda White for introducing me to Author House Publishing.

PROLOGUE

Approximately four years ago, I, a healthy, energetic, independent woman became so ill that I was practically bedridden. I needed assistance for the all the things I took for granted in my daily life.

Before my illness, I exhorted Sunday morning service, preached GOD's Word and ministered to the congregation.

I had always been considered hyperactive. I worked out four days a week.

I tried to be the dedicated wife and mother that GOD had instructed women to be.

I worked as a Public School Teacher, Executive Director of Sure Foundation Child Care Inc., maintained an immaculate house, and the Grace Cathedral International complex.

I Pastored along with my husband Bishop R.W. Harris. We were a team. We were visionaries. With GOD's help, I would make sure I encouraged and not hindered his visions for the ministry, and he did the same for mine. GOD moved in miraculous ways for us.

It was difficult for me to comprehend becoming suddenly so ill I could barely function.

This illness (that has yet to be completely determined) became what I thought at the time, a sour lemon in my life. I never asked GOD "why" but "what?"

What do you want me to do in this situation?" I was inspired to make sweet lemonade with my sour lemon.

GOD allowed me to write this book in my limited physical condition.

Since I was not able to stand and preach from the pulpit, I wrote a sermonette for the Sunday morning bulletin each week. Some of the Sermonettes were a series that covered several Sundays.

GOD has blessed me to use those weekly Sermonettes for this book.

STUFF HAPPENS IN THE GARDEN

"Thus it is written, The first man Adam became a living being (an individual personality); the last Adam (CHRIST) became a life-giving Spirit [restoring the dead to life]. [Gen. 2:7.]" (1 Corinthians 15:45 AMP)

Adam walked with GOD in the cool of the day. The sin of disobedience occurred in the **Garden of Eden.** "And to Adam HE said, Because you have listened and given heed to the voice of your wife and have eaten of the tree of which I commanded you, saying, you shall not eat of it, the ground is under a curse because of you; in sorrow and toil shall you eat [of the fruits] of it all the days of your life... "Therefore the LORD GOD sent him forth from the Garden of Eden to till the ground from which he was taken" (Genesis 3:17, 23 AMP) Once Adam sinned, his relationship with GOD was broken. From that point on, sin has separated us from GOD.

The Bible tells us that while the disciples were sleeping, JESUS was praying to the FATHER, "... if it is possible, let this cup pass away from ME; nevertheless, not what I will (not what I desire) but as YOU will and desire." (Matt. 26:39 AMP) It is in the **Garden of Gethsemane** we find JESUS agonizing over what HE would soon experience at the cross. HIS suffering is so intense that,"...HIS sweat was as it were great drops of blood falling down to the ground." (Luke 22:44 KJV)

Nothing stopped JESUS from going to the cross. It was prophesied that the Messiah would be crucified and would rise again on the third day.

GOD's unconditional love could not stand for a man to be separated from HIM because of sin. GOD made a way of reconciliation for us. In the Garden of Gethsemane JESUS prayed and received strength before HE would take on the judgment for all humankind. HE paid the price for sin. JESUS had to endure punishment, torture, and death for our sins.

"Now in the place where HE was crucified there was a garden, and in the garden a new tomb in which no one had yet been laid." (John 19:41 KJV) In Golgotha was the garden of victory. JESUS had just conquered sin and satan at the cross. In the Garden of Golgotha, JESUS becomes victorious over death by HIS resurrection. JESUS conquered death. "O Death, where is thy sting? O grave, where thy victory?" (1 Corinthians 15:55 KJV)

"He who has an ear, let him hear what the SPIRIT saith unto the churches. To him that overcometh will I give to eat of the tree of life, which is in the midst of the Paradise of GOD." (Revelation 2:7 KJV) The Paradise of GOD is the Garden of Eternal Life. The curse of the fall in the Garden of Eden is forgiven, and all true believers can walk with Christ through all eternity.

Stuff happens in the garden. We find sin, suffering, victory and finally eternal peace all happening in the garden.

SUCH AND SUCH

To reach the such and such of prosperity, fame, and fortune, we have to accomplish the such and such of preparation, experience and obedience to the will of GOD.

In 2 Samuel chapter 11, we read that David, in the Bible, committed adultery with Bathsheba. Bathsheba became pregnant. David had her husband, Uriah (one of his mighty men) killed so he could cover his sin and marry her.

Nathan the prophet came to admonish David for his sin. We read in (2 Samuel 12:8 KJV) "And I gave thee thy master's house, and thy master's wives into thy bosom, and gave thee the house of Israel and of Judah; and if that had been too little, I would moreover have given unto thee such and such things."

Immediately we all jump to the conclusion that such and such is what we all are striving for in life. Some even claim that they are already in such and such. Many interpret such and such as going beyond what we already possess, beyond our needs and acquiring all the desires of our hearts. We believe that money and possessions can buy us all the happiness we are seeking. It is true that money can buy us things that can temporarily make us happy but money and possessions can't buy us true love and peace of mind. Money and possessions can't keep us from experiencing poor health, heartache, heartbreak, and death; if that were so, Michael Jackson and Whitney Houston would still be alive today.

Often success comes with a price. Many find themselves working endless hours, spending sleepless nights, plotting and scheming to stay ahead. Some individuals sacrifice peace of mind to maintain the status that they have acquired and sometimes sell moral and ethical values to do so.

Spiritual success also comes with a price. The Bible tells us, "But seek ye first the kingdom of GOD and HIS righteousness, and all these things shall be added unto you." (Matthew 6:33 KJV) "Delight thyself also in the LORD, and HE shall give thee the desires of thine heart."
(Psalms 37:4 KJV) "Beloved, I wish above all things that thou mayest prosper and be in health, even as thy soul prospereth." (3 John 1:2 KJV) My acronym for such and such.

Such And Such

Suffer until change happens

Approachable not disagreeable

Stand under challenging circumstances

This such and such will lead us to the peace of mind that surpasses all understanding. This such and such will take us beyond this temporary life here on Earth to eternity with GOD. GOD possesses all the riches of glory.

To obtain such and such, we have to prepare ourselves. We need to obtain an education, acquire a skill, have a strong work ethic and apply ourselves passionately to what we have chosen to do. We must stop just trying to get by and presenting our finished product in a haphazard and not worthy of praise manner. Such and Such just doesn't happen automatically. It requires hard work, determination and lots of effort to achieve.

OUR PRAYER POSTURE

Have you ever heard people say, "It's not what you said, but how you said it?" So it is not so much what we say when we pray but our attitude and the respect we display when we pray. It baffles me why some Christians, especially those who have unanswered prayers or unmet needs just don't get it. I have learned that the posture in which I present my prayer requests to GOD is key to GOD answering me. We quibble over minute things. Should women cover their heads in the sanctuary? Are we supposed to lift our hands when we pray? Is it proper to kneel or lay prostrate when we prayer? How often should we pray each day? Do we set aside a special day and consecrate it totally to GOD? Why should it be necessary to wear respectable attire in the sanctuary? How significant is that to argue about when we want GOD to meet our needs in prayers?

When I went to the Vatican in Rome, I had my sweater around my shoulders, and the usher stopped me from going inside until I covered my shoulders. When Bishop and I traveled throughout Europe, the Cathedrals were a major part of our tours. We could not enter unless we were appropriately dressed. When we were in Israel, the same standard was upheld. On our recent trip to Abadabi, we visited the Sheik Mosque. I wore a long dress with lace-covered sleeves, but they would not let me in. I had to join the long line of other visitors and give my drivers license to get a borrowed garment that covered me from head to toe. The process was made more wearisome because I was in a wheelchair and Bishop was pushing me in 103-degree heat. I said to myself, "Is it worth all this? "Then I began to reprimand myself and say. "Wow look how much the people respect their place of worship." I could hear the prayers being called out during certain times of the day, and I watched the prayer posture.

We had to wait two days to tour the Mosque because you couldn't visit on the holy days.

I pondered over the years why individuals in some denominations genuflect when they pass the cross. I finally got it. It was a way of saying, "GOD I honor YOU. I am grateful to YOU. I magnify YOUR name. When I see the cross, YOUR place of suffering for me, I bow.

SCRIPTURES FOR THOUGHT WHEN PREPARING TO PRAY

"Let us lift up our heart our hands unto GOD in heavens." (Lamentations 3:41 KJV)

"Lift up your hands in the sanctuary and bless the LORD." (Psalm 134:2 KJV)

"I will praise YOU as long as I live, and in YOUR name I will lift up my hands." (Psalm 63:4 NIV)

"I will therefore that men pray every where, lifting up holy hands, without wrath and doubting." (1 Timothy 2:8 KJV)

"Therefore if thou bring thy gift to the altar, and there rememberest that thy brother hath ought against thee; leave there thy gift before the altar, and go thy way; first be reconciled to thy brother, and then come and offer thy gift." (Matthew 5:23-24 KJV)

"If I regard iniquity in my heart, the LORD will not hear me:" (Psalms 66:18 KJV)

"Now I beseech you, brethren, by the name of our LORD JESUS CHRIST, that ye all speak the same thing, and that there be no divisions among you; but that ye be perfectly joined together in the same mind and in the same judgment." (1 Corinthians 1:10 KJV)

Preparation is needed before we pray.

1. Respect

When we develop a mature relationship with GOD, we will respect and reverence HIS house. "Wherefore we receiving a kingdom which cannot be moved, let us have grace, whereby we may serve GOD acceptably with reverence and GODly fear: for our "GOD is a consuming fire."

(Hebrews 12:28, 29 KJV). The Bible gives instructions to the people of GOD. "Ye shall keep MY Sabbaths and have reverence for my sanctuary: I am the LORD." (Leviticus. 19:30, 26:2 KJV) "Be kindly affectioned one to another with brotherly love; in honor preferring one another;" (Romans 12:10 KJV) We should be respectful to everyone, whether we agree with them or not. Showing respect, even while disagreeing, is what we all must strive for. No one can take our self-respect from us. We have to give that away. Whitney Houston sang," No matter what they take from me, they can't take away my dignity. Learning to love yourself is the greatest love of all." The dress code for both men and women should show at least as much respect for GOD as we would expect to show in the presence of the president or the pope. Mature Christians will naturally show more reverence and respect for GOD's presence.

2. Choice of Music

The music we choose for worship should take into consideration the different generations that attend service. We must extend patient forbearance to music that is not our personal first choice. "With all lowliness and meekness, with long-suffering, forbearing one another in love; Endeavoring to keep the unity of the SPIRIT in the bond of peace. (Ephesians 4:1-3 KJV) The test of our selection of music in the church should be: are people being edified and drawn closer to the LORD. The mature saint is concerned about the worship experience of others as well themselves. We have an obligation to bring others to CHRIST. GOD's name should be mentioned in some form in every song that is used for ministry. We need to be clear on whom we are worshipping.

3. Honor The Sabbath Day

"If thou turn away thy foot from the sabbath, from doing thy pleasure on MY holy day; and call the sabbath a delight, the holy of the LORD, honorable; and shalt honor HIM not doing thine own ways, nor finding thine own pleasure, nor speaking thine own words: Then shalt thou delight thyself in the LORD and I will cause thee to ride upon the high places of the earth, and feed thee with the heritage of Jacob thy father: for the mouth of the LORD hath spoken it." (Isaiah 58:13-14 KJV)

4. Bad Attitude

"Let all bitterness, and wrath, and anger, and clamor, and evil speaking, be put away from you, with all malice: and be ye kind one to another, tenderhearted, forgiving one another, even as GOD for CHRIST's sake hath forgiven you." (Ephesians 4:31–32 KJV) Bad attitudes are easily identifiable because they are displayed on the outside. Everyone sees it except the individual with the attitude. Negative, critical, rebellious, defiant, impatient, rude, uncooperative, self centered, and disrespectful behavior are examples of bad attitudes, which Christians should reject. Attitudes are internal manifestations of our heart and thoughts. They are the hidden intentions, which will eventually serve as the basis for our outward actions. "For as he thinks in his heart, so is he..." (Proverbs 23:7 KJV) No one else really knows the thoughts of our heart, except GOD and us. A negative attitude is something that we can change with GOD's help. It is a change, which must take place inwardly.

5. Bodily Prayer Posture

A. Lifting Our Hands Towards Heaven.

"Solomon stood before the altar of the LORD in the presence of all the congregation of Israel, and spread forth his hands toward heaven." (1 kings 8:22 KJV) Lifting our hand towards heaven when we pray shows our reverence and worship. We extend our hands to heaven to receive the blessings that we believe are going to come down.

B. Bowing Before The LORD

"And it came to pass, that, when Abraham's servant heard their words, he worshipped the LORD, bowing himself to the earth." (Genesis 24:52 KJV)

"That at the name of JESUS every knee should bow, of things in heaven, and things in earth, and things under the earth;" (Philippians 2:10 KJV) We bow before GOD because HE is the KING of KINGs and LORD of LORDs. If we bow before kings and queens we owe GOD even more honor.

C. Kneeling Before GOD

"Solomon had made an end of praying all his prayer and supplication unto the LORD, he arose from before the altar of the LORD, from kneeling on his knees with his hands spread up to heaven Solomon was one of the wisest men that ever lived. I think we can follow his example in how to go before the LORD in prayer. (I Kings 8:54 KJV) So Ahab went up to the to eat and drink. And Elijah went up to the top of Carmel, and he cast himself down upon the earth, and put his face between his knees," (I Kings 18:42 KJV) It is a sign of personal humility. "O come, let us worship and bow down: let us kneel before the LORD our maker." (Psalm 95:6 KJV) How bad do we need GOD to answer us? The scriptures are clear on how we should approach the throne of grace.

D. Laying Prostrate Before GOD

This is my position when I find myself in desperate circumstances and I need GOD to do something for me right away. We can't get any lower to the ground than laying prostrate before GOD. It shows GOD how badly we need HIM when we are facing a crisis. It shows that we have used all of our resources and we need GOD's mercy.

When GOD speaks to us and gives us an awesome task to perform it is usually when we are laying prostrate before HIM. "And Abraham fell on his face: and GOD talked with him, saying..." (Genesis 17:3 KJV) "Then Job arose, and rent his mantle, and shaved his head, and fell down upon the ground, and worshiped, and said, Naked came I out of my mother's womb, and naked shall I return thither: the LORD gave, and the LORD hath taken away: blessed be the name of the LORD." (Job 1:20 KJV)

The scriptures have given great examples of how we should approach GOD in prayer.

SERMONETTE 4

ISHI

"And it shall be at that day, says the LORD, that thou shalt call ME Ishi; [my husband] and you shall no more call ME Baali [my Baal]." (Hosea 2:16 AMP)

Hosea a Godly prophet was commanded to marry a woman whom GOD told him was a prostitute and would not be faithful to him. Hosea's description in the book of Hosea of a relationship so ugly and yet so forgiving would not have been as effective for the man of GOD to write if he had not experienced it personally. Out of his anguish, Hosea shares with us a deeper understanding of the forgiving love of GOD. Hosea continues to love Gomer, and he forgives her when she runs away and sleeps with another man. Even though we do not worship GOD and appreciate HIM like we should GOD continues to love us and does not abandon us.

While Gomer was living in her adulterous relationship, Hosea found a way to make sure she had clothes, food, and money. Hosea finally realized that providing for Gomer's needs was not helping her. She needed to change her heart. Hosea made the decision to stop supporting her and eventually Gomer's lover sold her into slavery.

Hosea's love for Gomer is a picture of GOD's love for us. While many of us are unfaithful to GOD by not placing HIM first in our lives, HE keeps on providing for us. We often use GOD's blessings for our personal goals. However, it is important for us to recognize that just as Hosea never stopped loving Gomer, no matter how low she sank.

GOD never stops loving us even though HE has to stand by and watch some of us be given over to the terrible consequences of our sin.

When we recognize our state and desire to change, GOD is a restorer. We can call HIM Ishi, my husband, when we give ourselves wholly to GOD.

GOD cannot be recognized as our loving husband when our hearts and emotions are divided. We cannot call GOD Ishi when we allow the pleasures of life and selfish motivations to become more important than our love for HIM.

When we think of GOD's loving kindness and that we are alive today because of HIS grace; when we acknowledge that GOD's mercy kept us, we will embrace HIM as Ishi and never let go of HIS love.

HEAVY BAGGAGE/SURVIVING ON BROKEN PIECES

We cannot experience GOD's full blessing if we do not say we are sorry for the wrong things that we do. We must ask for forgiveness of GOD first, ourselves second and others that have hurt us. We need to understand and embrace the things we have experienced knowing that it has all been a part of GOD's plan and purpose. "And we know that all things work together for good to them that love GOD, to them who are the called according to HIS purpose." (Romans 8:28 KJV)

Is GOD willing to forgive us when we sin? GOD is a loving and forgiving GOD. HE is aware of our weaknesses. "For we do not have a High Priest who is unable to understand and sympathize and have a shared feeling with our weaknesses and infirmities and liability to the assaults of temptation, but ONE who has been tempted in every respect as we are, yet without sinning." (Hebrews 4:15 AMP)

"I, even I, am He who blots out and cancel your transgressions, for MY own sake, and I will not remember." (Isaiah 43:25 AMP)

Everyone wears a mask of some form that covers our insecurities, our failures, our hurts, our disappointments, our struggles and most importantly any unforgiveness we have in our hearts.

We all need to take off the masks we wear, be real, get delivered and experience the peace of GOD that surpasses all understanding.

When we pray, let us seek GOD's advice and direction on when, where, how and with whom we should share the things we find ourselves facing.

Forgiveness is the key to releasing the heavy baggage we are carrying. Forgiveness is the main ingredient that will enable us to stop surviving on broken pieces.

BLESSED

Everybody is looking for a blessing. Everybody has unfulfilled needs and desires. A financially successful life and fulfilling career just don't happen. Do you know what it means to try and live a champagne life on a beer man's salary? It means buying designer clothes, getting the best weaves in town, buying expensive cars that can't be maintained, investing in timeshares instead of the stock market, taking trips to Africa and Europe and only making $20.00 an hour. To be fruitful and productive not just efficient in every area of life some natural and most importantly spiritual things have to be in place. The world calls it success or luck but we who know GOD, call it blessed.

The key to life's greatest accomplishments lies inside of us. We do not have to walk in another man or woman's shadow. GOD has given us all our own shadow, and our potential, our purpose in life to fulfill.

We need a passion for whatever we do. We need to learn to be proactive, leaning on the door of opportunity so that we fall in when that door opens. Too many today want to live the life of Beyonce and Jay-Z, Michele and Barack Obama, T.D. and Sarah Jakes but don't want the heartache, pain, sacrifice and humility it took to get where they are. Whatever our career choice, we need preparation, determination, and relentless endurance.

Laziness, lack of motivation, love of sleep, avoiding the struggle, bypassing the dirty work, are major hindrances that prevent many from the things most desired in life. It takes humility, hours of practice, education and most importantly a real relationship with GOD to achieve the goals we set for ourselves.

Wisdom from the Word of GOD can only help those wise enough to follow it.

We can always find a scripture that emphasizes how to be blessed and what those who are blessed by GOD can expect. We need to take a moment and consider why those in the world are lucky to have fame and fortune, but many don't appear satisfied. People who are considered lucky very often lack contentment and inner peace. It is evident in the multiple sex partners, drug abuse and the suicide rate that has become increasingly newsworthy among the rich and famous.

Blessed people of GOD learn to be content and have peace that surpasses all understanding. Holy people of GOD know that GOD will make a way of escape so we can be triumphant when we feel overwhelmed and can't bear the heartache and pain that everyone endures at one time or another.

As we read GOD's word, let us be encouraged in knowing that life has not just handed us a lucky break, but GOD blesses us.

Listed are some scriptures that should become part of what can be called a daily lesson plan to read and eventually memorize and internalize. After reading the scriptures, pray. They will help guide us into GOD's blessings.

"Now therefore thus says the Lord of hosts: Consider your ways and set your mind on what has come to you. You have sown much, but you have reaped little; you eat, but you do not have enough; you drink, but you do not have your fill; you clothe yourselves, but no one is warm; and he who earns wages has earned them to put them in a bag with holes in it." (Haggai 1:5-6 AMP)

"Will a man rob or defraud GOD? Yet you rob and defraud ME. But you say, In what way do we rob or defraud You? [You have withheld your] tithes and offerings. You are cursed with the curse, for you are robbing ME, even this whole nation.

Bring all the tithes (the whole tenth of your income) into the storehouse, that there may be food in MY house, and prove ME now by it, says the LORD of hosts, if I will not open the windows of heaven for you and pour you out a blessing, that there shall not be room enough to receive it." (Malachi 3:8-10 AMP)

"IF you will listen diligently to the voice of the LORD your GOD, being watchful to do all His commandments, which I command you this day, the LORD your GOD will set you high above all the nations of the earth. And all these blessings shall come upon you and overtake you if you heed the voice of the LORD your GOD. Blessed shall you be in the city and blessed shall you be in the field. Blessed shall be the fruit of your body and the fruit of your ground and the fruit of your beasts, the increase of your cattle and the young of your flock. Blessed shall be your basket and your kneading trough. Blessed shall be you be when you come in and blessed shall you be when you go out. The Lord shall cause your enemies who rise up against you to be defeated before your face; they shall come out against you one way and flee before you seven ways. The LORD shall command the blessing upon you in your storehouse and in all that you undertake. And HE will bless you in the land which the LORD your GOD gives you. The LORD will establish you as a people holy to HIMSELF as He has sworn to you, if you keep the commandments of the LORD your GOD and walk in HIS ways. And all people of the earth shall see that you are called by the name [and in the presence of] the LORD and they shall be afraid of you. And the LORD shall make you have a surplus of prosperity, through the fruit of your body, of your livestock, and of your ground, in the land which the LORD swore to your fathers to give you. The LORD shall open to you HIS good treasury, the heavens, to give the rain of your land in its season and to bless all the work of your hands; and you shall lend to many nations, but you shall not borrow.

And the LORD shall make you the head, and not the tail, and you shall be above only, and you shall not be beneath if you heed the commandments of the LORD your GOD which I command you this day and are watchful to do them. And you shall not turn aside from any of the words which I command you this day, to the right hand or to the left, to go after other gods to serve them. But if you will not obey the voice of the LORD your GOD being watchful to do all HIS commandments and His statutes which I command you this day, then all these curses shall come upon you and overtake you," (Deuteronomy 28:1-15 AMP)

"Blessed (happy, to be envied, and spiritually prosperous—with life-joy and satisfaction in GOD's favor and salvation, regardless of their outward conditions) are the poor in spirit (the humble, who rate themselves insignificant), for theirs is the kingdom of heaven!

Blessed and enviably happy [with a happiness produced by the experience of GOD's favor and especially conditioned by the revelation of His matchless grace] are those who mourn, for they shall be comforted! [Isa. 61:2.]

Blessed (happy, lithesome, joyous, spiritually prosperous—with life-joy and satisfaction in GOD's favor and salvation, regardless of their outward conditions) are meek (the mild, patient, long-suffering), for they shall inherit the earth! [Ps. 37:11.]

Blessed and fortunate and happy and spiritually prosperous (in that state in which the born-again child of GOD enjoys HIS favor and salvation) are those who hunger and thirst for righteousness (uprightness and right standing with GOD), for they shall be completely satisfied![Isa. 55:1, 2.]

Blessed (happy, to be envied, and spiritually prosperous—with life, joy and satisfaction in GOD's favor and salvation, regardless of their outward conditions) are the merciful, for they shall obtain mercy!

Blessed (happy, enviably fortunate, and spiritually prosperous-possessing the happiness produced by the experience of GOD's favor and especially conditioned by the revelation of HIS grace, regardless of their outward conditions) are the pure in heart, for they shall see GOD! [Ps. 24:3, 4.]

Blessed (enjoying enviable happiness, spiritually prosperous—with life-joy and satisfaction in GOD's favor and salvation, regardless of their outward conditions) are the makers and maintainers of peace, for they shall be called the sons of GOD!

Blessed and happy and enviably fortunate and spiritually prosperous (in the state in which the born-again child of GOD enjoys and finds satisfaction in GOD's favor and salvation regardless of his outward conditions) are those who are persecuted for righteousness' sake (for being and doing right), for theirs is the kingdom of heaven! Blessed (happy, to be envied, and spiritually prosperous–with life-joy and satisfaction in GOD's favor and salvation, regardless of your outward conditions) are you when people revile you and persecute you and say all kinds of evil things against you falsely on MY account. Be glad and supremely joyful, for your reward in heaven is great (strong and intense), for in this same way people persecuted the prophets who were before you."[II Chronicles. 36:16.] (Matthew 5:3-12 AMP)

MAY THE WORKS I'VE
DONE SPEAK FOR ME

"For we are HIS workmanship, created in CHRIST JESUS unto good works, which GOD prepared before ordained, that we should walk in them." (Ephesians 2:10 KJV)

Genuine faith in CHRIST will exhibit itself in our good works, and the godliness displayed in our character."... And they were judged every man according to their works."(Revelation 20:11-15 KJV)

We are perceived by the quality of our works. We are treated, as GOD sees us and as well as people. How we perform our works is indicative of our faithfulness to GOD. We cannot expect to be praised, respected or rewarded for sloppy, have done, thrown together works. We cannot expect to receive the same kind of blessing from GOD when we are careless with our works, as those who show passion and great effort in what they do. It is true that our works cannot save us. "WHO hath saved us, and called us with a holy calling, not according to our works, but according to HIS own purpose and grace which was given us in CHRIST JESUS before the world began." (2 Timothy 1:9 KJV) GOD through HIS grace and mercy gives us salvation not according to our prior works. However, when HE saves us and gives us a purpose to fulfill, how we then perform our task represents the GOD in us.

I don't want to mislead you. We cannot work our way into Heaven, this is a gift of GOD. If we represent GOD than the works we do should correlate with how GOD would want them to be done. "The appetite of the sluggard craves and gets nothing, but the appetite of the diligent is abundantly supplied."(Proverbs 13:4 AMP) "And whatever ye do, do it heartily, as to the LORD and not unto men." (Colossians 3:23 KJV)

"For even when we were with you, this we commanded you, that If any would not work, neither should he eat." (2 Thessalonians 3:10 KJV)

"He becometh poor that dealeth with a slack hand: but the hand of the diligent maketh rich." (Proverbs 10:4 KJV) "He also that is slothful in his work is brother to him that is a great waster." (Proverbs 18:9 KJV)

"The desire of the sluggard kills him, for his hands refuse to labor." l(Proverbs 21:25 KJV)

We don't serve a lazy GOD. We serve a GOD, who is all-powerful. We serve a GOD, who is constantly repairing and cleaning up the messy and broken things in our lives. We are an advertisement for the GOD in us.

May the works we do speak for who we are, and who we represent.

BLESSED THROUGH OUR TEST

The book of Genesis, chapters 37-50 gives us a great example of how we can be blessed through the tests we go through.

Joseph, the favored son of Jacob, at seventeen, was too immature to realize that sharing his vision with envious relatives could lead to serious repercussions. Had Joseph been older and wiser he would not have been so hasty in sharing his dream with his brothers.

We must consider carefully with whom we confide our dreams and desires. The ones we think will be excited for us and encourage us very often become our dream killers. Every blessing must go through a testing process to see if we can handle it. So Joseph's test begins, and his brothers unknowingly become the catalyst that started his testing process. Through dreams, GOD was giving Joseph a preview of his future ministry. Joseph was young. His experiences were limited. He hadn't learned how to suffer yet. What a lesson to all of us. GOD will give us a glimpse of our future mission, but the vision is for an appointed time. Preparation has to take place first. The training will come through the tests we endure and conquer.

Joseph was a dreamer. We all have dreams. Without a dream or a vision, most of us would not make any advances in life. The Sure Foundation Child Care Inc. was first a dream, a desire. It had taken thirteen years of preparation before it became a reality. I had to get the proper background; the property had to be purchased, and a grant had to be secured. I didn't see a physical building, but I saved supplies and prepared my finances because I believed my dream would one day become a reality.

People will discourage you; circumstances will hinder your progress but don't give up on your dream. "For the vision is yet for an appointed time, but at the end it shall speak, and not lie: though it tarry, wait for it; because it will surely come, it will not tarry." (Habakkuk 2:3 KJV)

Jacob made Joseph a coat of many colors and created jealousy among his other sons. Jealousy grew into anger, envy, and hatred. GOD's divine plan was to put in motion the chain of events that would prepare Joseph for his ministry. When we find ourselves struggling and hindered in what we know GOD has called us to do, rejoice because the enemy doesn't want us to succeed. The enemy tries to block our progress at the same time GOD is training us to fulfill our destiny.

"My brethren, count it all joy when ye fall into divers temptations; Knowing this, that the trying of your faith worketh patience. But let patience have her perfect work, that ye may be perfect and entire, wanting nothing." (James 1:2-4 KJV) It takes prayer, fasting and a strong determination to survive the tests that will eventually lead us to the blessing that is awaiting us.

Joseph's brothers were living a rebellious and sinful life. When Joseph discovered it, he reported it to his father. He was labeled a tattletale. We don't like tattletales because they expose us. It bothered Joseph's brothers that Joseph refused to run into the same wages of sin as they did. The Bible tells us not to be partakers in another man's sin. We should not be willing witnesses of wrongdoing. If we keep silent and know of sin, we become partakers." Lay hands suddenly on no man, neither be partaker of other men's sins: keep yourself pure."

(1 Timothy 5:22 KJV) If we know someone is committing fornication, adultery or engaging in other sinful actions, and they are still singing in the choir, dance ministry, ushers, or ministering in any leadership capacity, and we don't inform the Bishop or Pastor we are a participating in their sin. The lives of Joseph's brethren were sinful and their doings deceitful. Some things their father needed to know, keeping silent would have been dangerous.

His elder brother's actions were risking the welfare of Jacob's tribe and

Joseph had to tell on them. In the church, one member's sin can bring a reproach on the whole church if it's allowed to continue. So exposing his brothers was another test in Joseph's journey to his destiny.

Many of us can say that I am already blessed, I have a house, a car, clothes, a job, my health but that is only the beginning of the major blessing GOD has in store for us. Many today are satisfied with just enough to get by. Why should we choose to settle for matchsticks when GOD owns the lumber yard? Great blessings require significant sacrifices. Those sacrifices often come in the form of the tests we triumph over.

Joseph had a good life, but GOD had so much more in store for him and before he could receive his major blessing he had to be tested. Envy and jealousy caused Joseph's brothers to want to kill him. "Then they took him and cast him into the [well-like] pit, which was empty; there was no water in it. Then they sat down to eat their lunch." (Genesis 37:24-25 AMP)

You can't get crueler than that. What did Joseph do to deserve that treatment? He had some dreams that he shared. His father openly favored him, which was not his fault. He was a good kid who didn't join in riotous living. None of those things deserved the severe punishment he received from his brothers. I am sure he cried and begged to be released. Joseph is thrown into a dried up pit and his brothers sit and eat lunch. The way Joseph was treated doesn't seem fair. It doesn't seem justified. When GOD has a purpose for us what seems cruel and unjust is only a test. Joseph's envious and jealous brothers throw Joseph into a pit. We all must expect to find pitfalls in life. Joseph's came suddenly. He was forced into his pit. He believed he did the right thing, but he suffered for it.

Circumstances in life, overpowering temptations, sin, lust, greed, ambition, spiritual pride, financial debt, depression, shattered relationships, interrupted dreams, and religious, and natural elevation can also become a pitfall. Many are drawn into pits by their carelessness, indifference, and neglect. Some find themselves trapped in a pit by the conditions of their birth and the environment they are raised in.

Those of us striving for a greater anointing in ministry often find ourselves in a pitfall situation by GOD's spiritual movement. HE wants to see if we can endure hardness and survive the trying of our faith. We need to stop giving the enemy credit for everything that seems to be going wrong in our lives. Sometimes what we perceive as negative situations or circumstances is part of GOD's plan for the divine destiny HE's preparing for us. There is deliverance from the deepest pitfalls. When we feel utterly helpless, and on the brink of despair, GOD is there to lift us out of the muck and mire of that temporary pit. "There hath no temptation taken you but such as is common to man: but God is faithful, who will not suffer you to be tempted above that ye are able; but will with the temptation also make a way to escape, that ye may be able to bear it." (1 Corinthians 10:13 KJV)

When Joseph was delivered from the pit, he ends up in the safety and security of Potiphar's house. Potiphar's house was blessed because of Joseph. When GOD's favor is upon us every place we dwell and everyone connected to us will share in it. Joseph was given control over all Potiphar's affairs. All that Joseph did prospered; everything he put his hand to thrived. That's what we can expect when we are delivered from GOD's ordained pit.

Our pitfalls are learning experiences. They are just tests that will lead us to the blessing awaiting us. We can't surrender our hopes and dreams while in our pit experience. We can't give up and wish for death while in our pit experience. When we recognize that our blessing depends on how we handle our pit experience, we can endure them with praise on our lips and joy in our hearts knowing that victory is on the way.

Everything Joseph put his hands to thrived. In the midst of the devastation and discouragement, Joseph was still experiencing prosperity. In the midst of the struggles we may be going through GOD still allows us to experience success. Prosperity is not always financial. Peace of mind, good health, a place to live, food to eat, knowing your family is secure, and a relationship with GOD can be our greatest prosperity.

We all want to move ahead and find favor in the sight of GOD and man so that we may prosper. The higher our spiritual desires, the greater the testing process to make sure we can handle all the responsibility fulfilling that desire will incur. In our secular pursuits timing, training, educational advancement, hours of preparation, and experience are prerequisites for obtaining what we are seeking. We can't just say GOD called me to preach, and we can't get along with people. We can't bring a quality word if we lack Bible School knowledge. "Study and be eager and do your utmost to present yourself to GOD approved (tested by trial), a workman who has no cause to be ashamed, correctly analyzing and accurately dividing [rightly handling and skillfully teaching] the Word of Truth." (2 Timothy 2:15 AMP)

If GOD calls us to be a musician or singer, it will not just happen without training and hours of practice. The call from GOD is advising us to prepare to sacrifice, struggle, educate ourselves and be tested to see if we are worthy of that calling.

Joseph had some personal characteristics that enhanced his prosperity. Joseph was observant, and he listened. He was diligent and conscientious. He did things on or before time. He gave his all and his very best in the performance of his duties. Whatever we do or display speaks for our character. We should not look for accolades or compliments when we just throw something together at the last minute. Joseph was faithful and devoted to GOD and his superiors. He displayed a passion when accomplishing the works entrusted to him. Success seldom comes to the lazy, negligent or the idle. His master trusted him. The fastest why to reach elevation is to gain the confidence of our master. Joseph was patient under suffering, faithful in service and content with his present circumstance. "Not that I speak in respect of want: for I have learned, in whatsoever state I am, in addition to that to be content."

(Philippians 4:11 KJV) A wealthy man or woman is one who has the LORD with them to give them favor with fellow men. Joseph was lifted up out of the dungeon and made to sit among princes.

"And the name of the second called he Ephraim: For God hath caused me to be fruitful in the land of my affliction." (Genesis 41:52 KJV) He was blessed through his test.

GOD gave Joseph the vision of his ministry when he was only 17, but it was at an appointed time. "For the vision is yet for an appointed time and Though it tarry, wait [earnestly] for it, because it will surely come; it will not be behind on its appointed day."[Hebrews 10:37, 38.] (Habakkuk 2:3 AMP) Joseph was thirty years old when his vision was finally realized.

Joseph's pit experience provided the way for his transportation to Egypt. His management of Potiphar's affairs was training for his final rule over Egypt. The unjust accusation caused him to spend about three years in prison. His experience in jail prepared him to be the deliverer of a nation and was the step that allowed him to stand before Pharaoh. Had Joseph not endured the prison experience, he would not have been able to help his family. He would not have been the instrument of fulfilling GOD's promise. GOD calls us, yes, but there's a training period, a learning period, a preparation period, a suffering period. We must all go through the process if we want our visions to be successful. There's a blessing in suffering wrongfully. "For what glory is it, if, when ye be buffeted for your faults, ye shall take it patiently? but if, when ye do well, and suffer for it, ye take it patiently, this is acceptable with GOD." (1 Peter 2:20 KJV) Everything that happens in our lives is ordered by GOD's infinite wisdom and love. We are often led through times of darkness, times when communion with GOD seems to be interrupted, temptation, opposition and difficulty in prayer make our souls feel sad. Know that GOD is not absent. "For I know the thoughts and plans that I have for you, says the LORD, thoughts and plans for welfare and peace and not for evil, to give you hope in your final outcome." (Jeremiah 29:11 KJV)

All through Joseph's years of struggle, GOD was guiding him. Every step of the way had its purpose. Potiphar, the jailer, Pharaoh, the Egyptian Nation and his family were all blessed through Joseph. His sufferings were blessings not only for himself but everyone connected to him.

Joseph's brother's plotted to kill him. He experienced being sold into slavery. He spent years in prison unjustly. In the end, Joseph was able to say to his brothers, "As for you, ye thought evil against me, but GOD meant it unto good, to bring to pass, as it is this day, to save much people alive."

(Genesis 50:20 KJV) GOD is a problem solver, a burden bearer, and trusting in HIS word can bring us through every situation in our lives. Our blessing is at the end of our test.

IMMEDIATE OBEDIENCE BRINGS INSTANT RESULTS

"...HE said to the paralyzed man, I say to you, arise, pick up your litter (stretcher), and go to your own house. "And instantly [the man] stood up before them and picked up what he had been lying on and went away to his own house...." (Luke 5:24-25 AMP)

"JESUS said to him, Get up! Pick up your bed (sleeping pad) and walk! Instantly the man became well and recovered his strength and picked up his bed and walked." (John 5:8-9 AMP)

"...HE then said to the paralyzed man, Get up! Pick up your sleeping pad and go to your own house. And he got up and went away to his own house." (Matthew 9:6-7 AMP)

In each of the above instances the individual received instant healing after immediately obeying GOD's command. There are times when we make promises to GOD but fail to follow through on what HE requires after we receive what we desire. I have often heard saints say if GOD would just give me one job making enough money, I will spend more time serving HIM. When GOD answers, they join a gym or outside club. I have prayed with individuals for GOD to help them with enough money to get out of debt and when GOD answers they take that money and buy a new TV or computer. LORD if you give me a new house I will serve you with all my heart and on Sunday they stay home to cut the grass and plant gardens. GOD if you just give me that new car I will use it to your glory. When GOD answers and they should be helping others to get to church, they go to the mall or visit relatives and friends. LORD if you just heal my body, I will witness to everyone I see. GOD answers and they have not brought one soul to the kingdom; in fact they stop attending church themselves.

Many return to the same condition they were in before receiving GOD's answer.

When GOD does something spectacular in our lives, HE places a condition or something we should follow up on to maintain what we have received. GOD wants immediate follow through on what HE asks us to do. HE is not accepting excuses and delay in our promise of duty under any circumstances. GOD also wants us to take the adverse situations we have survived in our life, pick them up, walk as a witness and an example of what once held us down and had us bound has now become our ministry. We can share with those going through and say with confidence, "GOD brought me through this and that. Look at me now I am a survivor. I have gained victory over my past and you can too." GOD is not going to bless us and not require us to use that blessing to draw others to HIM. GOD wants us to be walking advertisements of HIS power. GOD wants us to tell others that HIS grace and mercy brought us through, and we're living each moment because of the excellent, almost impossible things we have overcome. GOD wants us to tell somebody, "I was crippled by drug addiction, alcohol, sexually abused, unloved, and suffered depression. Prison became my home because of my life of crime. I was a whore, a prostitute, a womanizer, gay, a thief, a liar, a deceiver, a gang banger. Look at me now. I met JESUS and HE healed me. HE delivered me and told me to take the things that once enslaved me, pick them up and move forward in life. We are obligated to share the victory we have received. We must tell others about our deliverance. Use those things that once enslaved us to proclaim the mighty power of GOD. To maintain the things that GOD has for us and obtain instant results, we must immediately obey what HE will instruct us to do.

FAITH

Faith and salvation go hand and hand together. "But without faith it is impossible to please HIM." (Hebrews 11:6 KJV)

We all have a measure of faith; (Romans 12:3 KJV) we don't all have the same amount and our faith may be in different areas, but everyone has some faith.

It brings us into contact with GOD. It's the link that unites and binds us to JESUS. Faith is our hand stretched out to receive the gifts that GOD bestows.

We build out faith through love and trust. Love stays near and delights in the presence of the one that is loved. It is the same with all who love the LORD. We follow HIM, stay close to HIM, hold onto HIM, and we don't hear any other voice but HIS.

We don't listen to any other words but GOD'S words. GOD is not a GOD of I can't but, "I can do all things through CHRIST who strengtheneth me." (Philippians 4:13 KJV)

Faith is knowing, "No weapon that is formed against thee shall prosper;..." (Isaiah 54:17 KJV) Faith is to, "Delight thyself in the LORD; and He shall give thee the desires of thine heart." (Psalms 37:4 KJV)

Faith knows that whatsoever things I desire when I pray, when I have a meaningful, loving, empowering, intimate relationship with GOD, I just have to believe, and I shall receive.

WHAT DO YOU DO WHEN YOU DON'T KNOW WHAT TO DO?

How often have we been in the position of not knowing what to do?

When we realize that we have reached our extremity we have to know that it is GOD's opportunity to show HIS power.

If we keep our eyes on GOD, we will be triumphant. We must believe that GOD will take care of our issues and all will be well.

Let us leave our doubts, fears and mistrusting with GOD. Whatever our dangers, struggles or failures GOD has sufficient power to deliver us. It's not a question of our abilities but the power behind us.

In our spiritual conflicts, our victory and prosperity is accomplished through our faith, praise and worship.

Anybody can sing praises after the battle is over. It does not take much of a spirit to do that. The difference between an ordinary man of war and a Christian is this, a Christian shouts before victory because he knows it is sure to come. With GOD's help nothing will be able to stand against us.

In times of doubt or difficulty, we should never become so discouraged that we want to give up and stop the work that GOD has called us to do. Lamentations 3:22-24 KJV says...It is of the LORD's mercies that we are not consumed, because HIS compassions fail not. They are new every morning: great is thy faithfulness. The LORD is my portion, saith my soul; therefore will I hope in him.

GOD's faithfulness is a commitment on HIS part and is as dependable as the scheduled appearances of the sun and moon. When we wake up in the morning, GOD will always be there. Family and friends may disappoint us. The Pastor and church leaders may fail to live up to our expectations; nevertheless, GOD is always faithful.

GOD's presence is assured even if we are unaware of it.

We experience HIS faithfulness to us through HIS protection, mercy, preservation, love and discipline. Why don't we receive everything we desire?

1. We are not spiritually or naturally prepared to receive it.

2. GOD is preventing us from some future disaster or disappointment that may result.

3. GOD just doesn't want it to be.

No matter what we do, GOD cannot be unfaithful because HE cannot deny himself (2 Timothy 2:13).

GOD is steadfast and trustworthy and HE keeps HIS promises.

We have to learn to stop trying to force our will on GOD. It is difficult but we have to learn how to say, "LORD let YOUR divine will be done."

Thank GOD for a ministry of prosperity, the prosperity that (3 John 1:2) speaks of, "Beloved, I wish above all things that thou mayest prosper and be in health, even as thy soul prospereth."

We need to train ourselves to eliminate distraction and confusion.

We must compel ourselves to spend more time pleasing GOD.

Then HE will instruct us in what we need to do when we don't know what to do. GOD will be a source of strength, restoration and inspiration in all areas of our lives..

WHEN BITTER BECOMES BETTER

The book of Ruth is a great illustration of the mindset of people who say they believe and trust in GOD but in reality, rely on self-made plans. One of the main characters in the story is Naomi. The book of Ruth, is not a woman's story but a human one. For all intents and purposes, Naomi could be Nathan. Naomi means "my joy." Naomi had a nature corresponding to her name. Naomi had an innate beauty that gave her personality irresistible charm. We find this to be true later on in the story.

During the rule of the Judges, Israel suffered a serious famine. Elimelech was of Bethlehem. He traveled with his family to Moab. The food was more plentiful in Moab than Bethlehem.

It had to be a real sacrifice for Naomi to move from her native home. In taking the initiative to go to Moab, a foreign country, from Bethlehem, Naomi's husband appears to have stepped out of the will of GOD. If the famine was a judgment upon the nation, Elimelech should have repented and tried to help his fellow countrymen back to GOD. Elimelech was a Hebrew, and should have trusted GOD. But Elimelech left Bethlehem, "the house of bread", for Moab, to a land that was heathen in its ways.

Moab was about 30 miles from Bethlehem-Judah. The distance was not one of miles, but of the mind. The distance was not from one place to another, but from GOD.

Naomi had to be troubled by the move. How can I sing the LORD's song in a strange land? She was the foreigner in a strange land. She appears not have known anyone there. The Bible doesn't indicate that a home was waiting for her in Moab.

Some ladies would not have gone in the first place. "That's not part of my personal plan, so boy bye." That may be why so many women are without a companion today.

In the new and heathen land, Naomi found nothing but misfortune. The Bible says Naomi's husband dies. Elimelech had fled to Moab to escape death from famine. He lost his life in the midst of plenty leaving his wife a widow in a land of idolaters. Some of us would have taken our children and gone home, but Naomi didn't. GOD had a plan for her future.

Before the real purpose of GOD becomes evident in our lives we go through a process of suffering that may cause us to become bitter.

Naomi's two sons married women of Moab. It was forbidden by Jewish law to marry outside of the nation. Naomi's two sons who married foreign women die. Naomi finds herself out in the middle of nowhere, in a land of pagans and idol worshipers. She has lost her family. She must have felt like she had been left with nothing.

Have you ever felt like you had lost everything in your life that really mattered? Have you grieved so deeply that you felt there was no hope for the future? That is how Naomi must have felt. The Bible says she blamed GOD. "And she said unto them, Call me not Naomi, call me Mara: for the ALMIGHTY hath dealt very bitterly with me."

(Ruth 1:20 KJV) Naomi was old and struggling. Her widowed daughters in law, Ruth and Orpah, were heart broken also. Her husband and children were gone. She was in a land of strangers. Her heart and spirit were broken. Naomi becomes bitter. She decides to go back to the favor of GOD. Although broken and bitter she still maintained her powerful personality. Her daughter in law Ruth refused to leave her. When GOD attaches us to the right people who are part of our destiny, we must not let anything come between us.

Naomi and Ruth return to Judah. Poverty and affliction so changed Naomi that her old friends hardly recognized her. I went out full, and the LORD hath brought me home again empty. ..." (Ruth 1:21 KJV) Even though Naomi was bringing Ruth home with her, she felt that she was coming back with nothing.

Naomi's hope and restoration was right there with her in her daughter

33

in law Ruth. Naomi could not see GOD's plan of restoration... All she could see was her pain. So often when we face devastating times in our lives, all we can see is the dark. We cannot see the light of GOD at work. During those times we need to hold on to the word of GOD. "We are troubled on every side yet not distressed; we are perplexed, but not in despair; persecuted but not forsaken; cast down but not destroyed;" (2 Corinthians 4:8-9 KJV)

The beginning of Naomi's hope and journey to better was in Ruth. Naomi and Ruth arrive in Bethlehem during the barley harvest. Ruth asks Naomi's permission to, "go to the field and glean ears of corn after him in whose sight I shall find grace..." (Ruth 2:2 KJV) While working in the field of Boaz, Ruth was identified as Naomi's daughter in law. Boaz tells Ruth to work with the female servants and warns the young men not to bother her. At mealtime, Boaz invited her to share his food. When Naomi learns that Ruth has the attention and kindness of Boaz, a kinsman of her husband, she counsels Ruth to approach him directly. "Wash thyself therefore, and anoint thee, and put thy raiment upon thee, and get thee down to the floor: but make not thyself known unto the man until he shall have done eating and drinking, and it shall be, when he lieth down, that thou shalt mark the place where he shall lie, and thou shalt go in, and uncover his feet and lay thee down, and he will tell thee what thou shalt do." (Ruth 3:3-4 KJV)

Young women today need to find a Naomi who can teach them how to get and keep a man. Young men today need to find a Naomi who can give them wisdom in the search for the right wife. Stop taking advice from the wrong people or your bitter will never become better.

Ruth marries Boaz, and they have a son. "And the women said unto Naomi, Blessed be the LORD, Which hath not left thee this day without a kinsman, that his name may be famous in Israel. And he shall be unto thee a restorer of life, and a nourisher of thine old age; for thy daughter in law, which loveth thee, which is better to thee than seven sons, has borne him."

(Ruth 4:14-15 KJV) "And the women her neighbors gave it a name, saying, There is a son born to Naomi and called his name Obed: he is the father of Jesse, the father of David." (Ruth 4:17 KJV) Naomi's grandson was Obed, the grandfather of King David. He became an ancestor of JESUS CHRIST.

GOD did not leave Naomi bitter. GOD used her to be part of a blessing to the world. GOD had a plan, as HE always does. HIS plan is to give us beauty for our ashes. "To appoint unto them that mourn in Zion, to give unto them beauty for ashes, the oil of joy for mourning, the garment of praise for the spirit of heaviness, that they might be called trees of righteousness, the planting of the LORD, that HE might be glorified." (Isaiah 61:3 KJV).

GOD's plan is always to make our bitter become better.

DON'T GIVE UP THE FIGHT

I was tough on my natural children. They were taught a strong work ethic. Most importantly they were taught never give up on anything that they have had an opportunity to obtain. My motto is when things become difficult recognize that it is a test of your emotional, physical and mental strength. Fight with all you have to accomplish whatever you undertake to do. There will be opposition, and you will want to walk away but never leave when things are down or incomplete. I struggled to obtain everything I have today. People talked negatively about me. They said I would destroy the ministry and would never accomplish many of the things I tried to do. I made mistakes, but I have never walked away from anything. My dreams for my ministry and Day Care began to turn into nightmares, but I was determined not to leave until I made things right. I am a fighter and won't run away from a challenge or test. For my natural and spiritual children, I have the same standards.

We all have problems no one is unique in that. We all need to understand that the solutions to our problems are in GOD's hands, and while we are working for GOD, HE is working for us.

I have learned the secret to problem-solving, fast and lay prostrate in the prayer until GOD gives advice. Has GOD called us to serve Him? Is GOD confused? Is He a liar? To whom much is given much is required. We have to prove our calling.

Does GOD allow us to hurt and suffer if HE wants us to work for HIM? ABSOLUTELY!!!!

When we study the Bible, we will read that part of GOD's work is making better people out of us! GOD knows that the trials we overcome will build greater character in us. "In my distress, I called upon the LORD, and cried out to my GOD; HE heard my voice out of HIS temple, and my cry came before HIM, even to HIS ears." (Psalms 18:6 KJV)

"Let us, therefore, come boldly unto the throne of grace, that we may obtain mercy and find grace to help in time of need."

(Hebrews 4:16 KJV) When we find ourselves facing trials, the first source of help we should seek is GOD. When we feel beaten down by trials, GOD sees, HE knows, HE understands, and HE will never leave us alone. King David, a man after GOD's own heart, learned to look to GOD and depend on HIM.

"And let us not be weary in well doing: for in due season we shall reap, if we faint not." (Galatians 6:9 KJV) Don't get weary in well doing; faint not in well doing; don't lose heart in well doing. We should never get tired and exhausted in doing what is right and proper. Every good work; which is well done, according to the will of GOD, in faith, from a principle of love, in the name of JESUS and to the glory of GOD, is worth the struggle.

Remember if GOD gave us work to do, it is imperative that we don't give up the fight until it is accomplished.

CAN I HANDLE IT?

Can we handle what we are asking GOD for? Have we counted the cost? Sometimes we desire leadership but overlook the fact that all good leadership carries responsibility, sacrifice, anxiety and a willingness to see the situation through even if the leader has to do it alone. Leaders are often lonely because people envy who they are and find ways to confuse and sabotage their mission.

Our main prayer must always be for a clearer vision of GOD's purpose and for a readiness to obey HIS will, no matter what the cost is to our pride and expectations. It would help us to pray slowly thinking of each word as we speak it.

LORD this thing I desire from YOU, can I handle it or will it be more of a burden than a blessing in my life? We are to covet earnestly GOD's best gifts but we must first seek GOD for knowledge and wisdom in what we desire to do.

Sometimes we pray for what in itself is good but in the end could be harmful to us spiritually. LORD give me delight in this world and forgetfulness of THEE. That is what we're really saying. If everything always went our way, we would forget to pray.

LORD send me no more chastening and discipline. Remove from me all burdens and crosses. If GOD does that, we will find ourselves falling away from HIM and in danger of everlasting destruction.

Our petitions before GOD must be found in HIS will. GOD's will is that we be saved and draw others to HIM. To be in the will of GOD requires us to bear crosses and have restraints placed upon us. The word of GOD tells us that, "For whom the LORD loveth HE chasteneth..." (Hebrews 12:6 KJV)

Before we petition GOD for anything we need to realistically search ourselves and ask, "Can I handle it?"

WRONG ANSWER TO A QUESTION

"...wilt thou be made whole?" (John 5:6 KJV)

This passage in the Bible refers to a man who had lain by the Pool of Bethesda for 38 years was waiting to be healed. The Bible says in verse 2 of that chapter that in Jerusalem near the Sheep Gate was a, pool called Bethesda (house of mercy). There lay a great multitude of sick people, blind, lame, and paralyzed. Jerusalem is a place of peace, but there are multitudes of people who are not peaceful. It's a place of blessing but so many people are not blessed. It is a place of healing and deliverance, but some people are lying around in bondage. The pool Bethesda meant a house of mercy, yet there are people there who have not received mercy. Many people face this situation today. We come to the House of GOD for forgiveness and deliverance but often leave still bound by our circumstances. Many are still living unfulfilled lives. We have been stuck in one place for a long time and are too weak to do anything about our pitiful condition. We go through life from one weakness to another. Most of the time focusing on the illness, disability or negative situation that seems to paralyze us from making progress. How long are we going to fear and worry about battles GOD has already won? Our struggle can be lust, dishonesty, gossip, alcoholism, drug addiction, low self-esteem or a chronic illness. It seems we get over one negative situation just to find a bigger one to take its place. Whatever our situation, we need the assurance that we are not alone. Many of us can relate to this impotent man. The bible says when JESUS saw the man lying there in his condition. HE asked the man do you want to be made whole? Sir, the invalid replied, "I have no one to help me into the pool when the water is stirred. While I am trying to get in, someone else goes down ahead of me." (John 5:7 NIV) Now this was a simple yes or no answer. Tell me why does the man have a need to defend the system for failing to provide him with healing.

He blames his failure on others. There was no one to help him into the pool. Others beat him to it. The man's answer was a wrong answer to the right question.

The man had made no cry for mercy when Jesus approached. When Jesus asked if he wanted to be made whole, the man showed no evidence of faith. CHRIST in HIS mercy pronounced the life-giving word on HIM. If JESUS waited for us to recognize an appreciation of HIM while we were sinners, none of us would have gotten saved. Why did JESUS ask that question? We all need to come to the realization that we need to be made whole. We need to change our lifestyle and our focus on what is most important to achieve. It is not until we recognize, admit, we need spiritual, physical, emotional healing and are willing to accept the healing that GOD is offering, that healing will occur. Was the paralytic saying he wanted to be healed or not? The man's answer suggests that he didn't know whom he was talking to, or didn't have enough faith to believe he would be healed. Our weaknesses and disabilities sometimes become an addiction. We become comfortable with discomfort and order things in our lives around it. Sometimes it becomes easier to see that we can't be healed, or that healing can't improve anything than it is to have faith and trust in GOD. The man answered with self-pity. His answer seemed to indicate that he had no hope, and no one loved him enough to be there for him. JESUS knows our deepest desire. HE cuts through our weeping and puts us to the test. Get up, take your problem and move on. When GOD brings about changes in our life, we cannot let doubters convince us that the changes are only coincidence. The right answer would be, JESUS looked on my situation told me to rise and take that situation and use it to walk on to a prosperous future.

It appears that when JESUS arrived at the Pool of Bethesda the man lying there did not cry out for HIS help or try to get HIS attention. It is the LORD's awareness that the man had been in his condition for 38 years.

41

Our LORD seeks him out. The man is stuck on one thing only, the miracle of being the first one into the angel stirred waters. He isn't conscience that the healer of healers is in his presence.

When asked if he wanted to be made whole, he made excuses. It isn't his fault, no one will help him, and someone always beats him into the pool. We all find ourselves at one time or another making excuses for adverse situations that we encounter. When that happens, we need to recognize the presence of the LORD and apply the word of GOD as the only medicine for which we can expect a cure. The word of GOD tells us that HIS stripes heal us.. It says to cast all your cares on HIM for HE cares for us. It instructs us to take our burdens to the LORD and leave them there. It tells us to, "seek first the kingdom of GOD and HIS righteousness and all these things will be added to you." (KJV) We are encouraged by the word. It lets us know that GOD wants us to be prosperous and in good health as our soul prospers. The condition of many of us today is that we are waiting for something spectacular to happen. Many are waiting for some great emotion to engulf us so we can be assured that we are in the presence of GOD. Many are waiting for a great awakening to occur, waiting for a great business opportunity to open up, waiting to get rich quick, waiting for that perfect companion to share our life with. Too many of us are not making any progress in life because we are waiting. All we need to do is step out on faith and trust GOD. What are we waiting for? Waiting will not solve the problem. The man had been waiting for 38 years, and when asked if he wanted to be healed, he was not prepared to give the correct answer.

We are guilty today of giving GOD a wrong answer to the right question. JESUS said, "Wilt thou be made whole?" What a strange question to ask the man who apparently needed to be healed? Obviously being made whole would be the one thing desired above all others by a man who had suffered for 38 years? Sometimes people suffering in a situation are not always willing to be relieved. Sometimes it's easier to be dependent, rely on the sympathy and attention of family, friends, the medical profession or government agencies.

The first steps in overcoming problems whether they are physical, emotional or spiritual is to admit we are in need and desire a change. We need to care enough about our problem or our situation to do something about it. It will require us to perform some action, effort, sacrifice or even suffering. Wilt thou be made whole? JESUS wants us to be willing to put ourselves in HIS hands? Are we prepared to surrender all to HIM? Are we ready for GOD to do for us what we are not able to do for ourselves? When JESUS asked, "Wilt thou be made whole?", The sufferer did not promptly answer, "yes LORD." He failed to realize that GOD could cure him by a word. He had more faith in getting into the water than he had in GOD. He was fixed on the man, not GOD. He was relying on what he knew about healing when his deliverer; the healer was standing right there.

"JESUS saith unto him, Rise, take up thy bed and walk.." (John 5:8 KJV) Rise was the command. We must recognize HIS authority and immediately respond to his orders. Believe on the LORD JESUS CHRIST and we will be made whole. We have to take action against the thing that is keeping us from being productive. Take up thy bed. It requires work on our part. We must take the situation that had previously kept us down and use what we have come through to encourage someone else. Everything GOD allows us to suffer and delivers us from is not just for us. We must tell others about it and become a blessing to someone else. We have to become a walking testimony for what GOD has done for us.

SERMONETTE 16

GOD'S FAITHFULNESS AND MERCY

"It is of the LORD's mercies that we are not consumed, because his compassions fail not. They are new every morning: great is thy faithfulness. The LORD is my portion, saith my soul; therefore will I hope HIM. (Lamentations 3:22-24 KJV)

No matter what we do, GOD cannot be unfaithful because HE cannot deny HIMSELF. "If we believe not, yet HE abideth faithful: HE cannot deny HIMSELF." (2 Timothy 2:13 KJV). GOD is steadfast and trustworthy. HE keeps HIS promises. GOD will Prosper us if we apply HIS word to our daily lives.

"Beloved, I wish above all things that thou mayest prosper and be in health, even as thy soul prospereth." (3 John 1:2 KJV)

Everyone gets tired of financial troubles, disorderly children, relationship problems, and repeated physical ailments. We need to examine our spiritual lives to see if we are following the word of GOD.

When we willingly sacrifice without distraction and confusion and spend time in prayer, praise, and worship, the blessing we receive from GOD will be a source of strength, restoration and success in all areas.

We have to learn how to let GOD take the NOT word out of our vocabulary, CANNOT, HAVE NOT, DO NOT, WILL NOT and COULD NOT; and replace it with, "I can do all things through CHRIST which strengtheneth me." (Philippians 4:13 KJV)

"But seek ye first the kingdom of GOD, and HIS righteousness; and all these things shall be added unto you." (Matthew 6:33 KJV)

Each of needs to prepare ourselves to receive all the spiritual and natural things that GOD has stored up for us. We can begin each day by applying the principles listed below.

1. Thank GOD and worship HIM the first thing in the morning and the last thing at night.

2. GOD's money, that HE has allowed us to receive, should be our first commitment in tithes, offering and spiritual obligations.

Put aside our personal feelings, doubts and fears. Watch GOD move on our behalf.

IT'S TIME TO RELEASE FOOLISH DESIRES

GOD often wants us to give up some plan of our own. There are times when GOD requires us to be more humble. There are times when we try to retain a job, position or relationship and GOD tells us it is not for our family or us. Those are the times when we defeat GOD's plan for us.

Honestly searching ourselves, we must admit that we all have done something foolish at some point in our life. I remember a verse from an old favorite song, "Everybody plays the fool sometimes. There is no exception to the rule."

We are all foolish when we allow sinful passions and thoughts to find a place to linger within us. It is a sin when we act in opposition to what we know to be right. "Therefore to him that knoweth to do good and doeth it not, to him it is sin." (James 4:17 KJV)

The greatest and most difficult problem the Church has had to face in all the ages is how to prevent men and women from playing the fool. Education, position, and affluence are not enough to deter individuals from being foolish.

We must sincerely pray to see the highest and most divine aspect of every situation we encounter. Too often we prefer a moment of self-satisfaction to divine retribution, and that is foolish.

"The fear of the LORD is the beginning of knowledge: but fools despise wisdom and instruction." (Proverbs 1:7 KJV)

"Even a fool, when he holdeth his peace, is counted wise: and he that shutteth his lips is esteemed a man of understanding." (Proverbs 17:28)

The more we seek GOD's wisdom, the easier it is to release foolish desires.

ANGER

Anger is often an emotional response to a perceived wrong or injustice. Anger manifests itself when a person misinterprets circumstances, makes a mistake in judgment or has an adverse reaction because they feel threatened or hurt.

Unjustified anger is sinful. It denies the power of GOD to care for our needs and hurts and can even completely take over our life. Anger can destroy communication. Anger can tear relationships and families apart. Uncontrolled anger can affect our health. We often try to justify anger instead of accepting responsibility for it. We are all confronted with situations that make us angry. The Bible acknowledges anger; it says, "Be ye angry, and sin not: let not the sun go down upon your wrath: Neither give place to the devil." (Ephesians 4:26 KJV).

Anger can make us act or react. A person who can control anger acts with reason and a willingness to resolve the situation that caused the anger. They know who they are, value their image and has self-control. They not only know this information, but they choose to act upon it reasonably. The wise person controls their temper rather than be controlled by it. Another person's actions should not dictate our reactions, but rather we should rely on the wisdom of the LORD.

Anger can cause us to react foolishly. Undisciplined anger can control our lives. "Be not hasty in thy spirit to be angry: for anger resteth in the bosom of fools. (Ecclesiastes 7:9 KJV) "Wherefore, my beloved brethren, let every man be swift to hear, slow to speak, slow to wrath:" (James 1:19 KJV) "He that is slow to anger is better than the mighty, and he that ruleth his spirit than he that taketh a city." (Proverbs 16:32 KJV)

BEWARE OF THE SPIRIT OF KORAH

In the Book of Numbers 16:1-50 KJV; Korah along with Dathan and Abiram, conspired with 250 tribal leaders to challenge the authority of Moses and the priestly leadership of Aaron.

Korah was a leader in the rebellion against Moses and Aaron when in actuality he was rebelling against GOD.

When the spirit of Korah is in operation the following characteristics are evident:

1. They want others to submit to them, but they are not willing to submit themselves to those in authority.
2. They do not like change; they want to restore the old order of things.
3. They are critical of and not accountable to those in authority.
4. They are inconsistent in attendance and often will not show up unless they are in charge.
5. They will not participate or quit when they do not get their way; they are not in control or are challenged.
6. They will try to get others to rise against leadership.
7. They will campaign for their ideas and recruit others to help them defy leadership.
8. They will often meet in their homes under the guise of social gatherings when they are planning a Korah move.

9. They sneak off to other ministries without informing or getting the approval of the Bishop or Pastor.
10. They grumble against their spiritual leaders and their methods; not fully understanding or accepting the vision that GOD has given leadership.
11. They have a spirit of defiance; for example, if everyone agrees to wear pink they will come in black.
12. They entice others to follow rebellious suggestions.
13. They object to being counseled or corrected when in error.

The Consequences of the spirit of Korah

1. Unless there is deep repentance, those with the spirit of Korah become troublesome and worthless to the body of CHRIST.
2. They incur the wrath of GOD.
3. The spirit of Korah if not stopped will destroy individuals, families, and churches.
4. The spiritual blessing and activity of the Holy Spirit will be missing from their lives.

If we cannot submit to GOD'S delegated leadership, we cannot submit to GOD. We must be careful of how we let people affect us. Korah inspired the leaders, who should have been the watchmen, to join him in his rebellion.

We must beware of the spirit of murmuring and complaining; it can stop people of GOD from entering heaven. We all need to seek GOD for a gift of discernment of spirits when connecting ourselves to people. Stop blaming the church and the Pastor for problems. The problem may be with whom we are connected. "Now I beseech you, brethren, mark them which cause divisions and offenses contrary to the doctrine which ye have learned; and avoid them." (Romans 16:17 KJV)

THE WAY

"And they journeyed from mount Hor by the way of the Red sea, to compass the land of Edom: and the soul of the people was much discouraged because of the way." (Numbers 21:4 KJV) The season was one of the hottest making it more difficult for marching. The Bible says the people were discouraged because of THE WAY.

It was not only the heat and ruggedness of the route to test them, but the fact that they were marching away from Canaan, the very place they were trying to reach. They didn't know how they would ever get there. We are often discouraged because of THE WAY of life by which it pleases GOD to lead us. It sometimes seems so hard, so weary, and so unbearable.

It is because of THE WAY that things appear to be going that causes us distress.

The end is promising and desirable but THE WAY to arrive there is through trials and tribulations, which can be weary. "And let us not be weary in well-doing; for in due season we shall reap, if we faint not." (Galatians 6:9 KJV)

Many of us are grievously discouraged because THE WAY that life seems to be taking us is so hard and painful. It demands so much self-denial, especially when we feel like we are not making progress.

The children of Israel complained against Moses but were complaining against GOD. When we are suffering, and we must sometimes expect to suffer, THE WAY to our destination often takes us through disappointment and discouragement.

We are in great danger when we murmur and complain against GOD because of how hard the struggle is in reaching our goals. When that begins to happen, we must realize that we are digressing from THE WAY.

When we lose heart, faith, and start to complain, that is when we fall prey to deadly sins which war against the soul and block THE WAY. We must always have on the whole armor of GOD.

'Finally, my brethren, be strong in the LORD, and in the power of his MIGHT. Put on the whole armor of GOD, that ye may be able to stand against the wiles of the devil." (Ephesians 6:10-11 KJV)

We must be prepared to fight the enemy when he tries to stop and block THE WAY to our spiritual and natural destiny.

We must stay encouraged so that we do not lose THE WAY.

Our prayer must be for GOD to continue to direct THE WAY that HE would have us to go to obtain our spiritual and natural prosperity.

CONTENTMENT

We don't receive contentment at birth. It is painfully and tediously developed by walking with the LORD. We learn to be content. We have to make an effort to rise above our circumstances.

It does not mean we don't have drive, ambition or try to make wrong things right in our life. It does not mean that we don't face tragedy, hurt, disappointment and frustration. We have to program in our minds what the word contentment means as we face the challenges we encounter in life.

We learn not to be content WITH circumstances but IN circumstances. Reaching contentment is not easy. We have to allow GOD to transform our minds. It means to make every effort to "Trust in the LORD with all thine heart, and lean not unto thine own understanding" (Proverbs 3:5 KJV)

It means satisfaction when we have real unmet needs. It means praying and surrendering our worries to GOD when we face overwhelming concerns. It means having the patience to let GOD work when we have pressures weighing us down. It means praising GOD and sharing happiness despite our heartache.

These resources are found only in the indwelling of the HOLY SPIRIT. GOD wants us to learn contentment. It is not a gift.

Acceptance does not mean stagnation. GOD wants us to take our dissatisfaction to HIM and see what HE will challenge us to do.

The scriptures work together. "Not that I speak in respect of want: for I have learned, in whatsoever state I am, therewith to be content." (Philippians 4:11 KJV)) "And we know that all things work together for good to them that love GOD, to them who are the called according to HIS purpose." (Romans 8:28 KJV)

Perhaps we have murmured rebelliously under our affliction, the means of revival is to be silent and pray.

GOD lays crosses on us to admit us into the fellowship of his suffering. The Bible says if we suffer with him we shall reign with him. When GOD allows us to suffer affliction, HE has a purpose for it. These afflictions are not everlasting. GOD will not always reprimand neither keep HIS anger forever. Many times it is only a test to bring an anointing in our life.

The stresses that are removable and that we can reduce ourselves, we should endeavor to remove. Those which we cannot remove, we need to bear as much as we can.

In every situation in life, there are comforts. Find them and enjoy them.

When we indulge a discontented temper it will turn the displeasure of GOD against us. In order to correct these discontentments consider how little we deserve and how much we enjoy.

We can have contentment as we continuously depend on the LORD. We can have contentment when we allow GOD to move negativity out of our minds. We can have contentment knowing with certainty that GOD supports us as we pursue HIS goals for our life.

Contentment and satisfaction are rare and precious Christian gifts. Real satisfaction is a quiet restfulness in the midst of all kinds of changing events.

Contentment is rare and difficult to obtain because we depend too much on this world and its fortunes. The most important factor regarding our happiness is not what things we possess, but do we have contentment after obtaining the things we acquire..

Wealthy and Prosperous people are many times discontented, people. Obtaining wealth often brings a thirst for more wealth. Many wealthy criminals are in jail today because they resorted to all kinds of underhanded means to get more wealth.

SERMONETTE 22

GOD IS ALWAYS IN CHARGE

Job first appears before us as a man, not an angel, frail as a man, feeble, and fallible. No one is perfect; Job was not faultless, but he was not a hypocrite. His righteousness of conduct on the outside began with righteousness on the inside.

The Bible places tremendous stress on integrity. Job was an honest man, true to his word, fair in his dealings, trustworthy and honorable. GOD delights in the one that fears HIM.

The spiritual man/woman not only shuns evil, but he/she hates it. Though sometimes we may weakly succumb to what may be considered wrong, if we are serving GOD, we detest it. Job had a habit of divine worship; he prayed continuously. Job rose up early in the morning. Family worship should be done before the day starts. He interceded for his children, and he did so continually. GOD knew Job could handle whatever trial he would face and come out victorious. GOD does not cause things to happen to turn us away from HIM. GOD will step back and allow some things to happen to get our attention. When we come through our temporary suffering period and look back, we will find out that what we went through was necessary to make us more powerful in GOD's purpose for us. We can confuse the enemy when we take yesterday's negative experience and praise GOD for it. We have to know this, whatever we are going through, we are going to come out. If GOD has orchestrated our struggle, we are not coming out empty. "The lot is cast into the lap, but the decision is wholly of the LORD (even the events that seem accidental are really ordered by HIM." (Proverbs 16:33 AMP)

Job identified GOD as the one ultimately responsible for all his misery. He didn't blame satan from whose direct hand he received the suffering he was experiencing. "Then satan answered the LORD, Does Job [reverently] fear GOD for nothing? Have YOU not put a hedge about him and his house and all that he has, on every side? YOU have conferred prosperity and happiness upon him in the work of his hands, and his possessions have increased in the land. But put forth YOUR hand now and touch all that he has, and he will curse YOU to YOUR face. And the LORD said to satan (the adversary and the accuser), Behold, all that he has is in your power, only upon the man himself put not forth your hand. So Satan went forth from the presence of the LORD." (Job 1:9-12 AMP)

GOD permits HIS children to endure suffering. With all that he was enduring Job did not lose his greatest hope. Although his powers are impressive and extensive, satan can only act with GOD's permission. Satan limited by GOD and will be defeated. He roams the earth like a spy seeking whom he may devour. However, a believer need not fear satan; there is nothing satan can do that falls outside of GOD's dominion. GOD had a purpose in limiting satan's power.

GOD's intention in allowing testing is to prove the strength of character. Satan's goal is to demonstrate a lack of character. The LORD promises that believers will not be tempted beyond what they can endure and HE will make a way of escape so that we can bear whatever it is. "There hath no temptation taken you but such as is common to man: but GOD is faithful, who will not suffer you to be tempted above that ye are able; but will with the temptation also make a way to escape, that ye may be able to bear it. (1 Corinthians 10:13 KJV)

The lot is cast into the lap, but the decision is wholly of the LORD even the events that seem accidental are really ordered by Him" (Proverbs 16:33 AMP)

NEGLECT CAN BE DANGEROUS

"Ye have sown much, and bring in little; ye eat, but ye have not enough; ye drink, but ye are not filled with drink; ye clothe you, but there is none warm, and he that earneth wages earneth wages to put it into a bag with holes." (Haggai 1:6 KJV)

The Jews had been in captivity for many years in Babylon.

During that time they had wept, mourned and prayed that GOD would deliver them from their exile.

The scripture text takes place about 16 years after Cyrus decreed that the Jews could return to Jerusalem from the exile.

Haggai was a prophet who ministered to the people who returned from Babylon. The people had abandoned the repair of the temple and gave their attention to building their homes. They probably felt that there was plenty of time to build the sanctuary. They took care of their personal needs first. Their attitude displeased GOD and the prophet. Haggai watched as they worked ceaselessly to earn money and said. "You are putting your money into a bag filled with holes and working hard and getting nowhere!'"

The scripture does not indicate that the people said they would not build the temple, just not yet. How often have I heard people say? "I am coming to church, just not yet. I have to get myself together." People do not say they will never repent and become a Christian, just not yet. "I have to fix some things in my life first." I hear saints of GOD saying, "I am going to do more in the house of GOD, just not yet. I'm too busy on my job, in school, and I have too many family obligations." So the purpose we were sent into the world to do, is not done. The Jews returning from captivity neglected the building of GOD's house. They needed the time and money for personal commitments. If we want to have the comfort and continuance of temporal enjoyments, we must have the favor of GOD.

Unnecessary trouble and disappointment have allowed holes to form in our spirit and GOD's goodness; mercy and prosperity just pour right out. If we take time and analyze why we are progressing so slowly, we will discover that it is because the work we have to do for GOD and our souls is left undone, or partially done. We desire worldly things more than the things of CHRIST. Saints of GOD tell me that they cannot afford to give to spiritual events but, often lavish ten times as much in needless expenses on their houses and themselves. We all must be concerned about self-examination and look inside our hearts concerning our spiritual state. We all have to answer for our sins. If any of us has a a ministry that has been neglected, that is no reason why it should still be so. Thus saith the LORD of hosts, "consider your Ways." (Haggai 1:7 KJV) Whatever GOD will take pleasure in when it is done; we ought to take pleasure in doing it. GOD wants to see passion in our worship and service to H I M.

The poverty the People returning from Babylon tried to prevent by not building the temple, GOD allowed them to experience for not building it. Many good works have been intended but not done because men felt the time was not right. Thus too many believers neglect opportunities of usefulness, and sinners delay coming to CHRIST, till it's often too late. If we want to have the comfort and continuance of our temporary enjoyments here on Earth, we must have the favor of GOD. How often have I watched saints of GOD struggle year after year in the same situation?

Haggai reminded the people in chapter 2:14 KJV that refusing to support the temple building, every work of their hands was considered unclean. Haggai told them that if they would make a commitment and respond to GOD's plans for their lives that he would bless them from that day! I wonder how many of us are walking around with holes in our pockets. Do we love GOD enough to take time out of each day to pray and read HIS WORD, or are we going to continue putting our desires first into pockets with holes?

The Jews had misplaced their priorities. They were making excuses. Too many saints of GOD are doing the same thing today.

1. GOD wants us to take care of our families, doesn't HE? 2. The job is too big. We'll never finish it. 3. It's not our responsibility, we didn't cause this to happen, why should we have to fix it. 4. We don't have to rush it will get done. 5. We need to pray for more direction. 6. We want to build the temple, but we are overwhelmed with our other obligations. 7. It's not the right time. 8. GOD knows it's in our hearts to build the temple, but we are too busy!!! They were looking for a better time and an easier time. But the result was the same. They were neglectful. It's always easy to make excuses when we don't want to obey GOD.

When we find ourselves facing the same struggles year after year, and we have not shown any signs of natural or spiritual prosperity than we need to consider our ways. We become a bad representative for GOD.

Three things can keep holes in our pockets.

1. Failure to pay tithes.
2. Disobedience to leadership.
3. Lack of commitment to the will of GOD.

"I will praise and give thanks to YOU with uprightness of heart when I learn [by sanctified experiences] YOUR righteous judgments [YOUR decisions against and punishments for particular lines of thought and conduct]." (Psalm 119:7 AMP) "With my whole heart have I sought YOU, inquiring for and of YOU and yearning for YOU; Oh, let me not wander or step aside [either in ignorance or willfully] from YOUR commandments. [II Chronicles 15:15.]" (Psalm 119:10 AMP)

We often fix our expectations upon an abundant harvest, but we reap less than what we have sown because when we have stored up our profits, GOD blew on it.

He blew it away, and that's why we never seem to have enough. We are never satisfied with what we have. We are always looking for more. The ordinary occupations of life have more attraction for us than the duties of serving GOD.

We are more devoted to the earthly and material pursuits of life. We have difficulty in perceiving that it is not the time to seek our own ordinary desires and leave GOD out of the picture.

The time to build GOD'S house has come. I'm not just talking about a structural building, but the physical house of our souls. We are following our own interests rather than glorifying GOD.

We let the work that has only GOD'S glory as its motive drop and apply ourselves to that which feeds and nurtures our own material goals.

Some professing Christians cannot see beyond self. Some think that a man's chief duty upon earth is to do the best he can for himself. It should be to do the best we can for GOD.

Doing what we think is right in our own minds often leads to spiritual blindness, dissatisfaction and putting our money in pockets which have holes in them.

The time to seal the holes in our spiritual and natural pockets is now because Neglect Can Be Dangerous.

COME OUT OF HIDING

"Can any hide himself in secret places that I shall not see him? saith the LORD. Do not I fill heaven and earth? saith the LORD." (Jeremiah 23:24 KJV)

I laugh when I play hide and seek with my two-year-old granddaughter, Jammy. She thinks she is hiding, but I can plainly see her. So to give her a chance to play the game I pretend to look for her. Eventually, I say, "Oh, I found you!"

Many times we play that game with GOD, trying to hide our sins when they are clearly in HIS sight.

People build bomb shelters today to protect and hide them in the event of nuclear war. They would rather hide in a hole than to be found by GOD, seek salvation and go to heaven.

We can't hide from GOD, but we can hide in GOD. HE clearly sees everything we do and hears everything we say. If we hide in GOD, HE will protect us, lead us and guide us. HE will shield us from all hurt harm and danger.

Jonah tried to hide from GOD when he was sent to warn the city of Nineveh about their wickedness and impending destruction. (Jonah 1:3 KJV)

GOD knew where Jonah was; HE knew which ship he would be on, HE knew where to send the storm, and HE knew where to position the whale to swallow Jonah. When Jonah realized he could no longer hide he prayed. GOD delivered him and in obedience, he followed GODs instructions.

"Whither shall I go from thy spirit? or whither shall I flee from thy presence? If I ascend up into heaven, thou art there: if I make my bed in hell, behold, thou art there. If I take the wings of the morning, and dwell in the uttermost parts of the sea; Even there shall thy hand lead me, and thy right hand shall hold me. If I say, Surely the darkness shall cover me; even the night shall be light about me." (Psalm 139:7-12 KJV)

"But if ye will not do so, behold, ye have sinned against the LORD: and be sure your sin will find you out." (Numbers 32:23 KJV)

Today GOD wants someone to come out of hiding and cry out; I am a sinner LORD save me. GOD has HIS eye on you. GOD sees you. HE held back the death angels hand to give you a chance to come out of hiding from your sins and experience the spiritual high you can only get by knowing GOD intimately.

GOOD PARENTING SKILLS

In Matthew 20:20 KJV we find Salome, the mother of James and John, the sons of Zebedee, making a request to JESUS for her sons. Salome was one of the LORD's most faithful followers. She was even present at the cross. She prayed, not for herself, but with a mother's love for her sons that they might sit one on the LORD's right hand, the other on the left in the HIS Kingdom

Was she selfish and inconsiderate or ambitious, desiring the best for her sons? Mother's should dream of a great future for her children. It's a poor mother who does not look into her child's face and desire for him/her a high position, fame, financial gain and happiness.

A realistic mother, however, is aware that her child must be worthy of success and earn it. We can't just wish or ask for success, and it automatically happens. We all must meet certain conditions for success to occur. We must prepare not only our children but also ourselves academically, physically, mentally and socially for success to happen. The best role models for successful children are parents that are striving no matter what their social or financial status, to be the best at the things they try to accomplish in life.

We often don't know the consequences, disappointments or struggles that we may have to endure when we seek great things for our children or ourselves. The best prayer is not my will but THINE oh LORD be done. Salome did not think of the dangers, suffering, and temptations, which lie in making such a request. She wanted her sons to share the final victory, not conscious of the fact that they must share the conflict and suffering that would go before.

Many desire the blessings they see others possess without having to pay the dues they paid. They have no idea of what some of us had to endure to get where we are today.

An example of a parent who knew how to beseech GOD correctly on behalf of his children was Job. "And it was so, when the days of their feasting were gone about, that Job sent and sanctified them, and rose up early in the morning, and offered burnt-offerings according to the number of them all: for Job said, It may be that my sons have sinned, and cursed GOD in their hearts. Thus did Job continually." (Job 1:5 KJV)

Good parenting requires us to be good role models in our spiritual and natural lives. The Bible admonishes us to train our children. "Train up a child in the way he should go: and when he is old, he will not depart from it." (Proverbs 22:6 KJV)

PRAYER # 1

LORD, help me to remember YOUR WORD this morning, we know that all things work together for good to those who love YOU, to those who are the called according to YOUR purpose. Help me to hear YOU and pay attention to YOUR WORD always. Help me to meditate on YOUR WORD day and night so that I might not sin against you. Teach me to hear YOUR WORD and obey it.

LORD order my steps in your WORD, lead me and guide me every day. Dear GOD let your WORD be a lamp to my feet and light to my path. Make my way plain before me. Help me to agree with YOUR WORD and disagree with any thoughts desires or circumstances that are contrary to YOUR WORD.

LORD open my understanding and let me see the answers to my questions are in YOUR WORD. Give me wisdom and the assurance to believe that every WORD of GOD is true, that it will be a shield of protection for me if I put my trust in YOU.

LORD help me to put my faith and trust in YOU. I believe because of YOUR love for me; YOU will deliver me from every form of evil that comes my way. No one can show me greater love. YOU gave YOURSELF for me on Calvary. LORD, it is my desire to delight myself in YOU. Help me to make worshipping and pleasing YOU my priority. I need YOUR help as I strive to commit my ways unto YOU. GOD, I love YOU because YOU first loved me.

LORD, I put my trust in YOUR love. I believe that YOU do all things right because of YOUR love for me. I believe that YOU intend to work all things together for my good because I love YOU. Please stretch my faith. Remind me of YOUR love. Sometimes through the circumstances and trials of life, I forget how much YOU care for me. I get caught up in the burdens of my life forgetting that YOU will not put more on me than I can bare. Help me to meditate on all the ways YOU have loved me. I need to focus on all the great things YOU have already done for me, and I do not deserve. Help me to put aside my complaining spirit and replace it with an attitude of gratitude.

LORD, I pray for open eyes to see YOUR love working all around me. Thank you, LORD, for all YOU have done for me. Amen.

LET THAT DISOBEDIENT SPIRIT GO

Evil spirits are released when we are disobedient. Eve would not have been deceived (Genesis 3:13 KJV) if she had not disobeyed GOD. Her disobedience caused the spirit of fear to be displayed.

The spirit of disobedience can lead to a spirit of jealousy which leads to anger, in Genesis 4:5 Cane's anger resulted in murder.

If we find jealousy springing up within us, we need to check ourselves, go to GOD and seek a cleansing. With a new attitude, we can make adjustments to our behavior. We will no longer see our brother or sister as our enemy.

When we know we are wrong, we hide from the Pastor and other church members. We avoid eye contact, but we can't hide from GOD. Adam and Eve couldn't hide; Cane Couldn't hide his crime, and we can't hide any of our actions from GOD.

A curse or punishment will follow disobedience while blessings follow obedience.

The reason why change is not evident in our lives is that when we go to the altar to receive our healing; we want GOD to fix the symptoms at the altar before repenting for our sin.

We get depressed when change doesn't take place when we want it to. We ask GOD why HE does not hear us.

A reason why GOD can't hear us is the spirit of iniquity in our heart; the Bible says "If I regard iniquity in my heart, the Lord will not hear me." (Psalms 66:18 KJV)

To receive any kind of healing we are required to be obedient to GOD. We may need healing in our finances but refuse to bring our first fruits to GOD in our tithes and offering. (Malachi 3:9-10 KJV)

Being obedient to GOD means we must give up doing things our way and totally submit to the will of GOD.

We give the enemy authority over our lives when we are disobedient. We were created to worship GOD; we give the devil a foothold in our lives when we don't give GOD all the honor, glory and praise that HE is due.

To be free from the disobedient spirit, we need to put on the whole armor of GOD, (Ephesians 6:11-18 KJV), and use our weapons of warfare to fight the enemy and give GOD praise for deliverance.

DO IT FOR YOURSELF

And Joshua answered them, if thou be a great people, then get thee up to the wood country, and cut down for thyself there in the land of the Perizzites and the giants, if mount Ephraim be too narrow for thee" (Joshua 17:15. KJV)

For Joshua to give Ephraim what he wants would only increase their laziness. To let Ephraim get what he wants by his power would increase their courage discipline and self-respect.

We learn best when we learn ourselves. We profit more by our experience. Joshua's true kindness was to encourage the people of Ephraim to conquer the enemy for themselves. We must remember that greatness is not given to us to abuse and make others our servants but as a power to be of service to others. I have given some of our ministers a job to do and they intern designated someone else to do it. Who gets that reward? To keep them humble and prepared for a real anointing from GOD, I have assigned all ministers to clean the bathrooms, and pick up paper outside. I do it all the time. But there are those who think this task is beneath them.

And JESUS called them to him and said to them, "you know that those who are considered rulers of the gentiles lord it over them, and their great ones exercise authority over them. but it shall not be so among you. But whoever would be great among you must be your servant, and whoever would be first among you must be slave of all. For even the son of man came not to be served but to serve, and to give his life as a ransom for many." (Mark 10:42-45 ESV)

He is greatest who is servant of all, and he is chief who ministers to all. Not just when we have a crowd, and put on a performance but the ministers are assigned to minister in the children's nursery. We must use our greatness and power for the good of others.

We do not know the extent of our advantages, and what we can accomplish until we try them.

Joshua helped the people of Ephraim to see that if they cleared their forest, and so recovered the wasteland, their lot would thereby double.

If we make good use of the opportunities for service, we now possess these will develop new and better opportunities.

The more advantages we claim, the more obligations we will have. It is unworthy to look to personal favor to secure us a position in the world not earned by merit or work.

GOD will give us our inheritance, but we must conquer and cultivate it. HE helps us when we do our best, but never to justify our laziness.

"For we wrestle not against flesh and blood, but against principalities, against powers, against the rulers of the darkness of this world, against spiritual wickedness in high places. Wherefore take unto you the whole armour of God, that ye may be able to withstand in the evil day, and having done all, to stand. Stand therefore, having your loins girt about with truth..." (Ephesians 6:12-14 KJV)

No one is born a Christian. We all have struggles and trials. To be victorious and an overcomer, we must do it for ourselves.

EVERYBODY BECOMES SOMETHING

Everybody and everything in the world becomes.

We are becoming something from our birth to our death. We are changing continually and becoming something different from what we were a minute ago.

We can become stronger or weaker, better or worse, wiser or more foolish. Whatever our flaws, whatever our weaknesses, we can be successful with GOD and accomplish what HE has purposed for us to do.

Some of us need to be detoxed; get the poison of failure, rejection, disappointment and abuse out of our system.

We need to speak to the situations in our lives and tell them "I'm coming out of this situation, and I am not coming out empty. I am going to get whatever qualifications I need to be successful. I am going to master what is trying to hold me back from my destiny."

The qualification we need is faith, a positive outlook, determination, and a renewed mind. We have to tell ourselves, "I will accomplish my goals; I can do all things through CHRIST who strengthens me."

GOD wipes out the reproaches of our past and develops from our past experiences that will give us a rich and glorious future.

Everybody becomes something, it is up to us to believe GOD for what HE has purposed for us to be.

GOD IS DOING A NEW THING

Isaiah 43-18-19 KJV reads, "Remember ye not the former things, neither consider the things of old. Behold, I will do a new thing; now it shall spring forth; shall ye not know it? I will even make a way in the wilderness, and rivers in the desert."

Paul writes in Philippians 3:13-14 KJV, "Brethren, I count not myself to have apprehended: but this one thing I do, forgetting those things which are behind, and reaching forth unto those things which are before, I press toward the mark for the prize of the high calling of GOD in CHRIST JESUS."

The central theme of Isaiah 40-66 is a message of comfort and hope. Isaiah addressed GOD'S people in Judah; he pronounced judgments on the inhabitants of Judah not because they lacked religious activity but because they failed in moral and ethical living.

Isaiah also had a message of future comforts and hope for the exiles in Babylon. In chapter 43, Isaiah concentrates on comforting and encouraging the Israelites. He sets forth the revelation from GOD concerning the restoration of Israel. This recovery could only come about with a new covenant; an agreement between GOD and Israel had to be written in their hearts

Israel's condition was miserable because their sins were great. Israel had put aside her love for GOD and went seeking after the pleasures of life.

We often allow personal desires to come before our service to GOD. A lover, money, ambition, luxury, family or career all affect how we worship and praise GOD.

Before GOD can do new things with us, HE has to remove some old things that are hindering our progress. We can easily get distracted from our spiritual pursuits.

On our last retreat, we declared that we were blessed and in new growth. We vowed to forget the misfortunes of our past and press forward seeking new things from GOD. We must keep what we learned in our hearts and minds so that GOD can do new things in us.

FAITH AND SALVATION

Faith and salvation go hand and hand together. "Without faith, it is impossible to please GOD." (Hebrews 11:6 KJV)

We all have a measure of faith. "For I say, through the grace given unto me, to every man that is among you, not to think of himself more highly than he ought to think; but to think soberly, according as GOD hath dealt with every man the measure of faith." (Romans 12:3 KJV)

Everyone doesn't have the same amount, of faith and it may be in different areas, but we all have some faith.

Faith brings us into contact with GOD. It's the link that unites and binds us to Jesus. Faith is the hand stretched out to receive the gifts that GOD bestows. Faith will keep us walking in the way of salvation. Salvation is our deliverance from the sinful ways of the world. We need faith to keep our salvation healthy and active.

We build out faith through love and trust. Love stays near and delights in the presence of the one that is loved. When we love the LORD with all our hearts, mind, and soul, we follow HIM, stay close to H{M, and hold onto HIM. We don't want to hear any other voice but HIS. We don't listen to any other words but GOD'S words. GOD is not a GOD of I can't, but I can do all things through CHRIST who strengthens me. (Philippians 4:13 KJV)

Faith knows no weapon formed against me shall prosper.

(Isaiah 54:17) Faith is delighting myself in the LORD knowing HE will give me the desires of my heart. (Psalms 37:4 KJV)

Faith knows that whatsoever things I desire when I pray, when I have a meaningful, loving, empowering, intimate relationship with GOD, I just have to believe, and I shall receive.

Faith in GOD is the glue that holds our salvation together.

WHAT'S LOVE GOT TO DO WITH IT?

"If I can speak in the tongues of men and even angels, but have not love, that reasoning, intentional, spiritual devotion such as is inspired by GOD's love for and in us, I am only a noisy gong or a clanging cymbal." (1st Corinthians 13: AMP)

If we have sufficient faith that we can move mountains but have not GOD'S love in us, we are nothing.

Even if we give out all that we have to the poor and provide food and clothes but have not GOD'S love in us, we gain nothing. Love doesn't pick and choose who to like or dislike. Love doesn't show favoritism. Love is generous and giving. Love goes out of the way for others,

We need to understand that even though we can sing like a famous singer or preach like the greatest television evangelist if the love of GOD is not evident in us, we are wasting our time spiritually. If we want to minister to people we have to love GOD first, ourselves second and the people. When GOD resides in us, love is a first, not a second-hand emotion.

Love endures long is patient and kind. Love never envies or is jealous; it is not conceited, rude or acts unmannerly. It does not insist on having its way and is not self-seeking, touchy, fretful or resentful. Love tolerates the misunderstandings and harshness it faces.

Loves bear up under any and everything that comes up; it endures everything. Love can take down even when it feels wronged. When we have GOD'S love we don't pick and choose who to love; true love is shown to everyone.

We fool ourselves when we try to minister to others after we've been mean and indifferent. Love is caring and nurturing and feels the need in others.

Love doesn't try to retaliate when hurt. Love doesn't hold grudges. Love forgets the wrongs that it has endured. Love is forgiving.

If we want to prosper spiritually and be in GOD's favor, we need to have and show love.

What's love got to do with it? EVERYTHING!

STOP WASTING TIME

How many of you are wasting time waiting for a major crisis to come into your life before you look to GOD and give HIM yourself to HIM?

Why does GOD have to bring a tragedy or major illness into some of our lives before we acknowledge and serve HIM?

Until CHRIST has taken complete possession our lives, and the poison of sin is removed by HIS grace, there can be no real progress in our life. There is no real peace, only a drifting back and forth in the wilderness of drugs, alcohol, casual sex and unfulfilled relationships.

After CHRIST comes into our life, no matter how difficult the road or how many enemies we encounter we continue to move forward in the purpose GOD has chosen for us.

When we honestly look to GOD to help us, all things become new; there will be a success and happiness that had been lacking before. Our spirit and conduct will be altogether different. Our desires will be to please GOD and not self. Paul speaks of those who are justified by faith and have peace with through our LORD JESUS CHRIST. When CHRIST becomes apart of our lives we embark upon a course of satisfaction, peace and triumph.

GOD is waiting to give us clear directions in life. We don't have to repeat the same mistakes over and over again.

When CHRIST controls our life we are viewed as peculiar people. We have peace in situations that cause others who do not know the LORD to become mentally ill or commit suicide. With GOD in our life, we realize that when we reach our extremity, it is GOD'S opportunity to come in and take over and give us that peace and inner joy that surpasses all understanding.

Living a GODLY life will allow us to see a light in the darkness and that light is JESUS. HE leads us, guides us, protects us, carries us, picks us up when we fall, and encourages us to hold on and keep on moving forward.

Stop wasting time seeking temporary and frustrating solutions in life when JESUS is the answer to all our problems.

SERMONETTE 33

TONGUE OF A SLANDERER

The tongue of a slanderer is a devouring fire which tarnishes whatever it touches; wherever it passes it leaves only destruction and ruin.

Slanderers frequently attack the worthiest persons.

We must avoid false accusations and especially bringing charges against the innocent.

We must be aware of others inventing an untrue story, or giving any support to it when others have invented it.

We support a lie simply by listening to it.

To those of us who have been lied on or scandalized; we can overcome it by persisting in doing good and by prayer to GOD that HE would cure the minds and hearts of those who injure us with their lies and gossip.

When someone comes to us with a negative report about our brother or sister, we need to ask them, "Have you ever noticed the good things that the individual has done?

"Titus 2:8 KJV, emphasizes the need for sound speech and to avoid uncalled for criticism.

How can the Church be holy if its members are not holy?

Matthew 25:31-46 KJV, tells us that we will be judged by how we have treated one another.

We are condemned when people wonder if we are a Christian because of the way we treat and speak to others. We can't get so angry and upset that we forget to bridle our tongues.

We need to think about what we are saying or doing before we open our mouths and make others question our Christianity.

The book of James 3:8 KJV, lets us know how difficult it is to control the tongue. Before praying for GOD to bless us and change unwanted things in our lives, we need to fast and pray that GOD will control how we speak to and about other people.

We cannot use the excuse that I spoke to and treated him/her the way they talked to or treated me.

The Bible tells us in Matthew 5:16 KJV to, "Let your light so shine before men, that they may see your good works, and glorify your Father which is in heaven."

When troubles come we need to learn how to stretch out on GOD.

When Job heard all the distressing things that had come upon him, the Bible said he fell to the ground and worshiped.

On top of losing his wealth, children and health, Job had to endure the misconceptions and uncomforting ramblings of his friends.

satan can rise up in any of us if we give him space. I noticed that satan disappeared when Job's three friends entered the story; satan is not judged at the end of the story, but the three friends are.

When we are going through a test of slander, we need to get away from people. Seek some alone time with GOD, hear only His voice and stop asking GOD why instead ask him WHAT?

"What would you have me to learn? WHAT purpose or plan would you have for me to fulfill as a result of the slander I have endured.?"

satan can try to use the tongue of the slanderer to destroy us if we allow it to.

CAN I BE A LEADER?

We achieve success only by the Grace of GOD Paul accomplished great things, but he consistently gave all the credit to GOD.

A good leader must remain determined to witness positively for Christ no matter what the cost?

Paul endured some unthinkable hardships; beatings, shipwrecked and prison, but still he remained committed to doing the will of GOD.

No matter what came his way, he was steadfast in sharing the message of JESUS CHRIST. He kept his heart right and his attitude in check.

Paul was chosen by GOD to take the message of JESUS CHRIST to all people, and GOD gave him everything he needed to accomplish his purpose.

It is my firm belief that where GOD guides HE provides.

There is a soul winner crown for those who passionately tell others about GOD. We should all be striving to receive it.

Some of you have been in the Grace Cathedral Ministry for years but have not born any fruit by bringing a soul to the Ministry.

We often sing the song that we should live a life that is pleasing to our King but in actuality, we don't practice what we sing.

When leading others, it is important to demonstrate how the message of CHRIST has empowered us. Others should recognize that there is something different about us.

Some of us have an amazing conversion story, and we need to feel comfortable sharing that story with others. There is no situation that we have experienced that GOD can't use for HIS glory in a mighty way.

It can be hard for leaders to guide people down the right path without sounding pushy or judgmental. As an effective leader, our ambition is to achieve a relationship with GOD above all else.

JESUS doesn't require leaders to be perfect, but HE demands that we put our eternal goals first and leading others to salvation our priority.

Helping others recognize themselves as GOD sees them is just part of being a leader. We must teach others to see themselves according to GOD'S Word.

We must, as leaders, live each day to bring others into GOD'S eternal kingdom.

Hebrews 13:17 KJV says, "Obey them that have the rule over you, and submit yourselves: for they watch for your souls, as they that must give account, that they may do it with joy, and not with grief: for that is unprofitable for you."

As people of GOD, we must not get upset when leadership tries to instruct and correct us because that is their solemn responsibility to GOD. There are certain qualities that good leaders exhibit.

Good leaders need the call and gifting of GOD. GOD wants leaders to achieve goals that honor HIM.

GOD is our personal Guide and Teacher in this life. When GOD puts a call on our life, we must follow HIS specific instructions on how to proceed. In the 13th chapter of Numbers, GOD told Moses to send leaders to search the land of Canaan, not the regular people. Moses sent leaders so they could strategize, work together with GOD to gain the promise.

There are leaders, and there are managers, and we need to know the difference in their roles if we want to accomplish our goals successfully.

LEADERS VS. MANAGERS

- Leader designs   Manager develops the design
- Leader is the entrepreneur   Manager is the doer,
- Leader takes the risks   Manager seeks stability

The Manager complements the leader. We need both to achieve group tasks. Leaders need to study people's capabilities. When there is more than one leader type in the church and the world conflict will arise. So Moses sent leaders to scout out the land, but all the leaders didn't have the spiritual insight to excel. I believe there were too many negative leaders that went. Have you ever heard the saying too many cooks spoil the broth? Joshua learned from that experience. He only sent out two spies. "Joshua, son of Nun, sent two men secretly from Shittim as scouts, saying, Go, view the land, especially Jericho. And they went and came to the house of a harlot named Rahab and lodged there." (Joshua 2:1 AMP)

There's work to be done for GOD souls to be saved and that calls for tough, strong leadership that won't give up the fight. Someone who will make people man up, woman up.

FIVE THINGS THAT A STRONG LEADER NEEDS

1. You develop a strong back so you can tolerate being overlooked, under appreciated, misused and abused but never guit.
2. You become a goose, (a goose is greasy) let things slide off you; the criticism, negative and discouraging voices from people, the lack of cooperation but never quit.

3. Don't stop doing anything in ministry unless GOD has clearly shown you a higher calling and you are passionately working on it.

4. Endure some things and overcome some things, suffer some things, Some of us had to experience hurt, rejection, sexual abuse, physical abuse, psychological and emotional abuse, drug addiction, prison, death of a loved one, homelessness, unemployment, bad credit, bad marriage, illness, loneliness, homosexuality, and we survived. That's the real training. We can't help anyone if we haven't been through or overcome anything.

5. Give 100% of your efforts in becoming effective. If your calling is preaching or teaching study, study, study, pray, pray, pray, and fast. If your calling is music, dance, acting fast, pray, practice, practice, practice and practice some more.

GOD allowed the leaders to see exactly what they were going into before they actually went into it. They had one of two choices to make.

1. Either let fear or panic set in, and lose their chance to enter into the Promised Land or

2. Have the same strong faith and belief in GOD that Joshua and Caleb had and be willing to fight for what they wanted. Joshua and Caleb took their strong faith and belief in GOD entered the Promised Land, and achieved total victory in GOD.

If we can be strong, determined and believe GOD has chosen us, we can become great leaders.

IT'S NOT ENOUGH TO MAKE ME QUIT

"AND THE Lord said to Moses, Send men to explore and scout out [for yourselves] the land of Canaan, which I give to the Israelites. From each tribe of their fathers, you shall send a man, everyone a leader or head among them." (NUMBERS 13:1-2 AMP) There were twelve leaders one from each tribe. Of the tribe of Judah, Caleb and the tribe of Ephraim, Hoshea [that is, Joshua] son of Nun.

Their assignment was to see the land and whether the people there were strong or weak, few or many. They were to see if the land was good or bad and whether the cities were camps or strongholds. They were told to be of good courage and bring back some of the fruit of the land. The men returned from scouting out the land after 40 days. What they reported to Moses was, "we came to the land to which you sent us; surely it flows with milk and honey. "But the people who dwell there are strong, and the cities are fortified and large; we saw the sons of Anak, who come from the giants, and we were in our own sight as grasshoppers, and so we were in their sight." (Numbers 13:28 AMP)

Some of us are too quick to put ourselves down and walk away from what looks like a giant struggle we may not be able to overcome. Job situations, family struggles, educational pursuits, career goals, loneliness and health issues can become overwhelming. They become giants that we feel we cannot concur. We feel incompetent and too weak to address situations that seem problematic, so we let the blessing GOD has for us go and just settle and most walk away. We see the lumberyard, but we have to cut down some trees to get to it so we just settle for sticks. The Israelites lost the chance to enter the promised land because of fear and lack of faith in GOD.

GOD had miraculously delivered them from Egypt, separated the Red Sea and allowed them to cross it on dry ground with one of the greatest displays of HIS supernatural power that the world has ever seen. GOD never places us in a position to do a hard thing before HE allows us to see HIM deliver us from a prior hard thing. The Levites sing a song that says, "don't give up on GOD and HE won't give up on you. HE's Able.

This story should consistently remind us to walk in the spirit, not in the flesh! To trust GOD and believe in HIS promises. We need the passion for what we do in life. We need the determination to accomplish what we want to achieve. The Day Care was struggling. We lost our accreditation, clients, finances, and we couldn't pay all our bills. People said, "close it, rent it out, it's destroying your health." All I heard was negativity. I was already discouraged and wasn't getting the emotional support I was seeking. I wanted to give up and let it go because my dream was becoming a nightmare. I couldn't eat properly or sleep peacefully; it was impacting my personal finances, my health deteriorated. It looked like a giant, and I saw myself as an ant.

Having a school that would prepare children to enter the public school with a quality educational and social foundation was my passion, a vision. GOD had given me. So I made a decision that with all the negativity I was facing it was not enough to make me quit.

I stretched my faith in GOD's promise prayed and worshiped, prayed and praised GOD in my present circumstances. I knew how successful it had been so I put everything I had into making it what it should be. It took hard and long workdays sleepless nights, but I didn't quit. Sometimes we have to look back where the LORD has brought us and gain strength, encouragement and determination from what GOD has already done.

With renewed zeal we renovated our appearance, invested personal finances, received financial help from Grace Cathedral and donations from a variety of sources. Most importantly GOD sent assistance in the form of new ideas, and new personnel. We refocused on staff morale, encouraged enhancing our work ethic, pursued new and innovative ways for increasing our clientele. We regained National Accreditation, renewed our license, and got our BEDS Code. We successfully entered into the Grants Gateway vault and got grants. We joined the Shooting for the Stars program and recently became one of the centers accepted for the Quality Stars program. We are rising above our negative circumstances in spite of all the discouragement I faced; it was not enough to make me quit.

The Bible says, "Caleb quieted the people before Moses, and said, Let us go up at once and possess it; we are well able to conquer it." It is not enough to make us quit. (Numbers 13:30 AMP) "and all the congregation cried out with a loud voice, and [they] wept that night.2 All the Israelites grumbled and deplored their situation, accusing Moses and Aaron, to whom the whole congregation said, Would that we had died in Egypt! Or that we had died in this wilderness!4 And they said one to another, Let us choose a captain and return to Egypt.5 Then Moses and Aaron fell on their faces before all the assembly of Israelites.6 And Joshua son of Nun and Caleb son of Jephunneh, who were among the scouts who had searched the land, rent their clothes,7 And they said to all the company of Israelites, The land through which we passed as scouts is an exceedingly good land.8 If the LORD delights in us, then He will bring us into this land and give it to us, a land flowing with milk and honey.9 Only do not rebel against the LORD, neither fear the people of the land, for they are bread for us. Their defense and the shadow [of protection] is removed from over them, but the LORD is with us. Fear them not.10 But all the congregation said to stone [Joshua and Caleb] with stones. But the glory of the LORD appeared at the Tent of Meeting before all the Israelites.

And the LORD said to Moses and Aaron, 22 Because all those men who have seen My glory and My [miraculous] signs which I performed in Egypt and in the wilderness, yet have tested and proved Me these ten times and have not heeded My voice,23 Surely they shall not see the land which I swore to give to their fathers; nor shall any who provoked (spurned, despised) ME see it. [Heb. 6:4-11.]24 But My servant Caleb, because he has a different spirit and has followed Me fully, I will bring into the land into which he went, and his descendants shall possess it.30 Surely none shall come into the land in which I swore to make you dwell, except Caleb son of Jephunneh and Joshua son of Nun.34 After the number of the days in which you spied out the land [of Canaan], even forty days, for each day a year shall you bear and suffer for your iniquities, even for forty years, and you shall know MY displeasure [the revoking of MY promise and MY estrangement]." (Numbers Chapter 14 AMP)

Look what happened because the people quit and didn't fight for what GOD had clearly shown them was theirs.

Ten leaders saw how hard it would be and persuaded the people to quit. Two, Joshua and Caleb, saw the vision and encouraged the people to go forward it's not enough to make you quit. They were outnumbered and had to go through the 40-year wilderness experience with everybody else, but they were the only two that lived to see the promise fulfilled.

We need to develop some Joshua' and Caleb's, some warriors who will stand up and say we don't see anything positive in what we are doing right now. The pressure of the situation I am in is weighing me down. The discouragement is becoming overwhelming, but GOD you chose me for this task, and it is not enough to make me quit.

"And let us not be weary in well doing: for in due season we shall reap, if we faint not". (Galatians 6:9 KJV)

"Therefore, my beloved brethren, be firm (steadfast), immovable, always abounding in the work of the LORD [always being superior, excelling, doing more than enough in the service of the LORD], knowing and being continually aware that your labor in the LORD is not futile [it is never wasted or to no purpose]."(1 Corinthians 15:58 AMP)

Research some successful people in life, preachers, recording artists, TV. Personalities, politicians, business entrepreneurs, just to name a few. They did not get where they are on just lucky breaks. They had something deep down inside that kept encouraging them that no matter what they faced, it was not enough to make them quit.

In the armed forces, sports, boot camps, music world, politics and to move up the cooperate ladder, the training is rigorous, and there are many dropouts, but those who can take it will make it and go on to conquer greater challenges and succeed.

If GOD gave us a vision and calling on our lives, whatever giants and strongholds we may be facing at the moment, we must keep it in our spirit that it is not enough to make us quit.

HANDLING GREAT NECESSITIES

When our necessity is greatest, We need to go to GOD in prayer, and HE will supply our needs.

When our trials are hardest, let us go to Him in prayer, and He will ease it.

When our burdens are heaviest, let us go to HIM in prayer, and HE will lift it off our shoulders or at least enable us to bear it.

We want many things in life better jobs, better homes, better cars, better clothes a more comfortable place, less stress, more of the necessities of life in general.

We needn't desire these things more than we desire a relationship with GOD. The Bible reads in 3 John 1:2 KJV "Beloved, I wish above all things that thou mayest prosper and be in health, even as thy soul prospereth."

We need to ask with faith believing that we will receive but remember this one thing, that whatsoever you desire of the LORD, our hearts must be right; our spirit must be correct, and our petitions must be meaningful.

James 4:3 in the Amplified Bibles reads: "[Or] you do ask [GOD for them] and yet fail to receive because you ask with wrong purpose and evil, selfish motives. Your intention is [when you get what you desire] to spend it in sensual pleasures."

The Bible says in Psalm 66:18 KJV, "If I regard iniquity in my heart, the LORD will not hear me."

It also says that if we have ought against our brother, first reconcile with him and then present our petition. (Matthew 5:23-24 KJV)

The first thing we need to seek is the Kingdom of GOD and HIS righteousness, "But seek ye first the kingdom of GOD, and HIS righteousness; and all these things shall be added unto you." (Matthew 6:33 KJV)

WHAT IS WISDOM?

When I graduated from Jr. High School, Bishop Richardson, my uncle, wrote in my autograph book; Proverbs 4:7 "Wisdom is the principal thing; therefore get wisdom: and with all thy getting get understanding". (Proverbs 4:7 KJV)

At that young age, I asked myself, "What is he talking about?" As I grew older and began to study the word of GOD, I began to understand what Bishop Richardson was trying to teach me.

We must seek GOD before we embark upon any of our desires or plans. When we acquire wisdom from GOD, we must put it into action. "Trust in the LORD with all thine heart; and lean not unto thine own understanding. In all thy ways acknowledge HIM, and HE shall direct thy paths." (Proverbs 3:5-6 KJV)

As our relationship with GOD increases, we grow in wisdom. Wisdom is the key to successful living. When we keep our eyes on HIM instead of ourselves and remember that HE gives us all that we have, then we begin to acquire wisdom

Solomon in the Bible asked for wisdom, and it pleased GOD.

GOD granted his request. GOD also gave Solomon wealth, honor and long life because he did not ask for it.

That night GOD appeared to Solomon and said to him "Ask for whatever you want ME to give you."

Solomon answered GOD, "You have shown great kindness to David, my father and have made me king in his place. Now, LORD, GOD, let your promise to my father David be confirmed, for you have made me king over a people who are as numerous as the dust of the earth. Give me wisdom and knowledge, that I may lead this people, for who is able to govern this great people of yours?" God said to Solomon, "Since this is your heart's desire, and you have not asked for wealth, possessions or honor, nor for the death of your enemies, and since you have not asked for a long life but for wisdom and knowledge to govern my people over whom I have made you king, therefore wisdom and knowledge will be given you. And I will also give you wealth, possessions, and honor, such as no king who was before you ever had, and none after you will have." (2 Chronicles 1:7-12 NIV)

Wisdom is seeking first the kingdom of GOD, and all other things will be added unto us. Putting GOD first, above selfish desires and goals, shows that we are acquiring wisdom with understanding.

Proverbs 2:6-7 KJV reads, "For the LORD giveth wisdom: out of HIS mouth cometh knowledge and understanding. HE layeth up sound wisdom for the righteous: HE is a buckler to them that walk uprightly".

To see beyond the impossible is faith but, to see beyond the present is wisdom.

WHY SHOULD WE PRAY?

Prayer makes us fit to receive our blessing; it puts us in the proper position, that of humble dependence upon GOD. It brings us into conformity with GOD'S plan.

GOD'S purpose is that we must ask to receive, seek to find, and knock that the door of opportunity may be opened.

If we are going to worry there is no need to pray and if we pray in faith, believing, there is no need to worry.

We should say to ourselves; "I am not going to worry about this situation I believe the word of GOD and that settles it."

Yes, it's painful, rough and distressing sometimes, but we have got to hold onto our faith.

How do we do that? We have to glorify GOD in every circumstance. It doesn't matter how our situation looks right now; we have to continue to worship GOD.

Our physical and emotional strength may be drained, but we still have to hold onto our faith and our praise.

We need to stand still, not run away or turn our backs, and wait until our change comes. Faith and prayer work together.

We must believe GOD's word. "And we know that all things work together for good to them that love GOD, to them who are the called according to HIS purpose." (Romans 8:28 KJV)

Do we love GOD? Do we believe HE called us? Do we believe HE has a purpose for us in this life? Then we have to understand that everything we go through is necessary for advancement in GOD'S plan for us. We need all our experiences in life, whether they seem good or bad, to prepare us for the purpose that GOD has destined for us.

So we pray for faith and endurance, so we don't lose the blessing that is waiting for us.

DON'T BE TRICKED

When we substitute true Worship to the Glory of GOD with a need for recognition, and we work only for position and power in the church, it's a trick of the enemy.

Mica 6:8 reads "He hath shewed thee, O man, what is good; and what doth the LORD require of thee, but to do justly, and to love mercy, and to walk humbly with thy GOD?" (Mica 6:8 KJV)

We can't get so caught up and deeply involved in letting men see our works that we forget what GOD requires of us

And that is to "Delight thyself also in the LORD, and HE shall give thee the desires of thine heart." (Psalm 37:4 KJV)

We can't do as we want and think that GOD will be there to deliver us.

We are not indispensable. GOD was well served before us and if we fail HE will call others to minister.

"Set your affection on things above, not on things on the earth." (Colossians 3:2 KJV) and Colossians 3:23 reads "And whatsoever ye do, do it heartily, as to the LORD, and not unto men." (Colossians 3:23 KJV)

Don't be tricked by the praise of men and lose the gift and calling of GOD.

IT'S JUST A LITTLE THING

The Bible admonishes us to despise not the day of small things.

A great blessing can come from a small sacrifice.

We need to obey GOD'S command in difficult circumstances, a blessing will not just fall on us we have to do something ourselves to receive it.

How many times have we missed our blessing because we let pride get in the way?

We thought we were above doing certain things. We say to ourselves, it does not take all that; it's not worth all that. Most of the time it's just a small thing that GOD wants us to do.

It might seem unpleasant, but when we analyze it, it is just a small thing. We waste a lot of time when we delay what GOD wants us to do. It could take a short amount of time if we take self out of the way and obey GOD'S commands.

We have to learn to get over hurt feelings and hurt pride. Don't let people or petty differences get in the way of what GOD has for us.

We need to think about what is holding up our blessing. When we really look into the situation we will find it is just a little thing. We can survive it and get the blessing that GOD has in store for us.

TELL GOD ABOUT IT

A woman I admire in the Bible is Hannah; you can read about her in 1 Samuel 1st chapter.

This message is unique to any gender. It can apply to a Hannah as well as a Harold.

Hannah faced several serious problems according to the culture of that time. She had a raw deal in life. Hannah was barren. Even though she had the love of her husband and all he could give her, she was still devastated.

Her personal worth in the eyes of others was diminished. Hannah's husband was limited in how much he could comfort her. He could not enter into her suffering because he had children by his second wife.

Hannah felt she had no emotional support. We can sympathize with those who are facing a traumatic situation in their life, but we can't empathize because we may not have personally experienced what they have suffered.

Hannah used her pain as a catalyst to pray. GOD directly planned that she suffer in that way. "And she was in bitterness of soul and prayed unto the LORD, and wept sore." ... "Then Eli answered and said, Go in peace: and the GOD of Israel grant thee thy petition that thou hast asked of

HIM." ... "So the woman went her way, and did eat, and her countenance was no more sad." (1 Samuel 10, 17, 18 KJV)

Prayer is the most powerful and important tool we have which allows us to speak directly to GOD.

After her encounter with GOD, Hannah's attitude changed before her condition did.

Tell GOD about it. Contentment comes with believing GOD and resting in HIM

GOD WANTS US TO ASK FOR IT

In Mark 10:51 KJV, the LORD asked blind Bartimaeus, "...What wilt thou that I should do unto thee?"

The LORD didn't need to ask, everyone in the crowd could guess the answer to that question correctly.

The SAVIOR knew the thought that was most important to the blind man's heart because HE knows what is in all our hearts and minds; so why does he ask the question?

Just to give us the opportunity to present our petition and make our request in our words.

GOD already knows what we need before we ask HIM. HE wants us to come to him in prayer to make our petitions known in our words.

HE wants to hear how we are going to ask; are we asking amiss, asking in doubt, asking with right motivation or do we ask in faith believing that GOD will answer.

The blind man replied "LORD that I might receive my sight" and he asked with a determined faith that GOD could do it and immediately he received his sight.

Faith persevered, received encouragement, and got results. Before the results, Bartimaeus had to ask GOD for what he wanted.

I AM SAYS I CAN

"And GOD said to Moses, I AM WHO I AM and WHAT I AM, and I WILL BE WHAT I WILL BE; and HE said, You shall say this to the Israelites: I AM has sent me to you!" (Exodus 3:14 AMP)

We find in this passage of scripture Moses questioning his abilities and capabilities. Can I do what GOD is asking me to do? Am I qualified to accomplish the task that is set before me? Am I able to endure the trials and tribulations that will come as I endeavor to be faithful to my calling? Can I be victorious over the discouragement and disappointments I will face as I try to do GOD's will? Am I willing and able to overcome the shortcomings in my life to be what GOD wants me to be? Am I, can I, we all ask these questions when GOD places the challenge before us to go higher, go forward and do greater works for HIM. We need to know that the GREAT I AM says we can. We can do all things through CHRIST who strengthens us.

For 40 years Moses knew the pomp and pride of the Egyptian court. He was educated by the Egyptians, had the privileges and affluence of an Egyptian prince. He knew how to command and demand what he wanted. He was living large. Moses was raised in the Egyptian environment so he could learn and understand the temperament, culture, and ideals of the people he would have to negotiate with forty years later. Many today are in situations that are confusing and misunderstood. GOD places us in certain environments and circumstances to learn. HE has plans to use everything we face, later in ministry.

To understand what it is like to be an alcoholic, drug addict, prisoner, prostitute, homeless, the loss of a loved one, serious illness or major tragedy it has to be experienced personally so we can effectively help others in that situation. How can we tell someone GOD can heal a broken heart if we've never had one? How can we say GOD can deliver from drugs if we haven't a clue what it feels like to be an addict? When GOD has a purpose for our lives, to use us to HIS glory, HE gives us the strength to endure and succeed. We can say with assurance when faced with what appears to be insurmountable obstacles in life, "I AM says I can. GOD is the Great I Am and with HIM all things are possible.

Moses, a prince in Egypt, not by birth but destiny, killed an Egyptian who was abusing one of the Hebrews. Instead of praising Moses, the Israelites rejected him. He had been secure, courageous and brave before that incident. Moses fled Egypt in fear of the impending consequences he would face. He had spent forty years living an exalted life in the palace. GOD allowed Moses as HE does us to experience all the facets of life that we need for HIM to prepare us for the HIS work. Many of us have found ourselves facing situations we did not understand. We have been confused about why we had to experience the negative and painful things in our lives. GOD places us in all the areas of life that we need to learn, develop and grow. HE orchestrates the circumstances in our lives. We must become the vessel that will allow GOD to use us. Moses spent the next forty years as a shepherd leading sheep in the desert. He becomes a changed man. He knew pride, but he needed to experience humility before he could meet the I AM, (GOD). Moses had to move self out of the way. When Moses was told by GOD to go back to Egypt, the place he fled from in fear for his life, he was reluctant to do so. We cannot do great works for GOD until we are brought down from what we can do on our own.

Moses had justifiable reasons in his mind for why he could not be the one GOD wanted to use.

..."GOD called to him out of the midst of the bush and said, Moses, Moses! And he said, Here am I...And Moses said to GOD Who am I, that I should go ...I am not eloquent or a man of words...I am slow of speech and have a heavy and awkward tongue." (Exodus: Chapters 3 and 4 AMP). Moses initially answered GOD's call, "here I am." When given his assignment Moses uses "I am" to make excuses. I am ignorant of the proper name of GOD. I am afraid of being accepted by the people. I am not able to speak openly. Moses needed reassurance. He needed encouragement. He needed to know the I AM says I can GOD.

We find in this passage of scripture, the "I can't of Moses being contradicted by the "I can" of GOD.

"I can do all things [which HE has called me to do] through HIM who strengthens and empowers me [to fulfill HIS purpose––I am self-sufficient in CHRIST's sufficiency; I am ready for anything and equal to anything through HIM who infuses me with inner strength and confident peace." (Philippians 4:13 AMP)

Moses had not been near Egypt for forty years, and GOD requires what Moses considers an almost impossible task from him. GOD had chosen him to be the agent of deliverance to people who had already rejected him.

Moses asked the question "Who am I"? I can't do this job. It's too awesome.

It requires qualifications that I do not have. Moses was considering the difficulties he would encounter, but the one thing he had yet to learn was that GOD knew him better than he knew himself. When we are chosen by GOD to do work for HIM, HE qualifies us. HE already knows our destiny.

Moses expected that one of the first questions the people would ask is, who sent you? What is his name? Moses asks GOD "who shall I say sent me?

GOD replied tell them "I AM" sent you. "I AM" the one who has always been and always will be. "I AM" the EVERLASTING FATHER, the PRINCE OF PEACE, the GREAT ETERNAL WONDER, HOLY COUNSELOR. Before the foundations of the Earth were formed, "I AM." Tell the people the Great "I AM" sent you.

We need to know the name of who is calling us. When the "I AM" GOD calls us; it is evident in the success of whatever ministry or mission we undertake.

WATCH WHAT YOU SAY

The Bible emphasizes the need for sound speech and to avoid uncalled for criticism. "Sound speech, that cannot be condemned; that he that is of the contrary part may be ashamed, having no evil thing to say of you" (Titus 2:8 KJV)

We bring a reproach on the Church and scorn from the world, which is justified when there are Christians who are not careful to maintain sound speech.

How can the Church be holy if its members are not holy? We are condemned when people wonder if we are a Christian because of the way we treat and speak to others. We can't get so angry and upset that we forget to bridle our tongues. "Therefore all things whatsoever ye would that men should do to you, do ye even so to them: for this is the law and the prophets." (Matthew 7:12 KJV)

We need to think about what we are saying or doing before we open our mouths and make others question our Christianity.

The book of James talks about how difficult it is to control the tongue. "But the tongue can no man tame; it is an unruly evil, full of deadly poison." (James 3:8 KJV)

Before praying for GOD to bless us and change unwanted things in our lives, we need to fast and pray that GOD will control how we speak to and about other people. We cannot use the excuse that I spoke to and treated him/her the way they spoke to or treated me.

Often we encourage a negative report, it's in our nature to want to hear more. It's easy to splash mud, saints of GOD; we need to learn how to help our sister or brother keep his or her coat clean.

What would happen if we stopped the gossiper and said "lets pray right now for this individual" negative conversations would soon starve and die of itself if no one took it in and gave it a place to live.

A person's name can be scandalized when a slanderer begins to whisper, and another makes it a report, another adds to it and finally another presents an original lie as truth.

An innocent man or woman's good name acquired over many many years of sacrifices and hard work is lost in an hour; and so secretly that it's hard to find out who the true villain that started it was.

A false accusation, even though it is proven wrong can injure a man or woman for life, and they may never be able to recover from it.

GOD is going to hold us accountable for what we do and say. I always tell the children I work with who are about to do or say something that would cause them to be reprimanded to "stop and think and then don't do it."

Exodus 23:1 KJV reads "Thou shalt not raise a false report: put not thine hand with the wicked to be an unrighteous witness."

"Let your light so shine before men, that they may see your good works, and glorify your Father which is in heaven." (Matthew 5:16 KJV)

Applying that scripture in our lives is almost impossible to do if we don't watch what we say.

WE CAN LIVE HOLY

The Greek translation for the word Church is Ekklesia, which means "the called out one".

Christians should become separated from the world of sin and unrighteousness and dedicate our lives to GOD.

When we commit our lives to GOD, it does not mean to isolate ourselves and not function in the world today. I believe GOD would have HIS church be insulated, separate from the sins of this world and dedicated to living a holy life which will represent HIM. (John 17:15, 1 Peter 2:9-10 KJV)

When we read our Bible, it admonishes us to repent and be baptized in the name of JESUS, and we shall receive the gift of the HOLY SPIRIT.

(Acts 2:38 KJV) "Howbeit when HE, the Spirit of truth, is come, HE will guide you into all truth..." (John 16:13 KJV) The grace of GOD is our instructor in holy living. It teaches us to reject ungodly, and worldly lusts. GOD's grace and mercy lead us to the path of righteous living.

When things get right on the inside of us, the condition will be evident on the outside to everyone. The Spirit of GOD fills our lives with HIS desires and HIS holy aspirations. Through the Spirit of GOD that resides inside of us, we can live free from hatred, bitterness, pride, jealousy, malice, lust and wrath.

It does not mean that because we serve GOD, we do not have battles or conflicts. We have a power within that will enable us to overcome things that would destroy those who don't fully know GOD. "Now we have received, not the spirit of the world, but the spirit which is of GOD; that we might know the things that are freely given to us of GOD." (1 Corinthians 2:12 KJV) The GOD within us will affect our lifestyle making it conform to a holy life free from sin and its activities.

In the very beginning of creation, GOD created men and women equal in their authority.

Joel makes it clear that GOD does not discriminate because of gender. Paul emphasized that there is neither male nor female, but we are all one in CHRIST JESUS.

No holiness is unique to men and another that is designated for women. Holiness has no gender we are all required to live holy.

The Bible says in Hebrews 12:14 KJV "Follow peace with all men, and holiness, without which no man/woman shall see the LORD."

We can listen to all the TD Jakes, Jackie McCullough and Bishop R.W. Harris tapes we like. We can run around behind all the famous preachers of today. We can watch all the religious programs on TV every morning and listen to gospel radio all day long, but we will not profit from any of it if we don't receive help to live holy.

When can't live holy only when it is convenient, it is a lifestyle. We must be ruled by it and obey its requirements. We must submit to its authority, regulate our tempers and attitudes and live by its precepts.

Some teach very strictly and concerning dress and jewelry and lay

111

down hard fast rules governing such. The best policy is for us to remember that we are Holy constantly.

We are representatives of JESUS in a carnal world; remembering this let us examine our dress to see if it portrays a Holy life. We must cultivate sensitiveness to the leading of the HOLY SPIRIT and let it guide in such matters.

How do we receive Holiness? Repent and be Baptized, and we shall receive the gift of the HOLY SPIRIT. The grace of GOD is our instructor in Holy living, and it teaches us to reject ungodly and worldly lusts and leads us in the path of right living.

When things get right on the inside, the condition will be evident on the outside. The spirit of GOD fills our life with Godly desires and Holy aspirations. Through the Spirit of Holiness that resides in us, we can keep ourselves free from hatred, bitterness, pride, jealousy, malice, lust and wrath.

It does not mean that the child of GOD has no battles or conflicts, but we have power within that will enable us to be an overcomer.

"Now we have received, not the spirit of the world, but the spirit which is of GOD; that we might know the things that are freely given to us of GOD." (1st Corinthians 2:12 KJV)

Heartbreak and disappointment come when we are in a battle of wills; our will against GOD'S will.

When we are in a fiery trial, it is our faith and our will that is on trial. Surrendering to GOD'S will allow our faith to grow and we can survive whatever trials we face.

The astonishing thing about the three Hebrew boys in the fiery furnace is that they overcame what had destroyed other men. GOD did not take the heat out of the flames because it burned the guards that went near the furnace. The Hebrew boys were able to walk in the midst of the flames. If we live holy and believe GOD, we can walk in what other men burn in.

When I think of Blind Bartimaeus, he could not see JESUS he just heard that JESUS was passing. Here was an opportunity for him to be healed and delivered; he didn't care about GOD'S gender. It didn't matter if JESUS was a man or a woman. All he knew was that JESUS was a holy person who could heal.

We need to stop looking at whether or not it is a male or female who prays for us, preaches to us, or counsels us. It does not matter the gender, what is important is that they are holy.

It doesn't matter whose prayer line you are on. If it's a male GOD will give him more power? Not so, the Word says that GOD has poured out HIS spirit on both genders. Joel 2:28 "And it shall come to pass afterward, that I will pour out my spirit upon all flesh; and your sons and your daughters shall prophesy, your old men shall dream dreams, your young men shall see visions:"

What we need to do is not allow our negative thoughts of people to get into the way of our blessing.

Holiness calls for perseverance and determination no matter what. We need the HOLY SPIRIT inside of us and not just on us.

It's the inner man that controls the outer actions. When GOD is in us we can't help but walk right, talk right, live right and do right.

So when JESUS gets inside of us, HE renews our mind and cleanses our hearts. We begin to look at other people and circumstances in our life with the mind of CHRIST.

Drinking water cleanses and purifies us and quenches our thirst. We must allow CHRIST to clean and purify us with HIS holiness. We must not profess to believe in GOD or just admire Him but trust HIM, love HIM and live for HIM so that HE becomes one with us.

The Grace of GOD will continually quench our spiritual thirst. HE is a well of living water (John 4:14) always there always in operation.

Is the HOLY SPIRIT in us today? Does it quench our spiritual thirst?

Do we walk, talk and live Holy because GOD is controlling the inside of us? Or do we take our holiness off with our Sunday dress?

Do we have a form of Godliness but deny the power thereof (2nd Timothy 3:5). Are we putting on a holy show in Church so others can admire how saved we are or is it evident that JESUS is real because we can feel him deep in our soul?

We can live Holy if GOD resides in us.

SERMONETTE 46

DON'T PARTAKE

"Lay hands suddenly on no man, neither be partaker of other men's sins: keep thyself pure." (1ˢᵗ Timothy 5:22 KJV)

We should all be striving for heaven. It is better to go to heaven alone, or with a few, rather than with a multitude to hell.

We need to learn to be an individual not merely a member of the crowd. Don't take part in destroying the innocent or covering the sins of others. We are going to be judged by our LORD as individuals. GOD is not going to accept the excuse that everyone else was doing it.

Many are following the wrong crowd in disobedience, all disobedience is sin; it doesn't matter who the people are, church leaders, missionaries or deacons.

Many are crying and going through, waiting on a blessing that won't come because they are following a crowd into the sin of disobedience and rebellion.

GOD doesn't just bless any behavior and spirit. We need to recognize that the group may have succumbed to the seducing spirit that is bringing them fashionably to hell.

GOD blesses us as individuals for the right things that we do. There is one who judges us, and that is GOD, and HE will surely call us to account for all our wrongdoings.

We can't excuse ourselves by saying, "I do as I see others do" or "I didn't want to get involved" when you see others doing wrong.

Let us be aware of the company we associate with and be strong and firm in our mind. "Let this mind be in you that was also in CHRIST JESUS" (Philippians 2:5 KJV)

Following the crowd is easy, but separating from it requires lots of courage and a deep devotion to GOD.

There are secret sins, and there are open sins. Some men's sins are obvious and evident to everyone. Then there are others whose wickedness does not appear unless someone tells it or GOD reveals it.

If we are aware that a leader or member of the ministry is committing sin and functioning at the Church and we keep quiet about it, we have become a partaker in that other individual's sin.

TIME IS WINDING UP

The clock of eternity always keeps time. We are failing to discern the signs of the time. We prefer the material and temporal to the spiritual and religious.

Having the Spirit of GOD in us is the best defense against hard times. Repentance and prayer are the best resources in bad times.

We should all be preparing for our future by the deeds we are doing in the present. Each of us should be considering how we want to proceed in life.

We need to examine our spiritual condition carefully. No one can travel along securely or comfortably in life that does not think and plan the course they will pursue.

In planning for our future, we must not forget that life here on Earth is only temporary. In all our endeavors we must include preparation for meeting GOD one day.

"For we must all appear before the judgment-seat of CHRIST; that every one may receive the things done in his body, according to that he hath done, whether it be good or bad." (2 Corinthians 5:10 KJV)

Many of us frequently pause to ponder how life is progressing. Many of us contemplate on where and how our life will end.

There is a guarantee of ultimate success. The individual who perseveres wins in ordinary life, most of the time, in our spiritual life all of the time.

Those of us who know CHRIST personally have encouragement in the fact that GOD is with us; to help us with needed strength. GOD is there to protect and defend us against the plans of the adversary. HE is there to assist us in keeping our sanity when situations overwhelm us.

Tomorrow is not promised to any of us. In preparing for the future we must be aware that time is winding up for us to make sure our future leads us to heaven.

JESUS IS THE MAN

JESUS is the man who covered our back when we were in sin.

JESUS is the man who received us back from our backslidden state.

JESUS is the man who blessed us anyhow when we thought the world was our stage and allowed the devil to be our manager.

JESUS is the man who can empathize with our loneliness and will hold us and caress us.

JESUS is the man who can dry the tears we shed in our pillow at night.

JESUS is the man who sticks by us when we question why our husband, wife or children won't seek GOD.

JESUS is the man who comforts when people don't appreciate us and we are treated poorly.

JESUS is the man who can gives us strength when we lose a loved one or when our children don't act right.

JESUS is the man who protects our loved ones when they get involved in things in the world that may cause them to end up in jail or dead.

JESUS is the man who calms our spirit when our employers and co-workers mistreat us.

JESUS is the man who encourages us when the church members give us a hard time.

JESUS is the man who understands our desires and our secret yearnings.

JESUS is the man who is calling us to serve and worship to HIM.

JESUS is the man who has allowed us to experience all we have in our past and present life so that we can be a better witness for HIM.

JESUS is the man who soothes our doubts and calms our fears.

JESUS is the man who can supply all our needs according to HIS riches in glory.

JESUS is the man who can prosper us and give us the desires of our heart.

JESUS is the man who is worthy to be praised.

JESUS IS THE MAN

LOOKING BACKWARD

Looking behind us can sometimes be destructive; sometimes it is not productive to look back.

Lot's "no name" wife didn't have to die; she was given a choice, obedience, and life or disobedience and death. She was aware of the LORD and his dealings with Abraham, but the lifestyle of Sodom had a firm hold on her. GOD wanted to save Lot's wife; HE sent angels to warn, to escort and finally to physically pull her out of harm's way.

She had the same problems the Israelites did in the wilderness; when in their hearts, they turned back to Egypt. Because of their disobedience a journey which should have taken 11 days took 40 years.

GOD used Lot's wife as an example of someone who started the right way but looked backward because she was not completely willing to give up her old ways to follow GOD in obedience. She was one look away from reaching safety with her family.

She was thoroughly human, and like her, we often receive explicit instruction from GOD, yet still feel frightened and uncertain as to where GOD is taking us.

When we are following GOD in new directions the awareness of our former dreams and goals going up in flames behind us may be a temptation to distrust GOD'S leading.

Are you looking back longingly at what you are leaving behind while trying to move forward into a deeper relationship with GOD? In spite of what we fear we have to trust GOD. We cannot progress with GOD if we are longing for what might have been.

"I will lift up mine eyes unto the hills, from whence cometh my help. My help cometh from the LORD which made heaven and earth." (Psalms 121:1 & 2 KJV)

In every situation look to GOD. When we look backward, it can be discouraging but sometimes it can be encouraging. We need GOD's guidance in how we view our life. Positive looking says I survived my past and it is propelling me to my future. Negative looking says my past experiences were miserable failures and my future looks just as bad. We can look at a glass of water as half empty or half full. I choose to look at my glass as half full. I've learned that my past experiences were a training ground; they made me what I am today. I survived the negative things, but I thrived on the positive. But every experience taught me something. I know the mistakes I made and didn't want to repeat. I know that the things I thought were too hard or impossible, with the help of GOD, I mastered.

So looking backward isn't so bad when we do it with a positive attitude. When we look forward, we can have visions of what we want to do, and the strength from our past will enable us to live the scripture, "I can do all things through CHRIST that strengthens me."

Yes, we have fears about what the future holds and how our past may impact it. The desire to make our life better spiritually first and then naturally will move those fears aside, and we move forward. Whatsoever things are lovely, positive, holy and pure, think on them.

Aretha Franklin sang a song that I applied to my relationship with the LORD JESUS CHRIST. Looking back in my life, I used to feel so uninspired often and I neglected a lot of opportunities. Before I met JESUS, life seemed unkind; now JESUS is the key to my peace of mind.

In the spiritual, we can look up, down, forward, to our left and our right. But we don't have to worry about looking back. GOD has our back, in times of struggle, misfortune and spiritual attacks by the enemy. In the natural we need to look back on the distance we have come. We need to look back on the many prayers that have brought us through difficult situations in our lives. We need to look back on the many dreams that have come to fruition. We need to look back and remember the many joys we have experienced.

I have asked Bishop if he remembered being an infant, a toddler, a teenager and the things that happened during that time. I asked could he remember how we felt on our first date. I wanted to know if he could remember when the children were little and old arguments we had. Some things in our lives there is no memory at all. Some things we vaguely remember but the genuine feeling from those moments are gone. Our minds can't fully remember every situation we've experienced in complete detail. That's life; we move on.

There are yet a few more trials, more joys, more real work, old age and if GOD should delay HIS return, death. Is it all over then? Not for the believers. We begin looking forward to a new life, the glory of GOD and the fullness of eternity with HIM.

So you didn't get the promotion, the new house, the new car. Your marriage plans didn't work out. We need to stop looking at what should have, could have, and might have been. Look at what can, will, and shall happen in the future.

PRAYER # 2

LORD, I put my trust in YOU. I believe that YOU have control over everything. No matter what comes my way I know YOU are always in control. Although circumstances may come upon me unexpectedly, I believe that YOU always knew about those things before they happened. There are times I am surprised by the trials that happen in my life, but YOU are never surprised. YOU are all powerful and knowledgeable about all things especially those concerning me. It can be easy to waver in my faith when the trials I face are extremely hard.

LORD open my understanding to your word in Provers 16:33 AMP, where it says, "The lot is cast into the lap, but the decision is wholly of the LORD [even the events that seem accidental are really ordered by YOU."

YOU are the LORD of time and chance, nothing that happens or has happened in my life was accidental or a lucky break. LORD, YOU already know what life has for me. YOU had made plans for my life before I was conceived in my mother's womb."

When I don't understand why negative things are happening to me, help me to remember that YOU are in control of my life. Help me to remember YOUR WORD where you assured me that YOU would not put more on me than I could bear and that when the pressures of life begin to overtake me, YOU will make a way of escape so that I could take whatever it is I am going through for the moment. GOD, I thank YOU for choosing to test my faith. I thank YOU, for allowing me to trust YOU more fully. If I always knew how to control and fix everything and knew the outcome of everything I face, then I would never increase my faith in YOU.

The Bible says faith is the substance of things which are not seen. True faith means I believe that YOU are always in control even when the circumstances of life appear otherwise. I don't always know what YOU are doing, but I trust YOU.

Dear GOD someone besides me needs YOU to strengthen their faith. They can't see their way out of the situation they are in the right now.

They are on the verge of giving up. Dear GOD I'm asking YOU to send YOUR guardian angels to strengthen them and bear them up. Help them right now my SAVIOR to trust in you with all their heart and lean not to their understanding. I praise YOU right now for victory for my brother, my sister who is feeling YOUR strengthening power. Thank YOU for increasing our faith and placing a determination deep down in our souls that no matter what we are going to trust GOD. Help us this morning to thank YOU for the victory that is already taking place in our situation, even though we don't see it right now with our natural eyes.

I praise YOU for increasing my faith and belief that all things work together for good to those who love YOU and are called according to YOUR purpose. Amen

WHEN GOD SEEMS TO LOCK DOWN

Sometimes in our lives everything seems to go smoothly. Again there are times when changes come and a whole year of joy or sorrow feel like they may be concentrated into one single day.

The day starts out with joy, then tragedy; we know not what a day may bring. It's not what we have learned, what we possess, who we have become or who we know that will ease the pain and anguish when GOD seems to lock down.

We can't hear GOD or we don't understand what's going on and we can't find a solution; no matter how hard we pray, fast, cry and meditate.

When GOD seems to lock down, we feel overwhelmed with immeasurable distress. It is in those difficult times that we need to rely on the WORD of GOD. "I will lift up mine eyes to the hills, from whence cometh our help." (Psalm 121:1 KJV). When GOD seems to lock down; pray, shut the door to your situation and don't talk to anyone but those rightly connected and know how to pray. Then run to the house of GOD, find the prayer room and don't settle until you triumph over your situation.

GOD will answer you; HE will deliver, restore and give you strength to endure. If the LORD JESUS CHRIST is precious to us and we are walking in the newness and righteousness of life, our hearts are free of all evil.

I know it is hard to do, but at those times we need to force out "FATHER, if thou be willing remove this cup from me: nevertheless not my will, but THINE be done." (Luke 22:42 KJV).

SERMONETTE 51

GOD'S BLESSING IS A GIFT

The blessings of GOD are abundantly bestowed upon all those who follow HIM. GOD'S blessings are not only a reward for Godly living but a gift from a loving father.

GOD promises personal blessings to those who follow HIM in obedience. HE wants HIS people to be a blessing to others.

Provision, protection, and salvation are among GOD'S greatest blessings. Health, family, friends and ministry are among GOD'S choicest blessings.

The same gracious GOD who forgives sin heals diseases redeems lives and bestows mercy also promises abundant blessings. Deuteronomy 28:1-15 proceeds to list every blessing we could desire, but the key words in that scripture are that we obey the voice of our GOD.

The blessings of GOD are not an end themselves; they are the outcome of obedience for the purpose of glorifying GOD.

GOD is not concerned that we should make money or win applause, but HE cares that we should be wise, faithful and loving and these graces HE will not withhold from those who ask.

They bring the favor of GOD. Favor with GOD is the wrapping on the gift that is our blessing.

"Delight thyself in the LORD, And HE shall give thee the desires of thine heart." (Psalms 37:4 KJV)

How do we delight ourselves in GOD? By not doing our own thing on HIS day. Give GOD HIS time. Stop shortchanging GOD by easing our conscience with an hour and a half Worship to HIM once a week and doing our own thing for the rest.

We can receive GOD'S gift of a blessing when we serve HIM with all our minds, body, and soul and allow HIM to direct our path.

SERMONETTE 52

RELEASE NEGATIVE EMOTIONS

In the the book of Ruth, we find Naomi returning to her home in Bethlehem. When the people see her, they are astonished. She was so broken and her appearance so altered with affliction they could not believe it was the same person who had left so full of life

Grief, discouragement and stress will age you. It will destroy your health and your will to do no more than just merely survive.

Naomi was loaded down with sorrow and devastated by all that had happened to her. Thank GOD for the people of GOD who know how to pray. I believe those who really cared began to bear her up in prayer and GOD began to move in her life.

That dried up tree with no blossoms began to bloom again. Something down inside of her began to stir up. I believe I can hear her say, I feel like going on, though trials are oppressing me I feel like going on.

GOD can work through us when we move forward in the midst of tragedy and trials. When we feel we have lost everything, we must seize every opportunity that GOD provides us with to worship and praise HIM for what we have left.

Things will begin to happen, but first, we have to let go of negative emotions. Naomi had to let go of the negative, destructive things in her baggage so that she could find the positive, productive things that had gotten buried beneath all the junk.

The word of GOD says, "The sacrifices of GOD are a broken spirit and a broken and a contrite heart, O GOD, thou wilt not despise." (Psalm 51:17 KJV). HE will hear us in the day of trouble and send us help and strengthen us. Many times, what we consider evil turns out in the future to be a great blessing in disguise.

WHAT'S YOUR MOTIVE?

Men are governed in everything by motive. Selfish motives activate people. We judge each other from appearance, GOD judges us by our motives.

Motives keep the world in action; our character is developed from our motives. GOD is divinely inspecting our motives for what we do. Wrong motives breed dissatisfaction, discontentment and eventual loss of our happiness.

"Ye ask, and receive not, because ye ask amiss, that ye may consume it upon lusts." (James 4:3 KJV)

If our motives are depraved, then there is a necessity for reformation. If we seek knowledge, we should get an education. If we want refinement, we should study all the etiquette and social graces that are available. Learn about the social order and culture when striving for recognition and powerful positions. When prosperity is the goal, develop a strong work ethic. However, none of this will bring real satisfaction when our motives are wrong.

GOD says we must be born again (John 3:7). It is the key that opens the door to true motivation.

We can't see one another's hearts. We shield and protect our hearts. We can't see the heart of an individual because the heart is concealed. We only know each other after the flesh. If we were to take off the mask we wear to reveal our real motives, people would be running and hiding from us.

A man may realize the means which he thought would make him happy, but GOD will hinder it from happening.

One selfish person gains wealth and abundance another may acquire immense power in society; yet in all cases, there may still be unhappiness because they don't have the right motive and the peace of GOD which surpasses all understanding.

GOD smiles on the just and the unjust; but when HE takes that smile away, the unjust suffer because they don't have the power of GOD to fall back upon and their wrong motives will surface.

AFFLICTION

"And we know that all things work together for good to them that love GOD, to them who are the called according to His purpose." (Romans 8:28 KJV)

Perhaps you have murmured rebelliously under your affliction, the means of revival is to be silent and pray.

GOD lays crosses on us to admit us into the fellowship of his suffering. The Bible says if we suffer with HIM we shall reign with him.

When GOD allows afflictions to come upon us, they are not everlasting. "For our light affliction, which is but for a moment, worketh for us a far more exceeding and eternal weight of glory;" (2 Corinthians 4:17 (KJV)

GOD will not always reprimand neither keepeth HE HIS anger forever. Many times it is only a test to bring an anointing in our life.

The stresses that are removable and that we can reduce ourselves, we should endeavor to remove. Those which we cannot remove, we need to bear as much as we can.

In every situation in life, there are comforts. Find them and enjoy them.

When we indulge a discontented temper, it will turn the displeasure of GOD against us.

To correct these discontentments consider how little we deserve and how much we enjoy.

SATISFACTION REQUIRES DISCIPLINE

To be content or satisfied is literally to be interdependent upon GOD. We can't be independent of GOD we have to make an effort to do some things for ourselves. It takes discipline to do what is necessary to get what we want. If a job is needed; we must prepare a resume, look at the want ads and go online to see what is available. Satisfaction does not arrive by chance to us; any price does not purchase it. It is a product of discipline. The Bible says, "Not that I speak in respect of want: for I have learned, in whatsoever state I am, therewith to be content." (Philippians 4:11 KJV)

It is important that we learn to be satisfied with who we are and what we have accomplished. Our destiny in life is that which GOD has been pleased to choose for us. Satisfaction needs to be cultivated not only when we possess little, but likewise when we possess much. We need to maintain the right spiritual attitude while seeking satisfaction.

"Because he hath set his love upon ME, therefore will I deliver him: I will set him on high because he hath known MY name. He shall call upon ME, and I will answer him: I will be with him satisfy him and shew him MY salvation." (Psalms 91 14:16 KJV)

In a state of satisfaction, we must keep in mind that abundance neither exalts us neither are we crushed by want. Satisfaction is contentment. He that has found CHRIST will not be wholly cast down by outward troubles. Paul was content, satisfied. He was self-sufficient in the Christian sense, not with the independence of pride but resting on CHRIST.

The Apostle Paul speaks of this in the book of Philippians Chapter 4 "Not that I speak in respect of want: for I have learned, in whatsoever state I am, therewith to be content." (Philippians 4:11 KJV) He is content; satisfied even in the midst of hardship and captivity. His current contentment is an example of his spiritual frame of mind. He was disciplined.

Paul learned to be independent of external circumstances. His Joy in the LORD armed his soul against the trials of life.

The real Christian can bear misfortune and hardship with dignity, without ill humor and complaints. He can take riches and honor without arrogance, pride or ingratitude.

"We are troubled on every side, yet not distressed; we are "We are troubled on every side, yet not distressed; we are perplexed, but not in despair; Persecuted, but not forsaken; cast down, but not destroyed; Always bearing about in the body the dying of the LORD JESUS, that the life also of JESUS might be made manifest in our body." (2 Corinthians 4:8-10 KJV)

We must discipline ourselves to receive satisfaction.

FEAR GOD

"The secret [of the sweet, satisfying companionship] of the LORD have they who fear (revere and worship) HIM, and HE will show them HIS covenant and reveal to them its [deep, inner] meaning." (PSALMS 25:14 AMP)

It is when we reverence and fear GOD with awe at the power of HIS might that we will become acquainted with HIM.

The fear that we need to have will display so much respect and honor for who GOD is and what HE has and Can do for us that we will not make him ashamed by acting in ways that are displeasing to HIM.

Therefore, we must not be discouraged; or shrink from the battle against the evil we encounter in the world. We are indeed weak and helpless, even when we think we possess power and fortune; but the presence of GOD and in the strength of that presence we can do all things.

"Little children (believers, dear ones), you are of GOD and you belong to HIM and have [already] overcome them [the agents of the antichrist]; because HE who is in you is greater than he (satan) who is in the world [of sinful mankind]." (1 John 4:4 AMP)

It is very hard to work the prayer "THY will be done," into our lives.

"But JESUS beheld them, and said unto them, With men this is impossible, but with GOD all things are possible." (Matthew 19:26 KJV)

Contentment and satisfaction are that state of mind in which nothing can mess with the energy of the SPIRIT OF GOD. The secret of a Christian's ability is that we can undergo every trial, brave every sort of suffering, overcome every variety of temptation and perform every duty successfully when we fear GOD.

The Bible says I can do all things through CHRIST, who strengthens me (Philippians 4:13 KJV). By our union with CHRIST, we have access to the real source of strength. GOD infuses strength in us by HIS teachings, by HIS example of patience and forbearance, by the influence of HIS death as a real sacrifice for sin and by the abundant bestowal of HIS HOLY SPIRIT on us.

"Who is the man who reverently fears and worships the LORD? Him shall HE teach in the way that HE should choose.
He himself shall dwell at ease, and his offspring shall inherit the land." (Psalms 25:12, 13 AMP)

GOD'S SPECIAL PLACE FOR US

GOD has a special place for everyone to fill. Sometimes the child who is least thought of in the home ends up with the greatest destiny or blessing.

Esau was brave, manly, a great hunter and popular but his younger feebler brother Jacob became greater than he.

In Jesse's family, there were brothers tall handsome and heroic yet the shepherd brother David, who was thought of last was anointed to be king.

In David's family, the beautiful Absalom and ambitious Adonijah were not chosen. GOD selected Solomon the youngest and mild tempered brother to be king. Solomon's special place was to rule over one of the richest kingdoms in the world and to govern people at the time of their greatest prosperity.

David and Solomon ruled jointly for a short period.

David charged Solomon to be strong and prove himself a man. "When the time drew near for David to die, he gave a charge to Solomon, his son. I am about to go the way of all the earth," he said. "So be strong, act like a man, 3 and observe what the Lord your God requires: Walk in obedience to him, and keep his decrees and commands, his laws, and regulations, as written in the Law of Moses. Do this so that you may prosper in all you do and wherever you go 4 and that the Lord may keep his promise to me: 'If your descendants watch how they live, and if they walk faithfully before ME with all their heart and soul, you will never fail to have a successor on the throne of Israel." (1 Kings 2: 2-4 (NIV)

David instructed Solomon to walk in the ways of the LORD GOD, keep HIS statutes, HIS commandments and HIS testimony as it was written in the law of Moses. David wanted Solomon to understand these principles so that Solomon would prosper in all that he did and wherever he turned.

GOD has some charges that each of us must keep to thrive spiritually, naturally and to be blessed. We can't run away from responsibility and be blessed, we can't neglect our obligations to GOD and be blessed, we can't give up when the going gets tough and be blessed.

Psalm 1 (AMP) "tells us that blessed, (happy, fortunate prosperous and enviable) is the man whose delight and desires are in the law of the LORD and on the precepts (instructions and teachings) of GOD. He shall be like a tree firmly planted by the water, and everything he does shall prosper and come to maturity."

In our past, we may not have been thought much of or may have been considered the black sheep of the family and the one least likely to succeed. People may have told us that we were worthless and would never amount to anything. However, when GOD has chosen us, our past and even present conditions that men have made light of can't stand in the way of GOD'S blessings and destiny for us. GOD has a special place for us.

HOW DID SOLOMON DO IT?

We can only accomplish GOD's plan for us when we do as King Solomon began his reign in 1ˢᵗ Kings, and that is by listening to GOD.

How many of us have said, "I wish GOD would come to me and tell me my future now." "I pray, but GOD doesn't hear me".

"Men who don't serve GOD seem to have more or are blessed more than me."

GOD loves people who do not love HIM. While we were yet sinners, CHRIST died for us. We would not be here today if GOD didn't love the sinner. HIS purpose on earth was to call sinners to repentance.

Often you hear people say, "something made me come to church." It wasn't something, it was GOD'S love that motivated and compelled us to be in church. We have to understand that GOD is good to the unthankful and evil because of HIS love. Love begins with GOD. We love GOD because HE first loved us and we are grateful for HIS love.

Solomon had ascended to his father's thrown and was conscience of his responsibilities. He asked GOD to give him wisdom. Solomon started well by going up to the ancient tabernacle in Gibeon to offer sacrifices to the LORD. As Solomon slept, he dreamed and a happy night followed a holy day. The elements of a dream are in the mind before we sleep. Whatever we occupy our spirit with before sleep often initiates our dreams. Solomon had been thinking about his kingdom, the greatness of his father and the awesome responsibility facing him. He had a desire to rule wisely. He had spent the day in devotion to GOD and all these things reappeared in his dreams.

Solomon was not perfect before his dreams; the chapter opens saying he had married Pharaoh, king of Egypt's daughter. The marriage was profitable for Solomon, resulting in a treaty and territorial gain, but it also violated GOD'S prohibition of marriage with pagan unbelievers. But Solomon loved the LORD, that made the difference.

In 1 Kings 3: 3-10 (KJV), it reads, "And Solomon loved the LORD, walking in the statutes of David his father: only he sacrificed and burnt incense in high places. And the king went to Gibeon to sacrifice there; for that was the great high place: a thousand burnt-offerings did Solomon offer upon that altar.

In Gibeon the LORD appeared to Solomon in a dream by night: and GOD said, Ask what I shall give thee. And Solomon said, Thou hast shewed unto THY servant David my father great mercy, according as he walked before thee in truth, and in righteousness, and in uprightness of heart with THEE; and THOU hast kept for him this great kindness, that THOU hast given him a son to sit on his throne, as it is this day.

And now, O LORD my GOD, THOU hast made thy servant king instead of David my father: and I am but a little child: I know not how to go out or come in. And THY servant is in the midst of THY people which thou hast chosen, a great people, that cannot be numbered nor counted for multitude. Give therefore THY servant an understanding heart to judge THY people, that I may discern between good and bad: for who is able to judge this THY so great a people? And the speech pleased the LORD, that Solomon had asked this thing."

When our requests please GOD like Solomon's did we can expect more than we even thought would happen.

Solomon asked GOD to accept him and use him for HIS service. He offered a thousand burnt sacrifices.

Romans 12:1 KJV reads, "I beseech you, therefore, brethren, by the mercies of GOD, that ye present your bodies a living sacrifice, holy, acceptable unto GOD, which is your reasonable service."

As we continue to look at King Solomon and how he was abundantly blessed, there were things that prepared Solomon for listening to GOD and receiving HIS blessing.

Let us understand; Solomon had come from worship, the songs of praise and the united prayers prepared the young king for his dreams. Those whose hearts are uplifted by songs of praise who have been hearing about the love of GOD, who have been reminded of His mercy and forgiving unconditional love towards us, prepare the way for GOD to speak.

Those who bring sacrifices of praise into the house of the LORD and offer unto Him the sacrifice of thanksgiving can say as Samuel said in 1 Samuel 3:10 (KJV) "...Then Samuel answered, Speak; for thy servant heareth."

Solomon was alone with GOD. The crowd had disappeared. The shouts and songs and music were silenced. Let's look at some of the other characteristics of Solomon's prayer. 1) Gratitude – Solomon thanks GOD for what his father had been. David was far from a perfect man, but his son loyally overlooked his faults and praised GOD for what David had been to himself and others.

Whatever the impact others have had on our lives, parents, siblings peers, employers, lovers or friends, we survived them. We are here now so let's praise GOD for the experiences we encountered in our lives.

We need to stop looking at the mistakes that our natural or spiritual parents may have made raising us and focus on the positive. Too many of us are dwelling on past injustices, and we get stuck. We must forgive, forget and move on to the blessings that lay ahead of us. We need to do as Solomon did. He expressed gratitude for what David, his father, had been.

If we can say in our heart LORD, I want to become like YOU and always be obedient to YOUR will, I long to be earnest, humble, pure, loving and to live altogether for THEE. Then GOD says ask, and you shall receive and your joy shall be full.

HIDDEN IN A TENT

"Blessed above women shall Jael the wife of Heber the Kenite be, blessed shall she be above women in the tent." Judges 5:24 (KJV)

There should come the point in life when everyone needs to take a close look at themselves; not at our circumstances, not at what we did, not how unfair life is or who offended us. We need to acknowledge all our mistakes and imperfections. Have we ever admired a person who has been through significant changes in life and survived or do we see them as just messed up? Before we make that decision, we should consider the struggles and tragic situations in life that so many who have been chosen by GOD go through. "Confront the dark parts of yourself, and work to banish them with illumination and forgiveness. Your willingness to wrestle with your demons will cause your angels to sing. Use the pain as fuel, as a reminder of your strength." August Wilson, American playwright

Sarah, Esther, the Shuminite Woman, Moses, Job, the woman with the issue of blood, and Joseph we hear about all the time but not Jael. Who is she? I haven't heard anyone preach about Jael. She was hidden in her tent. Her time to shine hadn't come yet.

She couldn't come forward until it was her time. She had some things to experience, some things to go through, some things to overcome, some things to perfect first. GOD had to get her ready for her coming out.

Jael was overlooked. Some of us were ignored because people felt we were insignificant. They don't feel GOD can use us. They judge our background, how we dress and our lack of adequate education. They don't realize we are star quality; only GOD sees that.

GOD doesn't choose us because of our college education, how lovely we are, the designer clothes we wear, the expensive cars we drive. GOD is looking for survivors who can take a licking and keep on ticking.

When we started our ministry over 30 years ago, everything in me now was in me then. As a new pastor's wife, I was often ignored. People expressed the fact that I would destroy the ministry. They didn't feel I had the capability, nor the qualifications to help the ministry to grow. I already had low self-esteem from the abuses I had suffered growing up. It made me doubt myself, who I was and more importantly who I could and would be. People watched to see how long it would take the ministry to fail because of me. They had an opinion of what characteristics they thought I lacked. Some of the people smiling in my face today were tearing me apart 30 years ago. I have learned that GOD will hide our qualities sometimes until HE's ready to use us. It takes a lot of time to develop a woman or man with real potential that GOD wants to use. When I hear my resume now, I say to myself, "is that me, the one people said wouldn't amount to anything the one they wrote off?" I almost allowed people to do just that.

We have a cotillion for our young women every three years. The whole church is involved. It entails months of sacrifice and preparation. Many girls drop out. Some who had waited for the opportunity to become a debutant couldn't go through the struggle and long training. Those who endured had a coming out before hundreds of people. They wore their white gowns and were presented qualified to society. If we want to receive the rewards and blessings we desire, we have to persevere over anything that tries to stop our progress.

How many people are asking themselves, "When is it going to be my time to be recognized?" We must stop comparing ourselves to what we see on the surface of other individuals. We don't know what they have been through to get where they are now. We all are unique and qualified if we allow GOD the time to mold and make us into what HE would have us to be. It will not be what other people choose or even what we may have in our minds to become. Some of us have had experiences that no one around us has experienced. We are designer originals. We have experienced some things that have taken others out, but we are still standing. We have survived some things that didn't break us in the past and won't break us now. The things that didn't break us made us strong. The word of GOD says, "There hath no temptation taken you but such as is common to man: but GOD is faithful, who will not suffer you to be tempted above that ye are able; but will with the temptation also make a way to escape, that ye may be able to bear it." (1 Corinthians 10:13 KJV)

Jael was not a Jew but a Gentile. GOD exposed her to the Jewish nation. When it came time for her to choose how to worship, she decided to worship with the people of GOD. We can't allow the circumstances of our birth to dictate how we live our life. The moment we were born satan knew we were destined for greatness. Our greatness is going to come out of the stressful situations we have survived.

If people look down on us, walk by us, won't let us join the club, won't call on us to do anything significant, we need to know that it's all a part of GOD's plan for our growth. When we depend on people to make us, GOD can't develop us into what HE wants us to be.

Even though they talk about us, scandalize our name it's all for the time when GOD unhides our potential to be used by HIM. Had Jael or I gotten out of the tent before the time it would have destroyed us. We have to stay faithful in the tent.

We can read the results of accomplishments in resumes but we don't know how a person's life story began. There is nothing wasted in our lives. The abusive childhood experiences, the things we suffered growing up, the tragedies we survived, the broken relationships, the mistakes we've made and struggles we are still facing are part of GOD's plan. We may not understand why we suffer some things, but the word of GOD encourages us, "... we know that all things work together for good to them that love

GOD, to them who are the called according to HIS purpose." Romans 8:28 (KJV)

GOD uses all our experiences for the position he has destined for us in our future.

Everything we have been through was making us strong enough to lay the blow to kill the enemy. They were designed to build up our spiritual muscles of faith and trust to believe the word of GOD that says, "I can do all things through CHRIST which strengthens me." (Philippians 4:13 KJV)

GOD is not going to do anything new with us that HE has not prepared us for.

Jael was preparing all her life to become blessed above women in the tent.

1. Prophecy

"Deborah a prophetess called Barak and told him that the LORD commanded him to go to battle with Sisera, Captain of Jabin's army. GOD would deliver Sisera into Barak's hand. Barak replied, if thou will go with me I will go but if not I won't go. Deborah agrees to go but informs Barak that the journey he takes shall not be for his honor for the LORD shall sell Sisera into the hands of a woman. It was a disgrace to die by the hand of a woman." Barak didn't appear to be concerned about that. Deborah was a mighty leader and had proven herself exceptional. So if Deborah killed Sisera Barak could save some face. (Judges 4: 5-9 KJV)

Watch out for prophecies that you don't have all the information on because the woman Barak thought would do the job wasn't the one GOD had planned on. Don't just run off with a half prophecy and begin to plan our life around something that might not be for us. A prophecy is a confirmation on what GOD has placed in our spirit.

2. Preparation

GOD prepares us in advance for the work HE calls us to do. Jael had kinship ties with the Israelites through her husband, Heber. Heber

145

was descended from Jethro who had been the father of Moses wife. Jael's tribe were metal smiths. It is possible that they assisted in making the 900 chariots of iron that Sisera and his men rode to battle. Her tribe was nomads. They traveled wherever they could find work. They moved from place to place and Jael was used to putting up and taking down tents. Wives had to pitch and maintain their tents. It was an eastern custom that when a guest came into your tent, you were responsible for his protection. Jael's tent was the ideal hiding place for Sisera.

Jael knew just how to set the hammer and the pin and just how powerfully to land the blow to pitch a tent. Jael had grown strong in muscle power over the years from pitching tents. She was prepared for the day she needed the strength to drive a nail through Sisera's head.

GOD doesn't ask us to do anything that he is not already in the process of preparing us to be successful at. If we are called to preaching, study the word. If our desire is to play an instrument it takes hours and hours of practice. When called to Pastor, it requires someone who is not lazy but willing to sacrifice family and personal pleasures for the people of GOD.

There was peace between King Jabin and the Kenites. The Kenites were metal smiths. Jael's campsite must have been close to the battlefield if her family was making and supplying weapons for the army of the enemy.

3. The Set Up

GOD makes our battles a fair fight. Sisera's whole army was defeated. GOD sent a storm and turned the river into mud holes, and Sisera's 900 chariots were useless, and he was running for his life. He got out of the chariot and was on foot. One man and one woman. Sisera was exhausted and scared and that made him as vulnerable as one woman. When we are called to a GOD ordained ministry, we may get tired and discouraged, but we will not be overwhelmed by the power of the enemy. I like to quote this scripture, "... When the enemy shall come in like a flood, the Spirit of the Lord shall lift up a standard against him." Isaiah 59:19 (KJV)

4. Internal Struggle

Jael had an internal struggle. Her obedience to GOD caused Jael to break from her husband's values. She was in an awkward position of conflicting loyalties. Her husband Herber the Kenite had made an alliance with the enemy of Israel. Jael takes the initiative and invites Sisera into her tent not only without her husband's consent but against her husband's wishes if he had known. It was the custom at that time that only a woman's husband or father could enter her tent. Heber was at peace with Jabin the King. Jael assumes the male role of the assassin in her service to the LORD. However, she is acknowledged by Deborah as blessed above women. Jael willingly put herself in danger. Jael put her life and her marriage at risk.

I believe she sent out an arrow prayer as Nehemiah did when he stood before the King in Nehemiah 2:4 KJV and the king asked him what do you request. And the Bible says Nehemiah prayed. It was a quick internal prayer, an arrow prayer, direct and to the point and then he answered. Are we prepared to obey immediately in any situation? We need to send some arrow prayers before we answer too quickly in any situation we face. Jael in the tent wins a richer blessing than Barak in the field. Sisera found an enemy when he expected a faithful friend.

5. Decisions.

Jael respects Sisera's position. No doubt she recognized him because the word says her husband and the king were at peace with each other. She appeared to act with honesty. In offering him shelter. She was probably in awe of his presence and a little frightened too. She invites him into her tent. She offers him the best hospitality. A place to lay down. A blanket to cover and warm himself. He asks for water and she gives him expensive buttermilk or cream. She served it on her best china.

Here is a man exhausted thirsty frightened and we all know that when you can't sleep and under a lot of tension we've been told to drink some warm milk. She applied her nurturing and nourishing skills that GOD has gifted women with. She made him feel secure. We don't know what her motives were at the time.

Did Jael plan to kill Sisera or protect him?

"He said unto her, Stand in the door of the tent, and it shall be when any man doeth come and enquire of thee and say, Is there any man here?

Thou shalt say, No." (Judges 3:30 KJV) Now here the word adds THEN. "Then she took the nail..." (Judges 4:31 KJV)

When Sisera wanted her to tell a lie for him, she wouldn't make such a promise. If you ask me to lie, you'll ask me to steal; you'll ask me to compromise my body, you'll ask me to kill.

We must not sin against GOD to oblige those whom we love or hold in high regard or fear. Her principals were compromised. Learn to say no when we know we ought to say it. There are always people around whose purpose is to speak confusion in our ear and encourage us to compromise our principals and commitment to GOD. Watch who whispers in your ear. Let us learn to respect our judgment and values. If we value our health, our reputation, our piece of mind and personal independence, sometimes we have to say no. Whoever would encourage us to go against GOD's program sets himself against GOD, and we must deny one or the other.

6. What If?

It was a divine power that enabled Jael to do what she did. It inspired her with a more than manly courage. What if Sisera should awake before she completed her task? The enemy was pursuing him, and the least noise would have awakened him. Even though asleep he was still on guard in fear for his life. What if her hand should shake? What if she should drop the hammer or the nail? What if she should miss his head? What if? Jael put aside the what ifs and having obtained help from GOD she did the job effectively.

What if I am not good enough? What if the people don't receive me? What if I mess up? We need to get rid of the what "ifs" that are keeping us from doing what GOD has called us to do.

7. The Fulfillment Of Prophecy

It had been prophesied that Sisera's death would be at the hands of a woman and GOD's word will not return void.

Sisera was not Jael's enemy because there was peace between her husband and the Canaanites. She had nothing to gain by his death. The Israelites were in pursuit and would soon have overtaken him. She could have left him to his fate. He was a doomed man, and there was no necessity for her to endanger herself to ensure his destruction. Why must she be the executioner, because GOD said so? The killing of Sisera was a dangerous undertaking for a lone woman, but she was led by divine impulse and obedience to a divine command to take away Sisera's life. She did not have time to go and find the Israelite troops. It was her moment. It was up to her, or it wasn't going to happen. Her moment had come. It was her time to get out of hiding in the tent. It was time for her to use what GOD had been preparing her for all her life. She had received a commission from GOD. Her faith triumphed over all her inhibitions and doubts. How could she have committed murder? How could GOD have commissioned this? Well if Sisera had died in battle or GOD had employed a flood or storm or fire to destroy the enemy we would have no questions. She was only the executioner of a GOD given order. To her, it was the battle of the LORD of hosts against the heathen who refused to worship HIM. Sisera was the LORD's enemy.

Murder is a crime that is forbidden, I'm sure she was confused. Is this GOD? But faith triumphed. Sisera's people were the oppressors of the LORD's people for twenty years. Their wickedness was marked for extermination.

The flood happened in Noah's time, and the world will be destroyed by fire when the LORD returns for HIS people. The enemy can't continue to harass GOD's people and try to destroy GOD's plans. GOD will send HIS terminators to put the enemy in his place. "..., Touch not mine anointed and do my prophets not harm." 1 Chronicles 16:22 (KJV)

Jael was the executioner of a righteous sentence. She left a pattern to be followed by those who face difficulties and sacrifices in the service of GOD. We must put to death the enemy of the flesh, with it's affections and lusts. We must strike down the things we have admitted into the tents of our heart that are not of GOD. We have to hit a nail through fornication, adultery, witchcraft, homosexuality, cigarets, alcohol, drugs, jealousy, envy, strife, backbiting, gossip, rebellion and disrespect for leadership. Depression, suicide, and failure to obey the will of GOD must die. One woman did what ten thousand men could not do. She ended years of oppression by exterminating the enemy of the Israelites. The honor for the final victory goes to Jael as Deborah had prophesied.

Conclusion

Sisera dies not in a bed of honor of old age, not on the field of battle with a great sword wound but in the corner of a tent at the feet of a woman with a disgraceful wound. He was killed with one nail through his head. He whose chariots were constructed with thousands of nails was destroyed by one, and he goes down in shame. The fate of a proud man. The triumph of a humble, obedient woman of GOD. If we compare the story of Jael and the young boy David, when he killed the giant Goliath, we see several similarities in their character.

Both Jael and David would appear physically weak and smaller than their opponent. They both used unlikely weapons. They used divine wisdom rather than military methods. David cut off goliath's head after killing him with a slingshot, and a stone and Jael pierced Sisera's skull with a nail.

Jael is an example of faith when obedience to GOD is beyond human comprehension. She could not do what she did without GOD's help and intervention. Challenging and extreme sacrifices have to be made in the service of GOD.

Jael had an idea of Sisera's character as an enemy of the GOD of heaven whom the Israelites worshiped. As human beings, we are responsible in some measure for our destiny. We have to make the choice to destroy what is keeping us hidden in our personal tents and trust GOD for strength and knowledge to bring us out.

WHY DID NOAH CURSE HIS GRANDSON?

"And Noah awoke from his wine and knew what his younger son had done unto him. And he said, Cursed be Canaan; a servant of servants shall he be unto his brethren." (Genesis 9:24-25 KJV)

We read in the Book of Genesis 9:22 KJV "And Ham, the father of Canaan, saw the nakedness of his father and told his two brethren without." The question of why Noah cursed his grandson, Canaan, when Ham had sinned, has been debated for over two thousand years.

The following are groups that we teach descended from Noah's son Ham: Chinese, Egypt, Libya, West Africa, Middle East (Canaan), Sinai, Hindu Kush many island nations of Asia, Ethiopia, and lower Africa, Babylonia, and some of the American tribes.

This passage of scripture has been used as an explanation for why African Americans were subjected to slavery.

In the book of Genesis, Ham himself is not cursed, and race or skin color is not mentioned. What we can be clear about is that Noah's curse had to do with a rebellious son, not skin color.

Ham observed his father's nakedness, but his other two brothers deliberately did not. (Genesis 9:23–24 KJV) states, "And Shem and Japheth took a garment, and laid it upon both their shoulders and went backward, and covered the nakedness of their father and their faces were backward, and they saw not their father's nakedness."

If Ham had accidentally seen his father's nakedness and covered him with a blanket and if Ham had also protected Noah by not speaking about it, then there probably would not have been a curse. Telling his brother's was gossip and disrespectful.

Noah could not curse his son since GOD had already blessed Ham. (Genesis 9:1 KJV) reads, "And GOD blessed Noah and his sons and said unto them, be fruitful and multiply and replenish the earth."

When we review the story of Balaam and Balak, it gives us incite into why Noah did not curse Ham.

And GOD said to Balaam, "You shall not go with them; you shall not curse the people, for they are blessed." (Numbers 22:12 AMP)

Ham, the father of Canaan, saw the nakedness of his father and told his two brothers outside. Noah exclaimed "Cursed be Canaan! (Ham's son), he shall be the servant of servants to his brethren!" (Genesis 9:25 KJV)

We can only surmise that Ham was making fun of his father's lack of dignity at the moment when he informed his brothers. In showing disrespect to his father, Ham brought on a generational curse that would start with his son Canaan.

So we see here the sins of the father passed to the son. Generational curses are curses passed from to generation to generation. Our children, grandchildren, and great-grandchildren will carry a curse that we may have received for things we have done wrong and not know why. Somebody in our generation has to meet the curse breaker, the LORD JESUS CHRIST.

"Cursed is he who dishonors his father or his mother. All the people shall say, Amen." (Deuteronomy 27:16 AMP)

"Honor thy father and mother; (which is the first commandment with promise." (Ephesians 6:2 KJV)

"Children, obey your parents in all things: for this is well-pleasing unto the Lord." (Colossians 3:20)

"Honor your father and mother. Then you will live a long, full life in the land the LORD your GOD is giving you." (Exodus 20:12 NLT)

"Obey them that have the rule over you, and submit yourselves: for they watch for your souls, as they that must give account, that they may do it with joy, and not with grief: for that is unprofitable for you." (Hebrews 13:17 KJV)

Honoring our parents, both natural and spiritual is an important part of what GOD requires. When we don't honor our physical and spiritual parents, we become susceptible for adverse situations to come between GOD and us. We place a barrier between receiving the best that GOD has for us and the unproductive, painful, destructive things many endure unnecessarily.

Parents are people. They are not perfect. They make mistakes. We must learn how to cover our parents as Ham's two brothers did and not expose them to shame, embarrassment, and ridicule. We need to Pray before we jump to conclusions..

We must be careful what we say. Words can be hurtful. There is an old saying "sticks and stones may break my bones, but words will never harm me." That is a lie. Hurtful words cut deeply into our spirit. It may be better to have some broken bones that will eventually heal, than hurtful words that leave deep down infected, unhealed wounds.

When there are unresolved issues with parents, have open communication about it.
It allows parents to know how we're thinking and gives them a chance

to share their life experience. It also helps the relationship to talk to parents about what's going on in our life.

We don't know if Noah ever forgave Ham, but we do know that curses can carry over from generation to generation. Learn to forgive. Forgiveness can break the generational curses that tear families apart. It's so easy to take parents and family for granted. Our parents will not always be there. We need to take some time to remind our parents that we love them. Break that generational curse now; don't let it move to another generation.

OUR ATTITUDE AFFECTS OUR ALTITUDE

JOHN 15:11 KJV- "These things have I spoken unto you, that MY joy might remain in you, and that your joy might be full."

An enthusiastic person is an energized person. The passion they have for the tasks they perform is evident by the joy they exhibit. You can feel the sincerity, love and excitement they feel. It captivates the audience. It shows in their faces and body movements. They easily draw you into the moment with them.

When you enjoy what you are doing in the natural and spiritual, no one has to pump you up or make you have to give your all. You don't need cheerleaders to make you praise GOD. If the song that was sung was off key and the words mixed up, just the fact that it is worship makes you forget the technicalities and fall without restraint into all out worship and praise.

I wonder why some saints join ministries and act like they are doing GOD a favor and give efficient (just to be doing something) service. GOD surely doesn't need any of us to get HIS program across. The mere fact that HE gifted us to minister in various areas is worthy of a performance that will leave us breathless and overwhelmed with gratitude to be chosen.

A father and child were once looking at a picture of CHRIST standing at a door knocking. After looking at the picture a while the father said to the child, "I wonder why they don't let JESUS in.?" The child thought for a moment and replied, "I know why! I bet they are down in the basement and can't hear HIM knocking." Too often that's where we are, down in the basement of half doing; down in the basement of just enough faith; down in the basement of too little gratitude; down in the basement of when I have nothing else that takes precedence.

When we open the door of our hearts to the joy of the LORD we receive the promises that GOD has waiting for us. Our altitude in GOD depends upon our attitude in how we serve HIM.

A FOOL CAN'T GO TO HEAVEN, FIVE ALREADY TRIED

Matthew Chapter 25 1:14 KJV This parable is about ten virgins. Ten is the number of perfection. Ten persons were required to form a synagogue and to be present at any official ceremony.

It was the custom sometimes used among the Jews in a marriage ceremony, that the bridegroom came with his friends late in the night to the bride's house where she and her bridesmaids were expecting him. When notice was given of the bridegroom's arrival they were to go out with their lamps to illuminate his way into the house with ceremony and formality.

In the parable of the ten virgins, the five foolish virgins failed to have a back up supply of oil. As we grow in faith and our walk with CHRIST, we need reserves of courage, insight, endurance and faith. We can't have just enough to live on through our ordinary experiences. We need to have a stored up supply to fall back on when tragedy, a crisis or disaster comes into our lives. We can't survive on having just enough. It is not enough to do good, we must get in the habit of doing good. It is not, enough to just believe, we must get into the habit of ever increasing our faith. It is not enough to do a virtuous act; we must adopt a life style of living virtuously. It is not enough to perform an act of obedience; we must get into the habit of being obedient.

As we look more closely into this parable, it appears that a major fault of the five foolish virgins was negligence and carelessness. They placed other priorities above being prepared to go further in GOD. When we make hair dresser appointments, Dr. appointments, baby sitting obligations, shopping trips etc. that coincide with a commitment we have spiritually and fail to attend to GOD's program; we become as one of the foolish virgins.

GOD is a jealous GOD. HE wants to be number one in everything we do. That includes prayer, fasting, worship, praise, studying HIS WORD, paying our tithe and attending HIS service. Negligence and carelessness will impact our preparations to meet GOD when He returns and most importantly how extensive our blessing will be.

It is good to be watchful but just as all the virgins, there will come times when we all get weary and tired and need to sleep. Sleep can be a means of restoration or sleep can be a way to escape reality. When we awake restored we have renewed energy to continue the purpose that GOD has designed for us. When we use sleep as a means to escape we will awake to find ourselves in our same situation or worse. If we have not prepared ourselves with back up prayer, praise and worship we won't have enough strength to move forward and overcome the obstacles that prevent us from becoming all that GOD wants us to be.

In this passage of scripture the foolish virgins had the same knowledge of the LORD as the wise virgins but they had only maintained a portion of it. Part of their foolishness consisted in thinking themselves safe. They trusted in their own hearts when nothing could be more deceitful. They didn't store up reserves in preparation to meet the LORD.

There are three kinds of Christians.
1. Those who know they are saved and are constantly refilling their oil of the HOLY SPIRIT.
2. Those who recognize that they are not where they should be but are making an effort to become stronger in the LORD.
3. The last group is the saddest of all. They are the Christians that think they are saved and are not making any effort to replenish their oil supply of the HOLY SPIRIT.

Oil will not mix with water. It will separate and float to the top. If we have the oil of the HOLY SPIRIT we can't mix easily with all worldly desires and habits. When we begin to think and handle the situations we face in life like those who don't know the LORD deep down in the depths of their soul, the oil of the HOLY SPIRIT will begin to separate itself from us and rise to the top and our spiritual life will sink to the bottom.

We need to look beyond our present status and the situations we are facing today. There is a tomorrow with GOD. There is a hope beyond the grave. There is eternal life promised to those of us who guard and maintain our HOLY SPIRIT. We refill our spiritual lamps through fasting, prayer, praise, worship, reading the WORD of GOD, soul winning, and the service we render unto GOD in the house of GOD.

Seeing that their oil was drying up, the foolish virgins ask their wise sisters to share their oil with them. The wise virgins were too smart to part with any of their precious oil. Their conduct appeared to be selfish at the moment. Wisdom had taught them to prepare and store up additional oil just in case they faced unforeseen circumstances. We can't share our brain or heart and continue to maintain our natural life and we can't share our HOLY SPIRIT or anointing without draining our spiritual life. We can't count on our mother's prayers or the preacher laying hands on us periodically to maintain a healthy spiritual life. We are all responsible individually for the preservation of our own spiritual lives.

The wise virgins refused to share their oil with their unprepared sisters. I can imagine they must have said, "we must not, we cannot, we will not share with you lest there not be enough for all of us. Go and buy for yourselves." We've got to have our own faith, our own power, our own joy. We can benefit by fellowship with the saints, their testimonies, and prayers but our blessings, power and strength are dependent upon our personal salvation.

The just shall live by his own faith. Every man shall give an account of himself to GOD and therefore let every man prove his own worth. This walk with CHRIST is personal. Our relationship with HIM is a one on one relationship. Our righteousness cannot be shared. We can't give our holiness to another; only GOD can do that. We can't buy salvation or blessings with money. We receive blessings from our prayers, works, tears and the sufferings and trials we have triumphed over. We need to stay in love with GOD, build ourselves up in faith, prayer and endure hardness as good soldiers in JESUS CHRIST. No human being has a supernatural abundant store of prayer or faith that they can just give some away.

In the scripture, we read that the door was shut. The door was shut first to secure those that were within and secondly to exclude those that were outside. A door is a barrier which can separate two different places. The door represents heaven. The persecutions of this world cannot get through that door. The bereavements in this life cannot get through that door. The fatigues of this life cannot get through that door. The stress of this life cannot get through that door. The heartache and heartbreaks of this life cannot get through that door. The financial struggles we face in this life cannot get through that door. Relationship problems with spouses, children, co-workers, and yes, church members cannot get through that door. Poor health cannot get through that door.

We hear closing doors when something which was once ours and we used freely, took for granted, is ours no longer. Age can close doors. Lack of education can close doors. Unavailable job opportunities can close doors. Disappointment can close doors. Shattered dreams can close doors. It is up to each of us to decide which side of the door we want to be on in eternity.

The wise and foolish virgins' lamps were evidently handheld lamps intended to be carried about the house. When they were required to burn for a considerable time, they needed to be replenished from a small jar of oil whenever the light grew dim.

The lamps of the foolish virgins once had light, or else they could not have gone out. The foolish virgins lit their lamps but made no provisions for refilling them. They are a warning to all those who think just being saved or having the Holy Spirit is enough.

Those who can remember the time when they had serious thoughts and a determination to serve GOD wholeheartedly, worked diligently, but are now relying on their past works to bring them to the kingdom of GOD. Those who are no longer refilling their Holy Spirit at the altar or making an earnest effort to fulfill the gospel. We are commissioned to go into all the world to teach and preach the life, death, and resurrection of our Savior. (Matthew 28:16-20 KJV). Those who have developed a selfish attitude. "I have to look out for me" or "I can't help anybody else because I'm wrapped up in my problems". Those who have lost the desire to maintain within themselves the spiritual life they had once began.

The wise virgins are those Christians who recognize that they must have within themselves the power that will enable them to endure until the end. They have right impulses and a desire to work for GOD. They are not sitting down on the gifts that GOD has given them.

The more we work for GOD, the stronger our beliefs and principles will become. We must consider both our outward and inner spiritual life. If we do not renew our supply of spiritual oil, carefully see the conditions of our spirit, stop looking at and pointing the finger at others and search ourselves to see if we are where we need to be in CHRIST our spiritual lamps will go out. If we are not careful and prayerful, the good works we once did will soon become less frequent, less sincere and less lovely. Without replenishing our spiritual oil, the HOLY SPIRIT will become lazy and dry up.

GOD needs to know that HE can count on us for service and that we will remain faithful. An inconsistent maybe I will, and maybe I won't performing child of GOD cannot be used. They are not dependable. GOD wants active, cheerful, willing, faithful workers in HIS vineyard. GOD wants workers that love HIM deep down in the depths of their souls. It's all right to wait for the vision that GOD may have shown us, but HE doesn't want us sitting by unproductive while we are waiting.

The foolish virgins were not necessarily hypocrites. As many Christians today, they were just too easily satisfied with professing holiness but denying the power thereof.

The foolish virgins had their lamps and they lit them. They had oil in them but failed to store up an extra supply. We can't just survive spiritually with just initially receiving the HOLY SPIRIT. We need to constantly seek a refilling by continuously reaching out to GOD at the altar.

If the bridegroom had not delayed his coming all would have been well for them. It was the delay that proved fatal for the foolish virgins. Time revealed the shallowness of the foolish virgins. The foolish virgins are like too many today who have not stored up enough prayer, praise and worship to fall back on when faced with difficult situations. They represent Christians who have a brief or temporary religious experience.

The foolish Christians are content to live on their experiences of today and yesterday; failing to make preparation for maintaining the spiritual strength needed for the future. It is alright to look back on past experiences for encouragement but to fail to build for the future places us all in the same category of the foolish virgins.

Struggles of some kind are sure to come into the life of every Christian. It may take the form of affliction, persecution, temptation or lack of endurance and commitment. We can't act like a child of GOD today and tomorrow leave a question in the minds of others about who we are serving. The Word tells us that GOD does not honor lukewarm Christians. (Revelation 3:14 KJV).

We've got to endure hardness as good soldiers of JESUS CHRIST. Endurance is the replenishing oil that will get us closer to the mark of the prize of a higher calling in JESUS CHRIST.

The bridegroom is OUR LORD JESUS CHRIST. The bride is the church. The virgins represent the believers, the members of the church, us. Let us make note that all ten of the individuals in the parable were virgins. They all had some regard for the bridegroom. They all desired to honor him by going forth to meet him. They were all outwardly the same. They were all provided with lamps that at the moment were burning. They were all prepared to perform the same duty. They were all moved by one desire to welcome the bridegroom and to partake of the banquet.

It can be assumed from this that they all had some form of love for the bridegroom. The ten virgins had many features in common. The difference in them could not be discerned, at least for the moment. The common likeness and resemblance between the wise and foolish virgins continued for a considerable amount of time. The difference was not detected until the arrival of the bridegroom. In all outward appearances the wise and foolish virgins were the same. The difference between them was internal.

Even today we cannot discern the difference among saints in the house of GOD. All of us who call ourselves saints are professing that we love the LORD, worship HIM, and are on a mission to lead others to CHRIST. We testify that we are sold out to GOD and giving HIM our all. We all profess that we are undefiled followers of the LORD, waiting for HIS coming, and will love HIS appearance. But some of us will fail. Just like the foolish virgins, when the time comes for us to actually go into action, we are not prepared to do the job. Are we really preparing today to meet the LORD when HE comes?

UNFORGIVENESS CAN BLOCK OUR PRAYERS

"But as for you, ye thought evil against me; but GOD meant it unto good, to bring to pass, as it is this day, to save much people alive." (Genesis 50:20 KJV)

"Forbearing one another and forgiving one another, if any man have a quarrel against any: even as CHRIST forgave you, so also do ye." (Colossians 3:13 KJV)

In this passage of scripture, Joseph is speaking to his brothers who had sold him in his youth to the Midianites. Joseph had shared his dreams and visions with his brothers and his father. We can't always share our dreams and visions with everybody. People may not understand, or become envious of where they think GOD is taking us. Joseph's father apparently favored him. Parents, we have to be careful not to demonstrate that we prefer one child over another.

Families often become disengaged when preferences are shown among siblings. Joseph's brothers became jealous. Jealousy will cause people to try to destroy or even kill someone.

As we delve further into this scripture, we find that GOD allowed Joseph to suffer. Patience, submission, endurance, long-suffering, and persistence in well-doing, are passive virtues that are harder to learn. We need to be courageous in situations that seem negative in our lives; they are only momentary if we are walking in the will of GOD.

GOD had a plan for Joseph's suffering.

Whatever sorrows and troubles that we are facing at this time, we need to understand that GOD has allowed them to come to give us the opportunity to prepare for the future that HE has planned.

We need to assure ourselves that GOD has a plan and a purpose for us in the situation that we are facing. We need to take the scripture at its word when it says "...weeping may endure for a night but joy cometh in the morning." (Psalm 30:5 KJV)

If we believe the word of GOD, we need to wipe the tears away so that we can clearly see the vision. GOD does not reward us for walking away from responsibility. We cannot abandon the gifts and the calling that we say GOD has given us when things don't go our way. We must pray for patience to wait on GOD. We need to repeat over and over again until we have victory, "this is going to work in my favor; this is going to work in my favor".

Don't be discouraged or give up the fight or be unfaithful in the very little. Be thankful that GOD has given us this time of discipline and soul searching. Remember GOD brings HIS chosen people to the brink of sorrow, trouble, and frustration then HE opens a path so that we can pass through untouched.

When we pray, we need to bind unforgiveness. When we pray, we need to bind anger. When we pray, we need to bind the desire to get even. When we pray, we need to ask GOD to help us to trust HIS Word. "Dearly beloved, avenge not yourselves, but rather give place unto wrath; for it is written, Vengeance is mine; I will repay, saith the LORD," (Romans 12:19 KJV). GOD will show us the way that we should take.

We need to command the enemy to release the stronghold that he has over our family, our finances, our health, our careers and our spiritual growth. Tell GOD in our prayer how much we love, worship and adore HIM. Tell GOD we give HIM all the glory. When we tell GOD that HE is our LORD, and HE is King of our life, the iniquity, anger and pain will begin to dissipate.

As we pray, let us not forget, the thorns that pierced our LORD's brow, the beating HE endured, and the blood that was shed on Calvary. Let us thank GOD for the privilege to go through our temporary trials. Let us be grateful that HE found us worthy to endure our present suffering. Whatever it is, it is not worth us getting a negative report when we stand before GOD at the judgment. We are all going to be judged by GOD. We want to hear HIM say, "...well done my good and faithful servant... enter into the joy of thy LORD." (Matthew 25:21 KJV)

There is no fate so terrible that we cannot overcome. Isaiah 54:17 KJV reads, "No weapon that is formed against thee shall prosper; and every tongue that shall rise against thee in judgment thou shalt condemn. This is the heritage of the servants of the LORD, and their righteousness is of me, saith the LORD".

When we are reviled and hated we need to carefully search our hearts to see if we have given any cause to those who hate and revile us. If we endure grief wrongfully as Joseph did we follow in the steps of our SAVIOR.

We need to recognize that the enemy wants us to hold on to past hurts and feelings of being abandoned and not supported. The blessings, we have right now we didn't earn. GOD gave them to us. How dare we stay home and reopen old wounds over and over again. Who do we think we are punishing? It is certainly not GOD. HE does not need us. We need HIM.

We cannot rewind the clock of life and go back and change anything. Our prayer should be according to Philippians 3:13-14 KJV, "Brethren, I count not myself to have apprehended: but this one thing I do, forgetting those things which are behind, and reaching forth unto those things which are before, I press toward the mark for the prize of the high calling of GOD in CHRIST JESUS."

Let us remember to ask GOD in the situations that we face, what HE wants us to learn from the experience? "We need GOD to help us not to walk away from a negative challenge until we have mastered it.

When we begin to realize that every time we let our bitterness and stubbornness keep us from Worship that we show our ungratefulness for what CHRIST endured on the cross. Our prayer should be, "LORD I want to anoint the wounds you suffered for me with the balm of my worship and praise."

We need to say, "LORD, YOU don't deserve my neglecting service because I can't get over a problem." We need to apologize for every time; we came up short because we allowed personal issues to get in the way of our service, our praise, and our worship.

ENOUGH IS ENOUGH

"On the seventh day, when the heart of the king was merry with wine, he commanded Mehuman, Biztha, Harbona, Bigtha, and Abagtha, Zethar, and Carcas, the seven chamberlains that served in the presence of Ahasuerus the king, To bring Vashti the queen before the king with the crown royal, to shew the people and the princes her beauty: for she was fair to look on. But the queen Vashti refused to come at the king's commandment by his chamberlains: therefore was the king very wroth, and his anger burned in him." (Esther 1:10-12 KJV)

In the Book of Esther, Queen Vashti's self-respect and moral values apparently meant more to her than her role as Queen. Queen Vashti accepted disgrace and dismissal. That meant not only giving up her husband but her luxurious lifestyle.

King Ahasuerus had unlimited power, his power was supreme, the lives of everyone in his kingdom depended upon his word. He ruled without resistance and control. At the feast thrown by King Ahasuerus, all his officers were allowed to do according to everyman's pleasure.

Let's look at the evil that was occurring at this feast. The king feasted but Vashti his queen suffered. The king made an impressive display at his feast. He showed his magnificence, his material nature, the narrowness of his point of view, and the wantonness of his spirit. When will we learn that a man's life consists not only in the things he possesses. Money can't buy you peace of mind; money can't offer you eternal health, and it can't buy eternal life. "For what shall it profit a man if he shall gain the whole world and lose his own soul?" (Mark 8:36 KJV)

The king was drunk. Drunkenness robs its victims of self-respect. What people would not think of doing when they are sober they shamelessly indulge in when they are intoxicated.

The king commands "fetch Vashti now and make a show of her beauty, for she is fair to look upon". The king was not only drunk, but he was selfish. When a man's heart is merry with wine, all that is sacred in humanity goes out of him. Noah got drunk after the flood, and his sons had to cover his nakedness. Lot got drunk after the destruction of Sodom and Gomorrah, and his daughters had sex with him to obtain children; he committed incest. Proverbs 20:1 KJV tells us that, "Wine is a mocker, strong drink is raging, and whosoever is deceived thereby is not wise".

Queen Vashti, aware of the drunken state of her husband the king, had reached a point in herself where she said enough is enough.

The WORD of GOD tells us that the husband is the head of the wife, but no husband has the right to command a woman to do that which is wrong. "So ought men to love their own wives as their bodies. He that loveth his wife loveth himself." (Ephesians 5:28 KJV)

What the king requested would have infringed upon her feminine modesty. Therefore Queen Vashti had every right to disobey her drunken husband. A wife need not and should not obey her husband in what opposes GOD'S laws and her feminine honor and decency. Queen Vashti put on a crown which is beyond the power of the king to give or take away. She put on the crown of decency and honor. She refused to exhibit herself Before drunken men.. Queen Vashti's personal, dignity was more important than material gain. Queen Vashti had a soul of her own and preserved her integrity.

If women today fail to honor themselves and their self-respect they will never win the best GOD has for them. In our modern world, women are not as careful as Queen Vashti in guarding the dignity of their body. Sexual satisfaction, money, fashion, popularity and prestige are a small price to pay for a loss of one's self-respect.

Divine favor rests upon those who have the courage to stand up for such high ideals. To remain refined in speech and actions when it is the style to appear hardboiled. To be dignified when everyone else pretends to be wild. To maintain true respect and a real sense of value in an irresponsible age is challenging. Your peers may tell you that your life is boring, you are not having fun, and you don't know what is happening. Living by the WORD of GOD will enable you to maintain self-respect and your faith in GOD. It is more important to have inner peace and emotional security than to satisfy the desires of others.

1 Corinthians 6:19-20 KJV says, "What? Know ye not that your body is the temple of the HOLY GHOST which is in you, which ye have of GOD and ye are not your own? For ye are brought with a price, therefore glorify GOD in your body and in your spirit which are GOD's".

Queen Vashti's motive for refusal to obey the king's request to come into his feast may have been mixed. Perhaps she was tired from her own party responsibilities or maybe she refused because her sense of decency was injured.

We all experience mixed motives at one time or another, and Vashti's may have been also. If calling Queen Vashti to display herself was positively immoral, it was her duty to resist, whatever the consequences may be. Now Queen Vashti wasn't perfect; she made mistakes. Instead of making a mild excuse, or sending a soft answer which turneth away wrath (Proverbs 15:1 KJV) she gave a flat refusal.

Queen Vashti disobeyed the king. She was right in her reasons for that, but it was how she did it that caused irreparable harm. We have to be careful of that. It is not always what we say that causes the problem, but how we say it. Colossians 4:6 KJV reads, "let your speech be always with grace, seasoned with salt, that ye may know how ye ought to answer every man."

We need to say enough is enough to getting loud, flying off the handle and losing our temper. Had force been used to bring Queen Vashti to the king, her responsibility would have ceased but since that was not the case she had a responsibility not to yield. Queen Vashti realized that the royal crown was a cheap price to pay for her self-respect. Single women, don't give into sexual pressure and don't return to immodest dress, excessive makeup, and jewelry to gain a man. Trust GOD to give you the best. That will happen when you "seek ye first the kingdom of GOD." (Matthew 6:33 KJV). Believe the Word "...what things soever ye desire when ye pray believe that you receive them, and ye shall have them." Don't' sell GOD short. HE has you single for this time, and your concern should be in pleasing HIM.

When you strive to make yourself a whole woman you will find yourself attracted to a whole man. In this day and age, a piece of man is not good enough. Say enough is enough to settling for less than you deserve.

We don't know if Queen Vashti the wife of King Ahasuerus suffered physical abuse, but psychological and emotional abuse is just as wrong. Queen Vashti said enough is enough to psychological abuse. Men, women, and children are being abused today in one way or another. They need to reach a point where they say enough is enough and do something about it. They need to learn to love themselves enough to withdraw from an abusive situation. When we learn to love ourselves, we will elevate our low self-esteem and make decisions that will make us a whole person that can function independently.

The king commands his seven chamberlains to bring Vashti the Queen before him with the royal crown to show the men her beauty. Queen Vashti refused to come. The king was embarrassed. His pride was wounded.

For Queen Vashti to appear before the King's court when he requested, with her face uncovered, would have shocked all oriental society. The men who agreed while drunk that Queen Vashti come into the king's feast would in their sober moments have despised her. Queen Vashti's sacrifice becomes the object of hostility and the subject of an emergency counsel. The great fear was that all the wives in Persia would get too rebellious to be governed.

The King agrees at once to the cruel and unjust advice which he receives from his chamberlains. The enemy will help us find people to give us information that is not of GOD. The enemy will help us to find people to agree with our unfair treatment that we may cause.

So the self-indulgent King finds himself involved in the grievous injustice and wrong, which was the result of his sin.

We need to say enough is enough to satan and his trickery. Our prayer needs to be "LORD help me to see the truth and be strong and courageous enough to do the right thing no matter what."

The Queen was the first lady in the kingdom. She should, therefore, show obedience to the king's pleasures. She was an example to her subjects and a role model for other wives to follow. If men expect obedience from their wives let them be reasonable in their demands, otherwise half the fault of the disobedience of their wives remains with themselves. Husbands should never impose a burden upon their wives which either feminine delicacy or her particular temperament, which he ought to know, makes it too heavy for her to bear. Ephesians 5:25 KJV says, "Husbands, love your wives even as CHRIST also loved the Church and gave HIMSELF for it."

I have not heard anyone preach about the sacrifices that Queen Vashti made to enable Queen Esther to come forth and save her people from destruction. Moses paved the way for Joshua; Elijah made way for Elisha, and Rev. Dr. Martin Luther King opened the door for President Obama. Queen Vashti had the jewels, clothes, servants, honor, respect and all the riches that her title afforded her. She gave it all up for personal honor, integrity dignity modesty, virtue, peace of mind and self-esteem. It is not necessary to have a palace and royal robes to be queenly. A woman with strong faith in GOD, a deep love for GOD, herself and GOD'S people, who says enough is enough to immorality, indecency, scandalous behavior and ungodly desires is a queen.

King Ahasuerus in the book of Esther gave into wounded pride and treated his wife severely. Later in his sober state, he may have repented of his harshness. People in their wrath speak freely and eloquently but never wisely. They work with decision and energy but who is benefitted by what they do? The King not only wronged Queen Vashti but also made himself a sufferer.

When we allow ourselves to be carried away by impulse based on anger, hurt, and frustrations, we commit acts that afterward cannot be changed and may cause us, even more, pain and injury. "Vengeance is mine; I will repay saith the LORD" (Romans 12:19 KJV) the Word tells us in Ephesians 4:27 KJV, "Be ye angry and sin not: let not the sun go down upon your wrath:"

People of GOD, we all need to say enough is enough to the snares and distractions that keep us from focusing on the visions of the church and the ministry that GOD has planned for us.

Enough is enough to the devices that lead us away from fasting prayer and the Word of GOD. It is fasting, prayer and the Word of GOD that will bring marriages and relationships together and keep them that way.

We need to say enough is enough to discouragements that keep us from the job, home, education, and achieving the dreams we have for our future. Tell satan I recognize you for what you are and I have had enough of you wrecking my home. I have had enough of you destroying my children. I have had enough of you holding me back from achieving my dreams. I have had enough of you trying to steal my joy. I have had enough of you messing with my peace of mind. Enough is enough. I won't allow you to let me focus on the negative instead of the positive. I won't allow you to replace my joy with sorrow. I won't allow you to replace my laughter with tears. I won't allow you to replace my peace with confusion. I won't allow you to replace my kindness with bitterness. I won't allow you to replace my compassion with vengeance. Enough is enough. I won't allow you to take my praise because I've learned that something happens when I begin to praise GOD. When we praise and worship GOD, the enemy has to move out of our way. Worship and praise to GOD are offensive to the enemy. When we learn to say what (what will YOU have me to learn) instead of why when we find ourselves in difficult situations we will achieve spiritual success.

SERMONETTE 65

EXCESS BAGGAGE

Jonah 1:15 KJV reads, "So they took up Jonah, and cast him forth into the sea: and the sea ceased from her raging."

On the ship, Jonah had become excess baggage. We need to begin to examine ourselves and take out the extras from our spiritual baggage before we become overweight and our soul is thrown overboard.

When we take a trip on a plane, there is a certain amount of luggage that we can carry free. When we exceed the weight limit, we have to pay for the extra baggage. It is the same in our spiritual lives. When we take on extra baggage, envy, anger, jealousy, backbiting, gossip, fornication, lying and deception, we have to pay for it. Usually, it begins to rob us of our joy, and the word tells us that the joy of the LORD is our strength (Nehemiah 8:10 KJV).

When we lose our joy, we lose the strength and power to fight the enemy when he comes against us. Jonah's call was directly and explicitly from GOD. Arise, I know you have difficulties in yourself, in your people, in the mission to Nineveh but gird up your loins, stir up your strength and go. It's not peculiar that Jonah made up excuses. Moses hesitated and used the excuse that he could not speak well. Jeremiah made the excuse that he was just a child. Amos's excuse was that he was not a prophet but a herdsman and gatherer of sycamore fruit.

How many of us use excuses today to delay the work GOD wants us to do? Some of the reasons we use are "my family, my job, my home, my education, my spouse, the pastor; the missionary board won't use me." Just like us Jonah felt he had enough cause to make excuses.

The Ninevites were merciless, cruel, and proud and practiced horrible cruelties on their captives. It was a bloody city full of lies and robbery. The assignment was disagreeable. Disagreeableness of duty is a stumbling block. It is excess baggage. It makes us unfaithful. We become neglectful, and the job we have to do is half done or not done at all.

Jonah rose up and fled to Tarsus and the presence of GOD. Sometimes we act as if GOD is in the church but not in our homes or on the job, Psalm 139:7-8 KJV reads, "Whither shall I go from THY spirit? Or whither shall I flee from THY presence? If I ascend into heaven, THOU art there: if I make my bed in hell, behold, THOU art there." GOD is everywhere. We can't hide from GOD.

Jonah goes in a direction exactly opposite in which he had been sent. GOD said go North East, and he went South West. I don't think Jonah hoped to get away from GOD, but he did expect to get away from the work that GOD had called him to do. He was determined not to be near the place that GOD sent him unless he was forced to do the job he was chosen to do.

Sometimes we make hairdresser appointments, decide to go grocery shopping or do the laundry a few hours before choir rehearsal, auxiliary worship, bible study or missionary worship begins, and we find ourselves late or not attending our service at all. The enemy is shrewd and smart; he has us doing necessary things but at the wrong time. We have the energy to shop, visit and gossip but as worship time approaches, we become exhausted, get headaches, leg aches.etc. When we neglect our spiritual obligations, we add excess baggage to our lives.

Our greatest difficulty in doing GOD'S will is within. We need to be obedient, don't hesitate, don't delay or argue against GOD'S will. Reluctant will is excess baggage. GOD loves a cheerful giver in everything, not just financially, but in doing the job that we have been assigned in GOD'S house. We need to give 100% in the Choir, Levites, Sunday School, Missionary, Usher Board and most importantly in the Ministerial Board.

We fall little by little as Jonah did. There are many steps to reach a spiritual catastrophe. Let's look at some steps that led to Jonah's downfall. 1) He feared a new kind of work, different from the work in Israel among familiar surroundings. 2) The work was far off, involving a journey of several hundred miles. 3) He would be a foreigner in a city of proud and violent people. Excuses are excess baggage. If Bishop Harris and the Missionaries that went with him had allowed excuses to take over, they would never have gone to India or Africa and accomplished the work they did there. They may seem like valid reasons to us, but no excuse is acceptable for neglecting what GOD has called us to do. I've heard Bishop Richardson say "an excuse is the skin of a lie stuffed with a reason" in other words; we give a reason for the lie we tell.

Jonah was in a backsliding condition. When we begin to backslide, circumstances seem favorable. Take Jonah's flight for example, no illness delayed him, the sea was peaceful, and he found just the right ship he wished and going where he wanted. There was room for Jonah on board, and he had enough money for the ticket. We see this today. Members running from church to church, program to program declaring how blessed they were. They emphasize that the place was packed out, but there was a seat just for them. However, they neglected a service or responsibility at their church. We can't' be blessed when we neglect our spiritual home where our responsibilities lie.

Jonah wished to divert his mind by travel. GOD does not forcefully stop us when we choose to do what we want to do. No accident prevented Jonah on his journey down to Joppa. When we want to leave the ways of righteousness, we do not meet with too many difficulties. Sometimes we may feel troubled with self-reproach, but meantime outward circumstances may even appear to favor our downward spiral.

GOD gives us free will. We can choose to obey or disobey. The choice is up to us. Had a pleasant voyage taken Jonah to his destination or a sudden storm just drowned him in the depths of the sea we would only have known of him as a disobedient prophet. GOD dealt mercifully with Jonah. GOD sent a storm which aroused Jonah from his sleep, brought his sin before him and provided him a means of escape. 1 Corinthians 10:13 KJV tells us, "There hath no temptation taken you but such as is common to man: but GOD is faithful, who will not suffer you to be tempted above that ye are able; but will with the temptation also make a way to escape, that ye may be able to bear it."

In spite of all that seemed favorable to Jonah, he was going against GOD'S will. Have you ever had success in the wrong way, only later to find out you were in a mess? Things are not permanently favorable if GOD is not pleased. Jonah was spiritually falling when naturally things seemed to be in his favor. The enemy will make things appear promising when we are going against GOD. Jonah went down to Joppa. He went down in the ship to sleep. He went down from his moral elevation as a prophet. He went down from fellowship with GOD. He went down from peace in his soul and mind. He went down from divine service. A man may go up in society, wealth, power and fame yet morally and spiritually be going down.

Jonah is prayerless. How can the backslider pray unless he repents? Jonah is prayerless when he should have been leading others in prayer.

Let's look at Jonah, while the sinners were praying; he could not. The word of GOD tells me "if I regard iniquity in my heart, the LORD will not hear me." (Psalm 66:18 KJV). A guilty conscience makes prayer impossible until a breakdown takes place and contrition comes forth. Psalms 51:17 KJV says, "The sacrifices of GOD are a broken and a contrite heart, O GOD, thou wilt not despise." You see guilt is excess baggage. It is horrible to be in a state of suffering and cannot pray.

Jonah had utterly exhausted himself in his struggle with GOD. The great storm occurring outside could not keep him awake. Sleeping to excess is a sin, it is excess baggage, and it hinders us from fulfilling all of GOD'S work. How awkward must this have a appeared? The sinners were praying, and the servant of GOD was sleeping. Sleeping the sleep of unbelief. Sleeping the sleep of backsliding. Romans 13:11 KJV, "and that, knowing the time, that now it is high time to awake out of sleep; for now is our salvation nearer than when we believed". Jonah sleeps through the storm which his sin provoked.

Jonah was impulsive, if he had reasoned out the situation before he started on his flight, he would not have started at all. Jonah didn't examine himself. He didn't turn his eyes inward and pray. Jonah needed to pray as David did in Psalm 139:23-24 KJV, "Search me, O GOD, and know my heart: try me, and know my thoughts: And see if there be any wicked way in me, and lead me in the way everlasting." Impulsiveness, when not checked by GOD, leads to excess baggage.

The sailor's prayers, and even Jonah's, if he tried, couldn't stop the storm. GOD'S purpose was not to be accomplished in that way. When we come short of the glory of GOD, we have to do our first works over (Revelation 2:5 KJV). Men and women of GOD mess up today; they are silenced for a few months and go right back to handling GOD'S word and ministering to GOD'S people before they are restored. They pick up their previous spiritual commitments before they repent and are filled with the HOLY SPIRIT all over again. I know GOD is not pleased.

Storms are instruments of GOD'S will to show men their helplessness and their dependence. Storms are often used to punish people for rebelling against GOD'S will. Storms can come in many forms in our lives, illness, frustration of our plans, or family problems. Storms are also a test to see if we can endure hardness as good soldiers of JESUS CHRIST.

The sailors on the ship were afraid. Fear drives men to pray. Prayer becomes an instinct. No man, it has been said, has denied that there is a GOD or didn't call on GOD in a shipwreck or plane crash. The sinful sailors on board the ship stopped swearing and cursing and started praying to their god.

How many times have we heard the saints of GOD lying prostrate on the altar and crying out to GOD because a storm has arisen in their life? In the midst of the storms of our life, we must make sure that our anchor holds and grips the solid rock. We must be able to say, "though the storms are raging in my life, my soul is anchored in the LORD. We need to do like Jacob, when he wrestled with the angel, grab hold to the altar and cry "I won't let go until you bless me."

GOD calls men to private prayer. We are conscience that it is a duty and a privilege yet many avoid prayer services. They often plunge into a fascinating book, television program, yield themselves to sleep or someone calls to gossip just when it is time to get on their knees. Let the phone ring, give GOD HIS uninterrupted time. If an emergency arises while we are in the midst of prayer GOD is taking care of it. When we stop praying to handle it ourselves, we will find ourselves in a catastrophic storm.

GOD did not force Jonah to go to Nineveh, HE merely commanded him to go, and Jonah resisted GOD..

GOD did not come to help until the prophet had faced the worst, but HE came on time. At the very moment of death, GOD stepped in as a deliverer. GOD defies natural laws. I've read in the Bible that the Ravens furnished Elijah with food. The Lions were tame while Daniel was in their den. The violence of the fire was gone when Shadrach, Meshach, and Abednego were in the furnace. The sea divided and became a wall for Moses and the Israelites. They walked through on dry ground when they fled from Egypt.

In Jonah's situation, GOD provided a whale to preserve his life when he was thrown overboard. GOD converted the sea monster into a protector. GOD can turn the destroyer into a preserver. Instead of killing Jonah, the whale saved his life.

In Deuteronomy 28th chapter it tells me that the enemy will come against us one way but flee before us seven ways, if we hearken to the voice of the LORD. We can't hear GOD'S voice if we don't pray. Lack of quality prayer time is excess baggage.

During the storm, while Jonah was on board the ship they had a prayer, but no calm followed. "… So they cast lots and the lot fell on Jonah." (Jonah 1:7 KJV) Jonah confessed his sin and repented yet still the storm raged. The sailors respected Jonah as a prophet and were slow to lay hands on him. Jonah, the stranger, got on their ship and mixed them up in his trouble. How many times have we involved ourselves in other people's problems to the downfall of our spiritual lives? We allow people to drain our strength and our joy.

Disobedient though Jonah may have been, the sailors still perceived that he was GOD'S prophet. Jonah urges them to cast him into the sea. Jonah, the coward, now becomes the hero. He showed a generous spirit. So they took up Jonah, and cast him forth into the sea: and the sea ceased from her raging." (Jonah 1:16 KJV) When cast into the sea Jonah must have imagined that it was all over for him. When Jonah discovered he was miraculously preserved, he had the opportunity to reflect on his wrongdoing and GOD's marvelous mercy. In the whale, he had time to think of his neglected duties and seek forgiveness and restoration through prayer. Jonah was cast out that he might learn through prayer to suffer and be strong.

Jonah slept in the ship but awake in the whale, he feels his misery and sees his sin. Many times we have to reach rock bottom in our lives to recognize where we are in GOD. Sometimes GOD has to allow us to feel our misery. Sometimes GOD has to separate us to get HIS message across. GOD calls men to private prayer. Jeremiah prayed when he was in the miry pit. Daniel prayed in the lion's den. JESUS prayed in the garden of Gethsemane and Jonah in the belly of the whale. Jonah's prayer became one of praise for deliverance and his life. Affliction will cause us to repent. Jonah slept calmly in the midst of the hurricane. He made no sign when the sinners called on their god. The word tells me that the death of Bathsheba's child did it for David after he committed adultery and had Bathsheba's husband killed. David hardened his heart for a whole year, but he poured out a prayer when chastening was upon him. The experience of the whale's belly did it for Jonah. It isn't until the second chapter of the book of Jonah that we read "and then Jonah prayed." There is no indication that he prayed after GOD commissioned him to go to Nineveh or before making the decision to flee. But affliction in one form or another will do it every time. Illness has come so suddenly, or death has seemed so near that a soul will cry out, "what must I do to be saved?" GOD has used the breakup of a love relationship, failure of business, death, illness, or forsaking of friends to make us think and save our souls from destruction.

A part of Jonah's excess baggage was pride. As the prophet of GOD, he predicted the destruction of the city of Nineveh, even to naming the day. His pride required that the prophecy should be fulfilled. When GOD changed HIS mind after the Ninevites repented Jonah's pride was hurt.

He felt his reputation as a prophet suffered. So Jonah went out of the city and made himself a booth. He sat under it to see what would become of the city. He was devastated when he found the city was to be spared. Jonah's booth proved insufficient shelter and GOD allowed a gourd (a fine leafy green plant) to grow. Jonah rejoiced in the gourds shade without considering it to be GOD'S blessing. Ingratitude is excess baggage.

Every Christian who works for his own credit or advantage and not for the salvation of men shares Jonah's emotion. He preferred that men should perish rather than he should be considered a failure. Jonah was a fault finder and that is excess baggage. A true prophet is a man or woman who speaks for GOD unquestioningly. They act for GOD obediently, without doubt and lay aside their personal feelings and desires. They accept constructive criticism and go on.

Jonah was also a complaining man and complaining is excess baggage. He complained about going to Nineveh and he complained about GOD changing his mind. When GOD gave Nineveh another chance Jonah became angry and the intensity of his anger became so intolerable that he wished to die. Anger is excess baggage. Why was he angry? Was it because of divine compassion being shown to the Ninevites? Jonah had proclaimed their destruction in forty days. The forty days passed and no destruction came. The city was preserved by GOD because it repented. It seems that Jonah would rather see Nineveh in ruins than have his reputation as a prophet questioned. He thought more of his reputation than the lives of thousands of people. He was angry with GOD for having compassion. When GOD blesses someone we don't think deserves it, we get angry.

Our best blessing many of us don't trace to our heavenly source. We take GOD for granted. One day Jonah reclined gratefully beneath the shade of the gourd and a worm came and it was gone. GOD gives us things in HIS mercy and when HE sees them either unappreciated or idolized, HE in further mercy takes them away. Lack of compassion is excess baggage.

GOD told Jonah "thou has pity for a flower which sprang up in a day and died in a day should I not pity this town with a large population of people and multitude of cattle?" Jonah 4:10, 11 KJV The things we have are not our own, we just hold them at GOD'S pleasure. The gourd was lost almost as soon as it was found. The gourd was not the object of any long term relationship but Nineveh had been in GOD'S heart since before the world became. Jonah's spiritual values were misplaced. He had more regard for appearances than souls. Misplaced values are excess baggage.

Jonah 4:3 KJV reads, "Therefore now, O LORD, take, I beseech thee, my life from me; for it is better for me to die than to live."
Jonah wished to die because his prophecy hadn't come to fruition. GOD sent a gourd (a fine leafy green plant) for his shelter. Glad of the shelter Jonah was willing to live. When the shelter was removed, and he was exposed to the blazing sun and burning wind, Jonah longed to die again. That's the reaction of many people of GOD today. We want the blessing without the sacrifice. We want success without work.

We can rejoice when things are going our way. When disappointment, struggle or chastisement come our way we are ready to give up and die in our present situation.

When we surrender to GOD'S will HE will replace the negative emotions with a positive and productive ministry.

Jonah, the disciplined servant, was an improved servant. The LORD loveth those whom he chastens. "For whom the LORD loveth HE chasteneth, and scourgeth every son whom he receiveth." (Hebrews 12:6 KJV) The severe discipline had done its work. Jonas rebelliousness is over, and the unruly servant is ready to do his masters will.

GOD wants us to be faithful in completing the task that HE sets before us.

Our hope cannot rest on sense, reason, nature or time these things can become excess baggage when we rely on them too strongly. GOD had pursued Jonah ever since he had turned his back on HIM. GOD caused the storm. GOD cast Jonah into the sea. GOD entombed him in the whale. GOD shut Jonah up in what was considered a distressful and isolated place. GOD caused Jonah to be in despair. Affliction brings a man to himself. It brings him from self-conscious to GOD conscious. Again, GOD puts Jonah in a position where he experiences utter despair. Sometimes GOD has to take us through situation after situation that we are not happy with until we get it. We may do part of what GOD wants, but until our attitude and personality ultimately resembles what GOD wants we will continue to be put in situations of despair.

When we shed the excess baggage in our lives and surrender to GOD'S will, GOD will make the darkness light before us. What is wrong GOD will make it right before us. All our battles GOD will fight before us. The high places, the unreachable goals, the insurmountable obstacles, and the unobtainable desires GOD will make available to us.

SERMONETTE 66

WAITING, WAITING, WAITING

I don't like using the same word twice in a paragraph. I especially have a problem with reading the same word twice in a sentence. In Psalms 27 the word wait is used twice is in one sentence. I pondered upon it. I asked GOD, what are you trying you tell me? Grammatically nothing appears wrong. It Just seems awkward. Psalms 27:14 KJV "Wait on the LORD: be of good courage, and he shall strengthen thine heart: wait, I say, on the LORD."

The Bible instructs us to "wait on the Lord." It is so difficult for us to do. We impatiently take matters into our hands.

We find ourselves waiting for hours in a hospital, but we don't leave because we want a diagnosis or relief from the systems that sent us there. Why do we find it so difficult to wait on GOD? In our society today we want everything right now. We want immediate solutions to our problems. Technology has been a large part of the impatience we exhibit. Computers, social media, microwave ovens, cell phones, fast foods, allows us to have things right away. We have been spoiled to receive what we want when we want it. So we find waiting tough to do.

When we find ourselves waiting in traffic, on lines in stores, we become annoyed and often argumentative.

Waiting on GOD for a spouse, job, position, healing or for a loved one to come to CHRIST, causes many of us to want to give up.

Isaiah 40:31 KJV encourages those who wait on GOD. "But they that wait upon the LORD shall renew their strength; they shall mount up with wings as eagles, they shall run, and not be weary, and they shall walk, and not faint."

We can trust that whatever GOD does HIS timing is always perfect. GOD tests our faith. HE makes us wait to see if we can handle what we ask. He makes us wait to see if we will remain humble and appreciate what HE gives us.

Waiting is hard, and we begin to wonder whether the LORD is listening to our prayer. We may be waiting for our companion or a son or daughter to come to CHRIST. We may be waiting for guidance on the right type of job. We may be waiting on a GOD honored relationship. We may be waiting on our time for elevation. While we are waiting for GOD to answer, HE gives us guidance through HIS WORD.

(Philippians 4:6-7 AMP). "Do not be anxious or worried about anything, but in everything [every circumstance and situation] by prayer and petition with thanksgiving, continue to make your [specific] requests known to GOD. And the peace of GOD [that peace which reassures the stands guard over your hearts and your minds in CHRIST JESUS[is yours]."

Proverbs 3:5-6 (AMP) "Trust in and rely confidently on the LORD with all your heart And do not rely on your own insight or understanding. In all your ways know and acknowledge and recognize HIM, And HE will make your paths straight and smooth [removing obstacles that block your way]"

"For the vision is yet for an appointed time, but at the end it shall speak, and not lie: though it tarry, wait for it; because it will surely come, it will not tarry." (Habakkuk 2:3 KJV)

THERE'S A SPIRITUAL BULLY IN ME

"I have pursued mine enemies, and overtaken them: neither did I turn again till they were consumed. I have wounded them that they were not able to rise: they are fallen under my feet. For thou hast girded me with strength unto the battle: THOU hast subdued under me those that rose up against me. THOU hast also given me the necks of mine enemies; that I might destroy them, that hate me. They cried, but there was none to save them: even unto the LORD, but HE answered them not. Then did I beat them small as the dust before the wind: I did cast them out as the dirt in the streets." Psalms 18:37-42 KJV

"Put on the whole armor of GOD, that ye may be able to stand against the wiles of the devil. For we wrestle not against flesh and blood, but against principalities, against powers, against the rulers of the darkness of this world, against spiritual wickedness in high places. Wherefore take unto you the whole armor of GOD, that ye may be able to withstand in the evil day, and having done all, to stand. Stand therefore, having your loins girt about with truth, and having on the breastplate of righteousness; And your feet shod with the preparation of the gospel of peace;

Praying always with all prayer and supplication in the Spirit, and watching thereunto with all perseverance and supplication for all saints;" (Ephesians 6:11-15, 18 KJV)

"There is no universal definition of bullying. However, it is widely agreed upon that bullying is a subcategory of aggressive behavior characterized by the following three minimum criteria: (1) hostile intent, (2) imbalance of power, and (3) repetition over a period of time.[11] Bullying may thus be defined as the activity of repeated, aggressive behavior intended to hurt another individual, physically, mentally or emotionally". https:// en.m.wikipedia.org/wiki/Bullying

In the natural, some articles suggest that one being bullied should learn to fight. back.http://www.today.com/parents/new-anti-bullying-trend-teaching-victims-fight-back-1C7397916 http://nypost.com/2013/10/20/the-bullies-will-keep-winning-if-kids-dont-fight-back.

Spiritually we must learn to do the same when confronted by the enemy.

The term bully brings to mind negative behavior. In my way of thinking I use that term in a more positive way as armor to defeat the enemy that is challenging us. When the enemy comes against us, and we have to overcome what has been designed to destroy our GOD given purpose the Spiritual Bully in some of us surface. The fight, determination, stamina, will power, courage, faith and the power of prayer allows us to withstand the wiles of the enemy. The Spiritual Bully in us will not allow us to give up or quit what GOD wants us to accomplish.

Sometimes what one sees as a bully is a person who was forced to be one to survive in what life handed them the best way they could. I can recall an incident in my childhood when I was bullied. I was chased and ran jumping a fence and bushes to get away. I stayed in the house for three days while being taunted to come out.

My Grandmother told me to get the switch (the braided one she put together). She said to go out and confront my antagonist, or she would give me a beating. Long story short I had a better chance facing my opponent than that switch. I learned something that day when I faced my adversary; they backed off. Bullies will rarely continue a battle with another bully. It is easier to pursue a passive, nonaggressive victim.

Being small in stature, growing up in Harlem I was often faced with some form of bullying. When it became known that I would come back aggressively, my reputation preceded me, and I was no longer a target.

I pursue my spiritual walk in the same fashion. The enemy has a fight when I am being forced to surrender my gift, my anointing, my purpose and my relationship with GOD.

We may not look like what other people want us to look like or how we wish to appear. We may not behave the way other people want us to act or even the way we want to behave in our own eyes sometimes. We may not say all the right things at the right time, and realistically we may not say right things at the wrong time. We may not wear the apparel others want to see us in even though we know that how we are perceived, we will be received. We often doubt our ability to accomplish and achieve all the things we desire.

How often have we looked in the mirror and wished our body shape, our skin color, our hair texture, were different? How often have we envied someone else's lifestyle or career choice? We allow what other people say about us and expect of us to dictate the course of our lives because of low self-esteem.

GOD said we are wonderfully and beautifully made.

"For YOU did form my inward parts; YOU did knit me together in my mother's womb. I will confess and praise YOU for YOU are fearful and wonderful and for the awful wonder of my birth! Wonderful are YOUR works, and that my inner self-knows right well. My frame was not hidden from YOU when I was being formed in secret [and] intricately and curiously wrought [as if embroidered with various colors] in the depths of the earth [a region of darkness and mystery]. YOUR eyes saw my unformed substance, and in YOUR book, all the days [of my life] were written before ever they took shape, when as yet there was none of them."

(Psalm 139:13-16 AMP)

Many of us search for something that will turn our unfulfilled life around, and that will give us all the things we desire. For some, that break may come from Wall Street, and it will be written in the Dow Jones averages. For others, the lucky break may originate from a record deal, sports career or contract. Most of us tend to think our success may come from some life-changing, momentous event. We are not all going to find that kind of success.

"May HE grant you out of the rich treasury of HIS glory to be strengthened and reinforced with mighty power in the inner man by the [HOLY] SPIRIT [HIMSELF indwelling your innermost being and personality]." (Ephesians 3:16 AMP)

It's time to recognize the Spiritual Bully in ourselves. The Spiritual Bully part of us that will stand up and come against the self-doubt and insecurities that hold us back from being all we can be. The Spiritual Bully part of ourselves that will say, "I accept how GOD has fashioned me and I will praise HIM." The Spiritual Bully part of ourselves that will say, "I give GOD all the glory despite my present circumstances." The Spiritual Bully part of ourselves that will say, "I love the me that I am and will be the best me I can be."

The Spiritual Bully part that will give us the courage to, "... endure hardness, as a good soldier of JESUS CHRIST." (2 Timothy 2:3, KJV) The Spiritual Bully part that will give us the strength to do what we have to do until we can do what we want to do. The Spiritual Bully part that will fight to accomplish our GOD ordained goals against all distractions, disappointments, discouragement and temporary failures. The Spiritual Bully part that will not allow ourselves to be defeated because "Ye are of GOD, little children, and have overcome them: because greater is HE that is in you, than he that is in the world." (1 John 4:4 KJV)

SERMONETTE 68

GOD'S TIME CLOCK

The clock of eternity always keeps time. We are failing to discern the signs of the time. We prefer the material and temporal to the spiritual and religious.

Having the Spirit of GOD in us is the best defense against hard times. Repentance and prayer are the best resources in bad times, consider your ways. Do we have time to make plans without including GOD in them?

Tomorrow is not promised to any of us. Our time clock is a misrepresentation of life. We make plans for next week, next month, next year but GOD's time clock may say, today is your last day on Earth. Are we preparing for our last day by putting off what we can due for CHRIST because we think we have time?

"For we must all appear before the judgment-seat of CHRIST that every one may receive the things done in his body, according to that he hath done, whether it be good or bad" (2 Corinthians 5:10 KJV)

We all have desires, dreams, and plans for what we want to do in the present and the future. GOD has given us free will to consider the way in which we proceed in life. It is up to us to make sure we align ourselves with GOD's time clock.

We need to examine our spiritual condition carefully. No one can travel along securely or comfortably in life and not consider GOD's time clock.

It is imperative in our plans that we ask GOD if it is HIS will that we proceed. We need to seek GOD to see if our plans will be beneficiary to us in eternity.

When this life is over, and we stand before GOD, we want to hear HIM say, "...Well done, thou good and faithful servant: thou hast been faithful over a few things, I will make thee ruler over many things: enter thou into the joy of thy LORD." (Mathew 25:21 KJV)

DON'T LOSE YOUR BLESSING

We need to remember that our parents cared for us in our infancy. They fed, clothed and protected us from harm. They provided an education and nursed us when we were sick.

Our parents, teachers, supervisors, lovers, friends, brothers or sisters; whatever their faults, have had an impact on our lives. We survived, we are here now so let's praise GOD for allowing them to nurture us as much as they did and not physically kill us as they may have wanted to in some cases, when we stepped out of line. We need to forgive, forget and move on to the blessings that lay ahead.

So Solomon expressed gratitude for what David, his father, had been.

In the Bible GOD offered Solomon a choice of blessings. The treasure house of blessings was opened and he was told to take whatever he wanted.

One of the first lessons a child learns is to grasp. The desire to take is a part of our being. It is a part of GOD'S being to impart, to give.

Solomon had to make a choice between pleasure and duty, between temporal and eternal blessings. He could choose glory, wealth, and renowned earthly prosperity or he could choose character, wisdom and goodness in other words heavenly and abiding treasures.

"For where your treasure is, there will your heart be also" (Matthew 6:21 KJV)

GOD gave Solomon wisdom because he asked for it and at the same time gave him wealth because he did not ask for it. "Give therefore thy servant an understanding heart to judge thy people, that I may discern between good and bad: for who is able to judge this thy so great a people? And the speech pleased the LORD, that Solomon had asked this thing. And GOD said unto him, Because thou hast asked this thing, and hast not asked for thyself long life; neither hast asked riches for thyself, nor hast asked the life of thine enemies; but hast asked for thyself understanding to discern judgment;

Behold, I have done according to thy words: lo, I have given thee a wise and an understanding heart; so that there was none like thee before thee, neither after thee shall any arise like unto thee.

And I have also given thee that which thou hast not asked, both riches, and honour: so that there shall not be any among the kings like unto thee all thy days. And if thou wilt walk in MY ways, to keep MY statutes and My commandments, as my commandments, as thy father David did walk, then I will lengthen thy days.(1 Kings 3: 9-14KJV)

"The fear of the LORD is the beginning of wisdom..." (Psalm 111:10 KJV) We need to ask GOD for wisdom. We must trust GOD and walk by faith. There is more wisdom in a whispered prayer than in all the colleges, theological seminaries we can attend or all the psychology counselors we can pay.

GOD will give wisdom, the word of GOD says if any man lacks wisdom let him ask of GOD. When we seek wisdom from GOD, HE also rewards us with a blessing that exceeds our expectations. "HE is able to do exceeding and abundantly above all that we ask or think." (Ephesians 3:20 KJV).

King Solomon's choice was for the good of others rather that for the advantage of himself. He was not asking for knowledge and wisdom so that he might be admired. He wished to rule GOD's people well and for their good.

Unselfishness is commended and exalted by GOD. CHRIST himself came not to be ministered to but to minister and to give HIS life as a ransom for many.

Favor with GOD is better than money, with GOD'S favor comes health, wealth. More importantly, HE gives us peace and contentment with what we have and where we are.

If our chief concern is to please GOD, we don't have to worry about natural things. If GOD feeds the birds, He will provide for us. If HE makes the rose the object of HIS care and HE guides the Eagles through the pathless air, then surely HE remembers us. Our heavenly FATHER watches over us.

Ask GOD for the higher blessing; pardon from sin, righteousness, reverence, greater worship and praise, a stronger prayer life, a greater desire to serve HIM, and wisdom to make right choices. Without GOD'S wisdom, all the money and fame that we acquire may be abused and misused, and we will find ourselves still discontented.

Although Solomon was given divine wisdom, obedience to the covenant law was still necessary for him to take advantage of that gift.

Solomon's prayer did not keep him from falling, what a shame to get what we ask for and then blow it. Solomon received the blessings of GOD, and he blew it.

When GOD blesses some of us, we get caught up in the blessing and forget to continue to honor and worship GOD as we should.

Let's take one more look at what happens to Solomon. He stopped caring for wisdom and stopped asking for it. He ceased to covet the best gift and cared only for the riches and fame and lost both. David, Solomon's fathers' last word must have been prophetic. I Chronicles 28:9 KJV says, "And you, Solomon my son, know thou the GOD of thy father, and serve HIM with a perfect heart and with a willing mind: for the LORD searcheth all hearts, and understandeth all the imaginations of the thoughts: if thou seek HIM, HE will be found of thee; but if thou forsake HIM, HE will cast thee off forever." Instead of correcting and perfecting the mistakes of his past, Solomon magnifies them. He focused on the lesser blessing of fame and fortune rather than the greater blessing of favor with GOD.

Solomon broke GOD's law by mixing with the pagans around him; rather than leading the Israelites in maintaining separateness from the other nations as GOD required, Solomon married foreign women, worshipped foreign gods with pagan kings and even built pagan places of worship.

When GOD blesses us, we shouldn't allow the blessing to destroy our relationship with HIM. "The LORD giveth and HE also takes away." We need to be mindful that the husbands, jobs, houses, cars, education and children we ask GOD for can be a blessing or become a curse. They can begin to interfere with our prayer life, worship, praise and especially our service to GOD. When we have fallen out of favor with GOD, we start pointing the finger and blaming others for our shortcomings

Deuteronomy, the 28th chapter verses 1-14 it talks about the blessings that we can receive if we listen to the voice of GOD. In that same chapter versus 15-68, the curses are multiplied more than three times.

It is my desire to live with the blessings of GOD rather than to fall out of favor with HIM and be cursed.

GOD has abundantly blessed me and I refuse to lose my blessing.

A MOSES BREAKDOWN

Often children of GOD are afraid to admit they are suffering because they feel it will be seen as a spiritual problem. There is no shame in admitting we are weak or we need help. Knowing that we are not the only one takes some of the power away from the guilty emotions we experience when we feel overwhelmed and powerless,

Depression is one of the most common human emotions. Many of us experience a period of depression at one time or another.

However, the Bible does not leave us without help.

For me to minister in this area, I had to experience "A Moses Breakdown" personally.

In Numbers 11:14-15 KJV, Moses cries out to GOD, "I am not able to bear all this people alone, because it is too heavy for me. And if thou deal thus with me, kill me, I pray thee, out of hand, if I have found favour in thy sight; and let me not see my wretchedness." Moses was worn out. He was weary. He had a lot on him.

A "Moses Breakdown." can happen to any of us.

We feel overwhelmed in a situation, and it makes no difference whose fault it is. It doesn't matter if we brought conditions on ourselves or something happened beyond our control; we can find ourselves at a point where a breakdown threatens us.

Discouragement and depression can be triggered by the death of a loved one, illness, loss of a job or status, divorce, leaving home, exhaustion or many other traumatic events.

Many people in the Bible who were used by GOD reached a point in their lives where they faced depression, Hagar, Moses, Naomi, Hannah, David, Elijah, Nehemiah, Job, Jeremiah, John the Baptist, Paul and JESUS in the Garden of Gethsemane. The Bible does not show GOD punishing HIS people for their "Moses Breakdown," rather HE acts as a loving Father and supports them through it.

What we learn when we experience and survive "A Moses Breakdown" may help other people later. Their need may be even greater than ours was. "Blessed be GOD even the FATHER of our LORD JESUS CHRIST, the FATHER of mercies, and the GOD of all comfort; Who comforteth us in all our tribulation, that we may be able to comfort them which are in any trouble, by the comfort wherewith we ourselves are comforted of GOD." (2 Corinthians 1:3-4 KJV)

"And now my heart is broken. Depression haunts my days.... My weary nights are filled with pain as though something were relentlessly gnawing at my bones." (Job 30:16-17 NLT)
"I cry to YOU, [LORD,] and YOU do not answer me; I stand up, but YOU [only] gaze [indifferently] at me. My heart is troubled and does not rest; days of affliction come to meet me." (Job 30:20, 27 AMP)

Job was experiencing "A Moses Breakdown".
Job suffered as a godly man. Even the holiest people can suffer a breakdown; it can be part of the normal Christian life.
GOD doesn't always explain the reason for our suffering.
We shouldn't blame and reproach ourselves because suffering is not necessarily the result of sin.
GOD gave the enemy permission to afflict Job because HE knew Job would survive it. Christians suffer but we overcome, when we trust GOD's word. "No weapon formed against you shall prosper, And every tongue which rises against you in judgment You shall condemn. This is

the heritage of the servants of the LORD, And their righteousness is from ME", Says the LORD Me", Says the Lord." Isaiah 54:17 (NKJV)

When people of GOD suffer, it has a purpose, even though we often don't realize it at the time.

Job suffered, JESUS suffered, and likewise, we suffer also.

If we persevere in suffering, we demonstrate our faith in GOD. "For you have been granted [the privilege] for CHRIST's sake not only to believe in (adhere to, rely on, and trust in) HIM but also to suffer in HIS behalf." (Philippians 1: 29 AMP)

Suffering develops endurance and perseverance. GOD's discipline and training help us towards spiritual maturity.

"Then JESUS went with them to a place called Gethsemane, and HE told HIS disciples, Sit down here while I go over yonder and pray. And taking with HIM Peter and the two sons of Zebedee, HE began to show grief and distress of mind and was deeply depressed. Then HE said to them, MY SOUL is very sad and deeply grieved so that I am almost dying of sorrow. Stay here and keep awake and keep watch with ME." (Matthew 26:36-38 AMP)

"For we have not an high priest which cannot be touched with the feeling of our infirmities; but was in all points tempted like as we are, yet without sin." (Hebrews 4:15 KJV))

Strong faith serves GOD in the tough times; when we can say to GOD, not my will, but YOURS be done.

"So David and his men came to the town, and behold, it was burned, and their wives and sons and daughters were taken captive. Then David and the men with him lifted up their voices and wept until they had no more strength to weep. .... David was greatly distressed, for the men spoke of stoning him because the souls of them all were bitterly grieved, each man for his sons and daughters. But David encouraged and strengthened himself in the LORD his GOD."

(1 Samuel 30:3-6 AMP)

David had no other choice but to turn to GOD when everything seemed to be going against him. His thoughts were on GOD for comfort and support and not suicide.

We need to encourage ourselves in the LORD our GOD because human help is often powerless. In the critical moments of "A Moses Breakdown," there seems little we can do for ourselves and not much others can do for us.

"Hear my cry, O GOD; attend to my prayer. From the end of the earth I will cry to YOU when my heart is overwhelmed; lead me to the rock that is higher than I. For THOU hast been a shelter for me, and a strong tower from the enemy." (Psalm 61:1-4 KJV)

It's good to smile and laugh. When we are discouraged, we need to do something that cheers us up. Helping others during "A Moses Breakdown" is imperative because it takes the focus off of us.

On Mount Carmel, Elijah defeated the prophets of baal.
(1 Kings 18:36-40 KJV). Instead of being encouraged, Elijah, fled for his life fearing Jezebel's revenge. He was weary and afraid.

We often face depression when we are particularly weak physically, and emotionally. Elijah must have felt this way when he sat down under a tree and wanted to die. (1 Kings 19: 4 KJV).

When we don't have enough rest and sleep, when our health is weak, when we do not make enough time for personal leisure, when we do not have meals at regular times are all-important factors that make us vulnerable for "A Moses Breakdown." GOD allowed Elijah to sleep. HE also gave him two meals. Then Elijah was able to continue his journey.

The enemy wants to take away our joy and peace in GOD.
he attacks us with depression when we are exhausted and overwhelmed. We should avoid making important decisions when we feel depressed because we do not see things as they really are. Our perception may be altered.

We must find some quiet place to meet with GOD and be still.
Rest and restore our physical, emotional and spiritual strength.

"We are troubled on every side, yet not distressed; we are perplexed, but not in despair;

Persecuted, but not forsaken; cast down, but not destroyed;

Always bearing about in the body the dying of the LORD JESUS, that the life also of JESUS might be made manifest in our body. For we which live are always delivered unto death for JESUS' sake, that the life also of JESUS might be made manifest in our mortal flesh. 2 Corinthians 4:8-11 (KJV)

Remember this, what we have learned from our "Moses Breakdown" experience can help other people later.

SERMONETTE 71

THE SPIRIT OF AN ARMOR BEARER

Jonathan says to his armor bearer, in 1 Samuel 14:1-8 KJV let's go over to the outpost of the Philistines. Maybe the LORD will help us defeat them.

The path to the Philistines was a treacherous one, and the Philistines were a dangerous army. Does the armor bearer tell Jonathan he is nuts? No. Instead, he says, do what you are inclined to do and I will put my heart and soul behind you. GOD called the leader. GOD gave the leader the vision. Many times what the leader proposes or suggests may seem unreasonable, irrational and maybe even a little crazy to us. It is not our job as the armor bearer to question, advise and impose our personal will on a plan that GOD has instructed the leader to follow. The armor bearer is an encourager when a leader becomes overwhelmed and discouraged. "We can do this." "I got your back." "If you can't complete the job don't worry, I will step in and see that it gets done."

Jonathan's idea in the book of 1 Samuel chapter 14 is to get close enough for the Philistines to see them and wait and see what they say. If the Philistines bid us to come forth, we shall go up, because the LORD has delivered them into our grasp. If they don't, we won't go. Jonathan wanted a sign from the LORD, a confirmation that he was in the will of GOD.

Before we rush into a situation, ask GOD for a sign that we are doing the right thing, that we are moving in agreement with GOD's purpose and plan for us.

Every thought and decision we make may appear to be leading us in the right direction, but if we have not received specific guidelines and strategies from GOD, we will find ourselves caught in a spiritual or natural mess.

Seeing Jonathan and his armor bearer, the Philistines say, come on up, and we'll teach you a lesson. Jonathan and his armor bearer climb to where the Philistines are and as the Philistines turned to flee from him, he cut them down, and his armor-bearer finished them off. Johnathan started the work, and his armor bearer finished it off.

Moses started the work and Joshua finished it off. Saul started the work and David finished it off. Elijah began the ministry and Elisha finished it off. The leader can start a process, and his armor bearer can finish it off. The first battle Jonathan and his armor-bearer slew about twenty men within the space of a city block.

It is important to note that Saul had 600 soldiers with him, but Jonathan and his armor bearer were working alone.

The scripture says that "...... And the people did not know that Jonathan was gone. ...." (1 Samuel 14: 1-8 KJV) What could have distracted the people that no one noticed that Jonathan was gone. When we become involved in idle projects and would rather attend services that entertain us and find excuses to spend time in prayer, praise and worship we won't be aware that the HOLY SPIRIT has left us. We must continually be mindful of the fact that we are losing the joy, worship, and praise we once had. Our spiritual strength must remain high.

We need to acknowledge to ourselves when the eagerness to come to the house of GOD and serve HIM fervently is diminishing. When we find our prayer time is getting shorter, find ourselves making excuses for not giving our all in ministry as we used to, and begin to miss vital services, we must recognize that the spirit of GOD is leaving us.

SERMONETTE 72

GOD'S CHOICE

When GOD chooses us and has plans for our lives it doesn't matter what people say. The positive as well as the negative things we encounter during our life's journey are there to prepare us to become GOD's Choice. We can only be effectual as GOD's choice when we listen to GOD's instructions and trust HIM especially when we don't understand why things seem to be going wrong for us.

How many of us have thought within ourselves, "I wish GOD would tell me right now what HE expects from me." "I pray but GOD hasn't shown me a clear picture of what I am supposed to be doing in my immediate circumstance." "I wonder if GOD hears me or loves me." "I seem to be stuck where I am." "Has GOD really chosen me to do anything for HIM?

(Matthew 5:45) "Fret not thyself because of evildoers, neither be thou envious against the workers of iniquity. For they shall soon be cut down like the grass, and wither as the green herb. Trust in the LORD, and do good; so shalt thou dwell in the land, and verily thou shalt be fed. Delight thyself also in the LORD: and HE shall give thee the desires of thine heart. Commit thy way unto the LORD; trust also in HIM; and HE shall bring it to pass.(Psalms 37:1-5 KJV)

The Word of GOD says, that Solomon loved the LORD; walking in all of the statutes of David his father.

Solomon was listening to GOD who said, "ask what I shall give thee." The freedom to ask anything can only be given safely to those who are like Solomon. He had just given himself up to GOD as a living sacrifice and had asked GOD to accept him and use him for HIS service.

If we can say in our heart, LORD, I want to become like YOU and always be obedient to YOUR will. I long to be earnest, humble, pure, loving and to live altogether for THEE. Then GOD says ask, and you shall receive and your joy shall be full.

We need to stop looking at the mistakes we have made. Too often we focus on the past instead of what GOD is planning for us in our future. Whatever our faults or our feeling of being treated unjustly or unfairly, we are here now. Let's praise GOD for experiencing and surviving our past and allow those things to propel us into the move of GOD HE has chosen for us us for.

Unselfishness is commended and exalted by GOD. CHRIST himself came not to be ministered to but to minister and to give His life as a ransom for many.

The prayer of selfishness and greed can never prepare us to be GOD's choice.

What will make us noble and righteous is more readily given by GOD than what will make us wealthy.

Favor with GOD is better than money, with GOD'S favor comes.

Let's take one more look at what happens to Solomon. He stopped caring for wisdom and stopped asking for it.

He ceased to covet the best gift and cared only for the riches and fame and lost both.

We find David, Solomon's fathers' last words to him in I Chronicles 28:9 says, "And you, Solomon my son, know thou the GOD of thy father, and serve HIM with a perfect heart and with a willing mind: for the LORD searcheth all hearts, and understandeth all the imaginations of the thoughts: if thou seek HIM, HE will be found of thee; but if thou forsake HIM, HE will cast thee off forever."

Instead of correcting and perfecting the mistakes of his past, Solomon magnified them. He focused on the lesser blessing of fame and fortune rather than the greater blessing of favor with GOD.

When God blesses us, we shouldn't allow the blessing to destroy our relationship with HIM. "The LORD giveth and HE also takes away." We need to be mindful that the husbands, jobs, houses, cars, education and children we ask GOD for can be a blessing or become a curse. They can begin to interfere with our prayer life, worship, praise and especially our service to GOD. We start pointing the finger and blaming others for our short comings when in reality we have fallen out of favor with GOD.

When you read Deuteronomy the 28th chapter verses 1-14 it talks about the blessings that we can receive if we listen to the voice of GOD. In that same chapter versus 15-68 the curses are multiplied more than 3 times.

GOD has chosen me and I am determined not to make HIM ashamed of me. I want to be GOD's choice.

GOD SEES ME

It's terrible to feel abandoned by GOD. Many of us may feel abandoned by GOD at some point in our lifetime. When we experience things in life that cause heartache, confusion, frustration, catastrophe or maybe all of the above, we wonder in ourselves "GOD where are YOU?" "GOD, do you see me?"

Hagar must have felt like that when she ran away from Sarai in Genesis chapter 16 (KJV)

Sarai was beyond the time in the life for bearing children. When Sarah saw that they had lived in Canaan for ten years, she proposed to Abram that he take another woman to produce a child for her. It was the custom of the day for a wife who was infertile to make arrangements for a slave girl to have sex with her husband so that the family could have an heir. The child would become Sarai and Abram's legitimate offspring.

Sarai had an Egyptian maid whose name was Hagar.

Sarai was aware of GOD's promise to produce Abram, an heir, and she decided to help GOD out.

How often do we hear a word about our future from GOD and decide to take matters into our hands to help GOD out? We need to have patience and learn how to wait on GOD's time. There's an old song that says, "We can't hurry GOD. We've just got to wait. We've got to trust HIM and give HIM time no matter how long it takes. HE's a GOD that we can't hurry.

HE'll be there we don't have to worry. HE may not come when we want him but HE's right on time."

3 "So Sarai, Abram's wife, took Hagar her Egyptian maid, after Abram had dwelt ten years in the land of Canaan, and gave her to her husband Abram to be his [secondary] wife.

4 And he had intercourse with Hagar, and she became pregnant; and when she saw that she was with child, she looked with contempt upon her mistress and despised her.

5 Then Sarai said to Abram, May [the responsibility for] my wrong and deprivation of rights be upon you! I gave my maid into your bosom, and when she saw that she was with child, I was contemptible and despised in her eyes. May the LORD be the judge between you and me.

6 But Abram said to Sarai, See here, your maid is in your hands and power; do as you please with her. And when Sarai dealt severely with her, humbling and afflicting her, she [Hagar] fled from her." Genesis 16: 3-6 (AMPC)

Sarai placed Hagar in a situation but did not foresee the outcome. When that meek, submissive maid became pregnant by Abram, she changed. Hagar became arrogant and began to feel equal or perhaps above Sarai. She had accomplished something Sarai could not. We must always remember where we came from and not get too caught up in our accomplishments in life.

Sarai knew she had Abram's love and could influence him.

She cunningly seeks Abram's permission to put Hagar in her place. Abraham responded that she belongs to you, do what ever you want with her.

The other woman, the mistress, needs to be conscience of the fact that if a man loves his wife, her position as mistress will always be secondary.

Sarai made life miserable and humbled Hagar by placing her back in the position of a servant. Hagar couldn't take the humiliation and decided to run away.

Hagar knew about Abram's GOD. She had lived with Abram's family for several years. I am sure she learned about the true and living GOD.

For Hagar to run away she must have been desperate. I can imagine that she wondered if GOD knew or cared about her situation.

The Bible says the Angel of the LORD found Hagar. GOD is omnipresent. HE is everywhere. There is no place we can go that GOD will not find us. "Whither shall I go from thy spirit? or whither shall I flee from thy presence? Psalms 139:7 (KJV)

7 "But [a] the Angel of the LORD found her by a spring of water in the wilderness on the road to Shur.

8 And He said, Hagar, Sarai's maid, where did you come from, and where are you intending to go? And she said, I am running away from my mistress Sarai.

9 The Angel of the LORD said to her, Go back to your mistress and [humbly] submit to her control.

10 Also, the Angel of the LORD said to her, I will multiply your descendants exceedingly so that they shall not be numbered for multitude.

11 And the Angel of the LORD continued, See now, you are with child and shall bear a son, and shall call his name Ishmael [GOD hears] because the LORD has heard and paid attention to your affliction to your affliction." Genesis 16-12 (AMPC)

We may not initially place ourselves in troubling situations. How we react to the circumstances we find our selves in, whether positive or negative determines the outcome.

. The Angel of the LORD called her by name, "Hagar." Then HE reminded her of who she was, "Sari's maid."

When GOD wants to get our complete attention there is a process. GOD makes us aware that HE knows our name and our status in life.

Then HE reminds us of where we came from and opens our eyes to where we think we are going.

Hagar had to recognize she was fleeing from a situation that was partly her fault. She was leaving a place of safety despite the difficult circumstances she was enduring. She was fleeing on a dangerous mission to a place that, if she arrived, might not accept her new lifestyle..

The Angel of the LORD instructed Hagar on what she had to do. Go back and submit humbly to Sarai. Get over your pride.

We can't solve our problems by running away from them.

We need to seek GOD and make every attempt to resolve the difficulties we encounter. Then "...stand still and see the salvation of the LORD..." Exodus 14:13 (KJV).

The Angel of the LORD encouraged Hagar by giving her insight into her future.

"HE would multiply her descendants exceedingly" Genesis 16:10 (AMPC)

Hagar was overwhelmed by the experience. She gave GOD a special name.

13 Then she called the name of the LORD who spoke to her, You-Are-the- GOD-Who-Sees; for she said, "Have I also here seen HIM who sees me? "Genesis 16:13 (NKJV). She called the name of the LORD "EL ROI," (EL raw-EE) "the GOD who sees.

GOD sees me. GOD sees me when I am misunderstood. GOD sees me when my finances are short and I can't pay my bills. GOD sees me when my companion walks out on me. GOD sees me trying to raise my children by myself. GOD sees me when my children disappoint me and don't appreciate all I have sacrificed for them. GOD sees me when I am crying in my pillow at night from loneliness and despair. GOD sees me when I have given my all and I am not recognized for anything I do. GOD not only sees me, HE cares and comes to see about me in my wilderness experiences. "EL ROI", the GOD who sees.

"EL ROI" is my comfort in my darkest hour. "EL ROI takes my hand and leads me on when I am tired, weak and worn. "EL ROI" guides my feet so that I won't fall. "EL ROI" lingers near when my way grows drear. "EL ROI," my GOD who sees me, gives me the strength to keep on trusting HIM when my rope is busting, and I am just hanging on by a thread. Because GOD sees me, I can endure. Because GOD sees me, I am more than a conquer. Because GOD sees me, I can survive and master higher heights and deeper depths in HIM. Because GOD sees me, I know somehow, I know some way I'm going to make it. With my confidence in

"EL ROI", my GOD who sees me, I am aware that all things are working together for my good.

Though the storms keep on raging in my life I can still praise GOD because HE sees me.

PRAYER # 3

Dear GOD deliver us from fear.

LORD, I am aware that whatever we fear will have power over us. Let not fear triumph over us. Help us to fight fear and not listen to our minds.

I put my faith in YOU. I know that YOU shall give us freedom from our fears. We try to have faith during difficult situations but sometimes our fears seem to overtake us I am not alone in my concerns today. There are others who fear failure. There are others who fear being disappointed. There is someone besides me who fears being alone. Someone else today is fearing the loss of independence. Someone is fearing the loss of good health. Plaguing so many souls is the fear of being misunderstood. We fear that our earnest desires may never come to pass.

GOD, we know that YOU are faithful and work in YOUR own time. In our humanness, we become anxious and impatient. LORD give us patience so that our fears don't overwhelm us and cause doubt to interfere with our faith in YOU.

Dear GOD, YOU said in YOUR word that "YOU have not given us the spirit of fear; but of power, and of love, and of a sound mind." 2 Timothy 1:7 (KJV)

LORD help us to trust and believe YOUR word. Help us to be conscience of the fact that whatever we fear will have power over us. Dear GOD, we surrender our fears to YOU.

LORD help us to fear only YOU and give you the authority to control everything that is not pleasing to YOU in our lives.

LORD help us to rebuke over whelming fear today. Help us to rebuke unnecessary fear today. LORD let the power of the HOLY SPIRIT reign down over fear today.

We thank YOU for the strength that is flooding our souls right now with the victory over our fears.

LORD, YOU said in YOUR WORD that 'There is no fear in love; but perfect love casteth out fear: because fear hath torment.

He that feareth is not made perfect in love." 1 JOHN 4:18 (KJV)

Give us perfect love for YOU and one another so we can come together on one accord and overcome the fears in our lives that are not of YOU. LORD help us to understand that where there is unity, there is strength.

Help us to understand that when we don't share love, fellowship, sympathy and empathy with our brothers and sisters that disunity and division will cause us to fail YOU.

Help us to understand that when we allow discord and iniquity to maintain a stronghold in our spirits that we delay the promise and deliverance from unnecessary fear.

YOUR WORD tells us "... That if two of you shall agree on earth as touching anything that they shall ask, it shall be done for them of my FATHER which is in heaven." (Mathew 18:19 KJV).

Thank YOU, GOD, for answering prayer today. Amen

SERMONETTE 74

MOUNTAIN CLIMBING FAITH

Faith means that we are confident that the things we hope for will come to pass. Through faith, we are convinced that we will receive what is not yet seen. GOD graduates the trials we face in life. HE gives us the opportunity of learning to trust HIM in small difficulties so that our faith can become stronger and stronger. "If thou hast run with the footmen, and they have wearied thee, then how canst thou contend with horses? and [if] in the land of peace, [wherein] thou trustedst, [they wearied thee], then how wilt thou do in the swelling of Jordan?" (Jeremiah 12:5 KJV)

We all have a measure of faith. There's a song that the children sing that says, "faith, faith, faith, all I need is just a little bit." Whatever our sorrows and troubles are at this time, GOD has allowed them to come to give us an opportunity to prepare for mountain climbing faith. Do not be discouraged, give up or become unfaithful in little things. We need to be thankful that GOD has given us the time for discipline and soul searching so that the small bit of faith we have can grow. We have to make a choice to go forward when we face the difficulties and uncertainties that everyone faces in life. No human being is entirely free of troubles and worries. If we could experience utopia here on Earth, there would be no need to desire heaven. If we don't allow our faith to grow, we will miss the greater discipline and blessing that will surely come.

So often in our Christian walk, we come upon situations with our minds already made up. Sometimes we are so focused on our preconceived ideas about how to solve the situations we face, that we are not open to what GOD is saying to us. Faith is the first step in pleasing GOD. Faith lets us know that GOD does exist. Faith gives us the assurance that GOD's word is completely trustworthy.

Faith will allow us to stand and face the trials of life with the peace that surpasses all understanding. As our knowledge of GOD and HIS infinite wisdom increases, our faith grows.

JESUS' disciple Thomas had a natural human faith. His faith required physical evidence. He would believe what he could see and touch, rather than believe what GOD said. Too many people today are trying to lead successful lives with only enough faith to believe what can be seen. Mountain Climbing Faith believes what we cannot see with the human eye.

In the book Of Genesis, Abraham had spiritual-faith. A faith that was based upon GOD's Word, not what he could see or feel. If Abraham had trusted his intellect and what his natural senses told him, he never would have received GOD's promise.

Too many people are trying to gain Abraham's blessing with Thomas' faith. Spiritual Faith starts with the inward man. The heart and spirit believe first, and the outward results follow. Abraham did not allow human reasoning to interfere with what GOD was saying to him.

Fear is the greatest hindrance to many Christians' faith. We need to understand that the things we experience and conquer in life allow us to have a greater knowledge and relationship with the LORD JESUS CHRIST. The greater our understanding of GOD and who HE is, the more mature our faith becomes. We must stop allowing the enemy to cheat us of our belief in GOD by keeping us from depending on the WORD Of GOD. There will be pain sometimes, there will be sickness sometimes, and everyone is not going to love us or even like us. We are going to have some lonely times and many nights we may cry ourselves to sleep. The WORD of GOD lets us know that "... weeping may endure for a night, but joy cometh in the morning." (Psalm 30:5 KJV) There is joy in knowing that we serve a faithful GOD who will not let us fail if we trust HIM

Abraham's wife Sarah had impatient faith. GOD told Abraham that his son would be of his body. Sarah believed in the promise of GOD and desired that her husband receive GOD's promise. Sarah was beyond the age of child bearing and did not have the mountain climbing faith to believe that GOD would use her body to produce that son. Sarah decided to help GOD out. She gives her Egyptian maid to Abraham to bear a child for her. How generous of her. When GOD promises us something the only help HE needs from us is faith to believe that it will happen. We can't use human strategy to make something happen faster when GOD is planning a miracle. When we try to make things happen our way, we open ourselves up to shame, humiliation and fault finding. Mountain climbing faith means waiting for GOD to do what HE has promised in HIS way and in HIS time. We can't hurry GOD; we have to Trust Him and give Him time no matter how long it takes. The husband, the wife, the job, the child, the home, the car, whatever it is, it's ours if we are living in the will of GOD. Mountain Climbing faith says, "GOD said it, I believe it and that settles it."

As we look into the book of Genesis we are introduced to Lot. Abraham, a faithful man of GOD, raised his nephew Lot and exposed him to areas in life that caused Lot to make poor choices. Those choices interfered with Lot achieving mountain climbing faith on his own.

Everyone can't be exposed to a life of opulence and luxury and not be affected by it in a positive, productive way. We can't indulge our children with everything they see others have when they are not responsible enough to handle it. When we give our young people whatever they want we deprive them of the opportunity to trust GOD to supply all their needs.

We spoil them to the point that thinking about making right choices on their own is difficult. Mountain climbing faith requires us to make spiritually good decisions. We can't do that if we are relying on someone else to have faith for us.

We spoil them to the point that thinking about making right choices on their own is difficult. Mountain climbing faith requires us to make spiritually good decisions. We can't do that if we are relying on someone else to have faith for us.

Abraham was forced to spend some time in Egypt, the land of plenty. Abraham came away with greater faith because of some of the circumstances GOD brought him through. Lot, a young man came away with visions of grandeur and undeveloped faith. He didn't need to strengthen his faith because he could rely on Uncle Abraham.

There came a time when GOD had prospered Abraham and the land was not large enough for Lot to remain home. Abraham allowed Lot to make the choice of where he wanted to live.

"And Lot looked and saw that everywhere the Jordan Valley was well watered. Before the LORD destroyed Sodom and Gomorrah, [it was all] like the garden of the LORD, like the land of Egypt, as you go to Zoar. Then Lot chose for himself all the Jordan Valley and [he] traveled east. So they separated." (Genesis 13:10-11 AMP)

We have to give our children the opportunity to learn how to have faith in GOD and acknowledge GOD in all their ways. They need to be prepared for mountain climbing faith when they move out on their own.

We would think that the younger Lot would have asked his older, wiser uncle for advise. When we have not made provision for our children to learn personal faith in GOD they will choose what they like, not what is right. Mountain Climbing Faith is something we have to learn. Lot made a wrong choice in choosing to dwell in Sodom. He relied on what he thought looked exciting and prosperous instead of his faith in GOD. He didn't have the faith to believe that GOD could change what appeared to be dull and mediocre into something beautiful and fulfilling.

Abraham had wealth but it did not have him. Material things possessed Lot. He got a glimpse of the good life during his stay in Egypt. Just a taste of the lifestyle of the rich and famous can be come so desirable for some, that obtaining and maintaining it will consume them.

Abraham was secure in GOD's promise to bless him. He was developing mountain climbing faith. Abraham wanted Lot to make the best choices in life. He had raised Lot and taken care of him, and I am sure he tried to instill some Christian values in him. Abraham wasn't perfect, he made some mistakes, but he lived a life of faith and obedience to the will of

GOD. As a good parent, we want the best for our children, and we also need to encourage them how to make right choices and depend on the will of GOD. Often we make our most important decisions at a time when we have the least amount of experience to guide us. Have you ever said to yourself, "If only I had known?" "If I had it to do over again"?

Lot appears to be like many Christians who depend upon another's faith for strength. Lot apparently depended upon Abraham's faith to cover him. We all need to prepare ourselves to develop our own mountain climbing faith. It's time that we stop leaning on the Bishop's faith, the pastor's faith, grandma's faith, our mother's faith and start climbing our own personal mountain of faith.

Angels informed Abraham that they were sent to destroy the wicked city of Sodom. Abraham begs that the town is spared if they could find at least ten righteous people there.

"And he said, Oh let not the LORD be angry, and I will speak yet but this once: Peradventure ten shall be found there. And he said I will not destroy it for ten's sake." (Genesis 18:32 KJV)

Abraham had mountain climbing faith. I believe he trusted that his nephew, Lot still maintained some of the faith in GOD that he had witnessed while living in Abraham's household.

The messengers find Lot sitting at the city gate alone. Sometimes when we make rash decisions without consulting GOD first, we try to make the best of it. We often find ourselves sitting by the gate of regret alone. We beat ourselves up mentally and emotionally for not having at least a measure of faith to follow GOD's plan for us.

Lot may have been contemplating how to reverse the poor decisions he had made. It is evening; Lot had to be aware that the men of the city of Sodom were preparing to have another night of ungodly pleasure. Somehow Lot had morally escaped becoming a part of the sins that were causing GOD to destroy Sodom and Gomorrah. Abraham's prayers had covered Lot. We can cover each other in prayer, but we all have to increase our measure of faith on our own. Apparently, Lot had maintained some of the social graces he had learned from his Uncle Abraham.

When the Angels arrived, Lot was respectful; he bowed himself to the ground. He was hospitable and offered accommodations to the Angels. He was sincere; when the Angels declined his offer, he implored them to come into the safety of his home. He wanted to protect the angels from the perils that they would encounter by being out in the open at night in that corrupt city. He knew what remaining in the streets meant. Lot was generous; he treated the Angels nobly. He made a feast for them. He showed good Christian qualities, but he had valley faith. The object of his deliverance was standing right before him, but he didn't have enough faith to realize it.

The men both young and old demanded that Lot give them the people that had entered their city so they could use them sexually. Lot tried to speak civilly, called the men brethren, and begged them not to touch the Angels that were in his home.

We don't know if Lot was aware that he was entertaining Angels but there was an urgency to keep them safe. When we are in the presence of righteous men and women of GOD, there is a sense that we can't allow any and everything to go on in their presence.

Lot's weak faith caused him to offer his virgin daughters in place of the Angels unjustly. Faith will never allow us to do evil thinking that good may come of it. The men of the city were drunk and would not listen to reason. We can't be rational with a drunk or a saint that needs deliverance and is operating out of the will of GOD.

All Lot accomplished by using natural means was to make the men of the city angrier. They were ready to tear Lot apart. We waste time talking to people instead of GOD. There was a powerful presence right in Lot's house. Lot again made a wrong choice. He relied on self as opposed to touching and agreeing in prayer with the Angels, who had the power to make miraculous things happen.

"But the men [the angels] reached out and pulled Lot into the house to them and shut the door after him." (Genesis 19:10 AMP)

The angels were sent not only to destroy the city of Sodom and Gomorrah but to spare Lot's life.

Saints of GOD are pulled, like Lot, into a house of safety, and the door is shut against the enemy that tries to come against us. Lot is instructed to notify his family that the city was about to be destroyed.

They didn't ask Lot if he knew any righteous in the city because they knew there were none. The Angels asked what relationships Lot had in the city that, whether righteous or unrighteousness, they would be saved with him. Unrighteousness people are often spared in this world because of the Abraham's with mountain climbing faith with whom they are connected. Lot's relatives laughed at him. He was a joke. When we do not remove ourselves immediately from bad circumstances, even though we may not be participating in them, preaching righteousness to others becomes a joke.

Lot lingered, he hesitated, and it would have proved fatal, had the Angels not interceded.

"And while he lingered, the men laid hold upon his hand, and upon the hand of his wife, and upon the hand of his two daughters; the LORD being merciful unto him: and they brought him forth, and set him without the city. And it came to pass when they had brought them forth abroad, that he said, Escape for thy life; look not behind thee, neither stay thou in all the plain; escape to the mountain, lest thou be consumed." (Genesis 19:16, 17 KJV)

We can have faith to go through the valley experiences of our lives, but it takes mountain climbing faith for GOD to bring us over the miraculous things we encounter. Climbing a mountain means we have to claw our way, search for secure places to put our feet and something to grasp to help us continue the climb. We can't look back to see our progress because we may lose our footing and the fear of the distance we have gone will cause us to fall. Mountain climbing faith means propelling ourselves forward, continuing in spite of the scared and bleeding hands and feet. The nursery children sing, "the bear went over the mountain, the bear went over the mountain, the bear went over the mountain to see what he could, to see what he could see, the other side of the mountain ..." We will never know what is on the other side of our mountains if we don't climb over the obstacles and impediments that we encounter on the journey to the top.

For I say, through the grace given unto me, to every man that is among you, not to think of himself more highly than he ought to think; but to think soberly, according as GOD hath dealt to every man the measure of faith. (Romans 12:3 KJV)

The prayer for all of us who have a genuine and growing relationship with GOD should be," LORD don't move my mountain but give me the faith to climb."

The angels told Lot to go to the mountain, but Lot appeared to have valley faith still. He begged to go to the nearest city of Zoar. Eventually, Lot was frightened out of Zoar, a refuge of his choosing. He probably found Zoar to be as wicked as Sodom and realized that it could be destroyed also. We often find ourselves becoming disappointed with our decisions when we follow our desires instead of GOD's directions.

Lot was finally forced to go to the mountains and live in a cave. Why didn't he return to Abraham's protection? Was it pride in admitting that he had made a mistake in what he chose to do? Was he too stubborn to follow orders from others? Was his faith still too weak to support the will of GOD? We cannot speak for Lot, but there are Christians today whose faith is not strong enough to follow GOD's commands. So many people of GOD are limited in personal, financial and spiritual growth because of poor choices and weak faith.

Lot was finally ready to flee to the mountain. Disappointment and frustration in doing what we think is right can force us to follow what GOD requires. We waste so much time, energy and progress when we don't seek and follow GOD's advice. We pay the price for delayed obedience. Lot, who did not have enough room for himself and his stock when he lived with his Uncle Abraham, finds himself confined in a cave on a mountain.

Lot didn't seek GOD's advice when he separated from Abraham.

He didn't obey GOD's directions when he was spared from the destruction of Sodom. When he was finally forced to obey GOD, he experienced deprivation instead of prosperity.

It takes a lot of faith to climb the mountains in our lives. When we remain weak in faith, we never reach the higher heights and deeper depths GOD has for us. We all need to stop just going through the valley of little faith and pray for the strength to climb the steep and challenging mountains we encounter. When we fail to climb to the top of our personal mountains, we will never know the blessing waiting for us on the other side.

SERMONETTE 75

AN AMBITIOUS MOTHER

In Matthew 20:20 KJV) we find Salome, the mother of James and John, the sons of Zebedee, making a request to JESUS for her sons. Salome was one of the LORD's most faithful followers. She was even present at the cross. She prayed, not for herself, but with a mother's love for her sons that they might sit one on the LORD's right hand, the other on the left in HIS Kingdom.

Was she selfish and inconsiderate or ambitious, desiring the best for her sons? It is a rare mother who does not dream of a great future for her children. What mother who does not look into her child's face and dream for him or her a high position, fame, financial gain, and happiness?

A realistic mother, however, is aware that her child must be worthy of success and earn it. We can't just can't wish or ask for success, and it automatically happens. We all must meet certain conditions for success to occur. We should prepare ourselves as role models to our children. The best role models for successful children are parents that are striving no matter what our social or financial status, to be the best at the things we try to accomplish in life.

We often don't know the consequences, disappointments or struggles that we may have to endure when we seek great things for our children or ourselves. The best prayer is not my will, but THINE oh LORD be done.

Salome did not think of the dangers, suffering, and temptations, which lie in making such a request.

She wanted her sons to share the final victory, not conscious of the fact that they must share the conflict and suffering that would go before.

So many desire the blessings they see others possess without having to pay the dues they paid. Many onlookers have no idea of the suffering that some of us have endured to get where we are today.

As ambitious mothers, the first thing we need to do is prepare our children spiritually by introducing them to GOD.

The Bible says, "Train up a child in the way he should go, And when he is old he will not depart from it." (Proverbs 22:6 NKJV)

The greatest lesson our children can learn is how to pray and seek GOD's advice and strength when they face obstacles and setbacks. They need to understand that life and success require sacrifice and struggle.

An example of a parent who knew how to beseech GOD on behalf of his children correctly was Job. Job had a habit of divine worship; it was constant. Job ".... rose up early in the morning, and offered burnt-offerings according to the number of them all: for Job said, It may be that my sons have sinned, and cursed GOD in their hearts. Thus did Job continually." (Job 1:5 KJV) Family worship should be done before the day starts. He interceded for his children, and he did so continually.

As ambitious mothers, we must encourage our children to strive to fulfill their dreams and not give up when the going gets tough.
As ambitious mother's we should seek GOD for what HE has in store for our children and not what we think they should become.

Let us not set our children up for failure because they don't have the ability or temperament to handle the burdens we place upon them as ambitious mothers.

It is alright to be an ambitious mother as long as we allow GOD to remain in control of our desires for our children.

223

GET READY BECAUSE A CHANGE IS COMING

We find in John chapter 4 KJV JESUS, as usual, doing the unexpected. HE left Judea on HIS way to Galilee. But HE did not follow the proper manner for Jews to travel which was to avoid Samaritan territory. The Bible says HE needed to go through Samaria. I believe HE said, "I've got a potential evangelist down in Samaria."

When there is a need to go through something GOD ordained we may have to defy custom, formalities and take risks to see that what is required will be fulfilled.

JESUS didn't take the wrong road by mistake; HE had a purpose. There was a problem with JESUS going through Samaria.

The Bible tells us that there was a bitter rivalry between the Jews and the Samaritans. There was a long-standing feud going on between the two races of people. Perhaps JESUS was seeking to remove the prejudice of HIS disciples by personal contact with the despised race. JESUS in the book of Matthew had admonished the disciples not to have anything to do with the Samaritans, but a change was coming. When something new takes place in ministry the one making the change has a need to go through somethings. Struggling with a need, people can get weary.

It can be exhausting trying to explain and reason with others about the change about to be made. The Bible says JESUS was weary from HIS journey. The attempt to accomplish HIS mission made HIM tired. HE had to overcome the obstacles, hostility, and repercussions HE would encounter.

The scripture opens with JESUS in a place where he knows HE is not welcome.

It's high noon and hot, and JESUS is thirsty, not just for water but with a thirst to deliver a soul from the bondage of sin.

Some things had to be in place before JESUS could minister.

HE had to get rid of HIS disciples. HE sent them to the city to buy food. It's hard to minister when there are distractions around. It is necessary to separate from people who may not verbally say anything, but in their minds try to figure out what change is taking place. JESUS didn't need questions or advice. HE didn't have time to waste with explanations and calming fears because HE was on a mission.

JESUS sat down by a well, and an unknown woman came to draw water from the well. She was obviously not well off because she had no servant to draw water for her. She arrived in the heat of the day, midday, rather than in the morning or the cool of the evening when it was customary for the women to gather around the well and share bits of gossip.

This immoral woman who had five previous husbands now lived with a man who was not her husband. Being a woman of questionable reputation made her unpopular in town. Perhaps she was trying to avoid being ignored and publicly slighted. She made a habit of going to the well at a time when she was certain no one else would be there. JESUS knew she would be alone, that was part of the plan.

HE did not choose one of the self-righteous, respectable women. JESUS wanted a woman who had a famine in her soul, a thirst for a more worthy life. HE chose a lonely, disrespected woman that men used for sexual purposes. She was looking for love in all the wrong places.

JESUS had gone out of his way on purpose and broke three major social rules of the custom at that time.

1. Women were considered greatly inferior to men in public. No middle eastern man spoke to women in public.

2. Jews didn't talk to Samaritans. Jews believed Samaritans had betrayed their faith because they had intermarried with foreigners.

3. No self-respecting man especially a teacher would ever speak to a woman of such despicable reputation. This woman was a well-known social outcast.

"There cometh a woman of Samaria to draw water:JESUS saith unto her, Give me to drink." (John 4:7 KJV)

With Jacobs well for a pulpit and its water for a text, JESUS is prepared to preach salvation to the Samaritan woman.

It was a surprise to her when JESUS asked her for a drink of water. By his clothes and accent, it was obvious to the woman that JESUS was a Jew. "Then saith the woman of Samaria unto him, How is it that thou, being a Jew, askest drink of me, which am a woman of Samaria? For the Jews have no dealings with the Samaritan." (John 4:9 KJV)

Many things must have been going on in this woman's mind.

A Jew is asking me a favor. A man is publicly speaking to me. He's a stranger so he can't be setting me up for sexual favors. Has my reputation gone that far? He doesn't know me. The nerve of him to think that me a Samaritan would respond to him anyway.

The enemy floods our minds with questions to distract us from hearing GOD.

I like the way JESUS took no notice of her comment; HE ignored it. Sometimes when we know, things are going to cause an argument we need to ignore them and look for the bigger picture.

JESUS response was if thou knewest thou would have asked me for a drink of water. JESUS skillfully turns the conversation from the natural water in the well to the blessings that HIS living water would provide. The living water is the HOLY SPIRIT. JESUS offered her what she needed, a clean heart, freedom from sin, a life of peace and joy in serving HIM.

GOD was giving her a second chance. HE saw her possibilities. HE was aware of her value. It was the living water of the HOLY SPIRIT that would raise her self-esteem and self-worth.

GOD wanted HIS healing virtue to break the link between this woman and her past. JESUS' words to the Samaritan were going to transport her to a new level of life. Her encounter with JESUS was going to change her present condition and bring her into spiritual worship.

In Samaria there was no winter, for the greater part of the year, there was burning scorching heat, therefore water was a precious commodity. JESUS had her attention because HE was offering her something that she needed, something that everyone needed to survive. Her mind was fixed on the natural water. Not only is JESUS offering her water but it would be a well of water springing up into everlasting life.

When we drink natural water, it cleanses and purifies; receiving CHRIST into our lives does even more. The grace of GOD continues to quench our thirst. HE is a well of living water, always there always in operation.

I can imagine the Samaritan woman thought that she wouldn't have to carry a heavy water pot every day in the hot sun to get water.

She was looking at the natural. Too many people want the best for less, something for nothing, especially sinners and immature saints.

"The woman saith unto HIM, Sir, THOU hast nothing to draw with, and the well is deep: from whence then hast THOU that living water?" (John 4:11 KJV)

JESUS wanted the woman to understand that HE was talking about everlasting life, a new lifestyle, an attitude change. She didn't have to be abused and misused anymore. She didn't have to continue to live a life of sin and degradation. She would no longer have to hang her head in shame. She could stop avoiding people because of the sinful life she had been leading. JESUS wanted to give her something that would satisfy her every need and yearning. HE was offering something that would heal every pain and affliction, something that would lift every burden and trouble in her life. I am sure the woman was ready for a change to come. She had been trying to find peace and satisfaction, and only ended up degrading herself, being used by men and despised by decent folk.

JESUS said unto her, first call thy husband and come back. HE made the woman face the facts of her life.

The gift of eternal life is free, but we must be worthy of it. We must confess our sins and JESUS is faithful and just to forgive us. We must repent first and then receive the gift. So JESUS opened the wound of guilt in her conscience mind. HE had to clean out the wound before HE could heal it. We need to stop putting clean bandages on infected wounds. GOD has to find a way of breaking into our sinful hearts and cause us to want to repent and make a change.

The woman is honest with JESUS. "The woman answered and said, I have no husband. JESUS said unto her Thou hast well said, I have no husband: For thou hast had five husbands; and he whom thou now hast is not thy husband: in that saidst thou truly." (John 4:17 KJV)

Now this woman who evidently had been the subject of so much gossip was bewildered. Here sat a man she had never seen before, but he was revealing her past. JESUS didn't rebuke her for her sins. HE didn't put her down. HE didn't demand her repentance. HE calmly and lovingly let her know that HE was aware of her reputation and her immoral life of sin and was still willing to give her a gift. All she could respond was, I perceive that thou art a prophet. How could HE know all this unless HE was GOD? She didn't say a lot verbally to JESUS but her soul was immediately filled with change, a new hope and her life took on a new interest. Going from man to man couldn't fill the void in her life. She realized the answer was not getting another man but getting in touch with 'The Man', JESUS. Forgiving ourselves and others will break the link between us and our past. There is no healing in blame.

The woman forgave the men who had used her, the women who had scorned her and she forgave herself for allowing so great a sin to prevail in her life. She released where she had been so she could receive what GOD had for her now. She was ready, and change came into her life. We pray for sinners to come to church then limit what they can do because of their past. JESUS allowed her to go forth She communicated at once to her neighbors what had taken place in her life. She became a missionary, an evangelist of JESUS to her countrymen. Her message was, come see a man, a man who changed her life.

She met a man who told her everything she'd ever done. HE gave her another chance in life and saw possibilities in her. She had encountered a man who discovered her value and emphasized her worth as a woman. HE had lifted her into equality with others. HE chose her, a woman with a past, to work for HIM.

JESUS reached out to her regardless of what she had done. GOD knows that there are those who have been abused, molested, tried to find satisfaction in illicit sex, drugs, and alcohol. Many have had babies out of wedlock, and some can hear the cries of the, dead babies that have been aborted. GOD calls on purpose people with a negative history.

JESUS knows the conditions we live under and the things we suffer. HE still covers our back when we find ourselves making bad decisions. He understands our loneliness and a need for someone to hold and caress us. HE dries the tears we shed in your pillow at night when we question why our companion won't seek GOD, and our children don't act right. JESUS will calm our spirit when the boss on our job is unfair, and the saints give us a hard time in church.

HE understands our desires and secret yearnings.

GOD chooses ordinary people, men and women, people who will do as HE commands. HE will use the homeless, the jobless, the uneducated, prostitutes, yes even the backsliders to build HIS ministry. GOD loves us in spite of who we are and where we have been.

This woman's story confirms the fact that GOD is no respecter of persons.

People of all types of backgrounds and experiences get ready because change is coming when we allow JESUS to come into our life.

JUST ANOTHER TEST

In the book of 1ˢᵗ Kings 17:9 AMP; Elijah is directed by GOD to "Arise, go to Zarephath, which belongs to Sidon, and dwell there. Behold, I have commanded a widow there to provide for you." So Elijah goes to Zarephath where he encounters the widow gathering sticks.

He requests her to fetch him water to drink; she readily obeyed. She did not object to the scarcity of water. She did not make an excuse because of the weakness she might have been experiencing due to the famine. She did not hesitate or stop to discuss the urgency of her affairs. As she was going to get the water, he called,

"And bring me, please, a piece of bread."

She didn't make any excuses about the water because evidently, she had enough water to share but when Elijah asked for bread, she began to make him aware of her limitations. "And she said, As the LORD your GOD lives, I have not a loaf baked but only a handful of meal in the jar and a little oil in the bottle. See, I am gathering two sticks, that I may go in and bake it for me and my son, that we may eat it and die." (1 Kings 17:12 AMP). She could have said do I take my meal and oil and give it to someone that I do not know. But she gets over her objections, and she obeys.

To deny herself and depend upon a divine promise was a great miracle in itself. To be asked to give a stranger a little cake from her handful of meal, that was left before she met the cravings of hunger in herself and her son, must have seemed like an unreasonable demand. It was more than a test of faith it was a test of trust.

The Bible says "he that loveth son or daughter more than ME is not worthy of ME" (Matthew 10:37 KJV). It goes on to "say seek ye first the kingdom of GOD and HIS righteousness and all these things will be added unto YOU." (Matthew 6:33 KJV). GOD asks little but makes a significant return. Because of her obedience, the barrel of meal did not waste. The meal and the oil multiplied, not in the hoarding of what she had but in the giving. When GOD blesses a little, it will go a long way, beyond our expectations. On the contrary, though there may be abundance in our life, if GOD blows on it becomes little. (Haggai 1:9 KJV).

There is nothing lost by being kind to GOD'S shepherd. When we step out of our selfish mode and give to the man and woman of GOD. GOD will take our little and abundantly multiply it.

GOD will not fill us until we are emptied of self. Sometimes we need to give away a portion of that cake that we intended to eat and die; if we bring our weak state to GOD, He will increase our strength.

This woman gave, and she got, but let us remember that she gave unselfishly and not to get. She gave her utmost and GOD gave her a divine material blessing when she thought all was lost.

There was a miracle of abundance because she was willing to give all that she had and was willing to believe there would be more.
There was a plentiful supply for a full year for herself, her son and the prophet.

GOD often demands the lighter sacrifices from us first and then as our faith and patience increases, HE requires greater sacrifices. This woman exchanged the certain for the uncertain and the seen for the unseen. When looking for a miracle, expect the impossible.

The widow in First Kings 17th chapter was a single parent who had been too focused on her present problem, and she could only see one option, prepare a cake and die.

The HOLY SPIRIT continues to provide alternatives for a woman raising children alone, when she focuses upon her trust in GOD instead of the problem. When she spends time in the word each day to receive divine direction especially during stress filled times. Thy word have I hid in mine heart, that I might not sin against THEE. (Psalm 119:11 KJV) She needs to be constant in Church attendance and active in service so that both she and her children can be nurtured spiritually and emotionally through fellowship with other believers.

After the widow exhibited faith in GOD'S providence she was tested again. The Prophet, who had demonstrated to her the LORD'S abundance, had to also miraculously demonstrate GOD'S power to heal. GOD employed her to sustain a great Prophet and she had strong reason to believe that the LORD would do her good always. It seems the child died suddenly or she would have asked Elijah for help while he was sick. We must not think it strange if we meet with very sharp afflictions when we are doing GOD'S work.

In the midst of all her satisfaction she was again afflicted. How calmly had she spoken of her child and her own death when she expected to die for lack of food, when Elijah first approached her. When her child died, and not so miserably by famine, she is extremely disturbed.

We speak lightly of affliction when it is at a distance, it's not reality, it has not happened yet. When tragedy happens suddenly it is a different story. It's hard to keep our spirit composed when troubles come upon us suddenly, unexpectedly and in the midst of our peace and prosperity.

The widow called Elijah a man of GOD and yet quarreled with him as if he had caused the death of her child. She is ready to wish she had never seen him forgetting past mercies and miracles. The mother overwhelmed with sorrow severely blamed Elijah and charges him with the loss of her son.

It is human nature that seeks to blame something or someone for any calamity that befalls us. Elijah does not resent, correct or rebuke her, as he could have done. He sympathizes with her and treats her with tenderness.

No one is exempt from the trials and sufferings of this life. Everyone suffers the pain of sickness and death. Money or fame cannot erase either of them. The widow began to wonder if the sins of her past were the cause. It's a true instinct that leads us to think of our sins in times of adversity. Time of trouble is meant to be a time of heart searching confession. David understood that when he prayed "Search me oh GOD and know my heart; try me, and know my thoughts" (Psalm 139:23 KJV).

The bible says Elijah cried unto the LORD for the child's soul to come into him again. And the LORD heard the voice of Elijah and the child's soul came to him again. (1 Kings 17:19-24 KJV) It was just another test.

DOES THE DEVIL HAVE AN ANOINTING?

Too many Saints find themselves listening to and following a spirit that is not anointed by GOD. It is so sad to see people of GOD following someone not possessing the GODly anointing.

Does the devil have an anointing? I believe so.

There are two types of anointing: The anointing of GOD and that of the devil. Anointing means the outpouring of a spirit causing an empowerment of the vessel on which it is poured.

There are those who are anointed with the Spirit of GOD, and some are anointed with an unholy anointing. In other words, the HOLY SPIRIT anoints true believers in JESUS CHRIST. False prophets and those used by the devil are anointed with an evil spirit.

In the Acts of the Apostles, Paul and Barnabas encountered a false prophet named Elymas Bar-Jesus on the island of Cyprus. (Acts 13:6- 12 KJV)

"Then some of the itinerant Jewish exorcists undertook to invoke the name of the LORD JESUS over those who had evil spirits, saying, "I adjure you by the JESUS whom Paul proclaims." Seven sons of a Jewish high priest named Sceva were doing this. But the evil spirit answered them, "JESUS I know, and Paul I recognize, but who are you?"

And the man in whom was the evil spirit leaped on them, mastered all of them and overpowered them so that they fled out of that house naked and wounded." (Acts 19:13-16 ESV)

"As we were going to the place of prayer, we were met by a slave girl who had a spirit of divination and brought her owners much gain by fortune-telling. She followed Paul and us, crying out, "These men are servants of the MOST HIGH GOD, who proclaim to you the way of salvation." And this she kept doing for many days. Paul, having become greatly annoyed, turned and said to the spirit, "I command you in the name of JESUS CHRIST to come out of her." And it came out that very hour." (Acts 16:16-18 ESV)

I don't allow any and everyone to lay hands on me. I believe that when a prophecy comes into my life, it is a conformation on what GOD is already revealing in my spirit.

People of GOD need to stop being gullible and susceptible to spirits that are not anointed by GOD. Saints of GOD are warned throughout the New Testament to be watchful and prayerful of both false prophets and false spirits. (Matthew 7:15–23 KJV) From the Sermon on the Mount: "Watch out for false prophets. They come to you in sheep's clothing, but inwardly they are ferocious wolves. By their fruit, you will recognize them."

"For thus says the LORD OF HOSTS, the GOD OF ISRAEL: Let not your [false] prophets and your diviners who are in your midst deceive you; pay no attention and attach no significance to your dreams which you dream or to theirs, For they prophesy falsely to you in MY NAME. I have not sent them, says the LORD." them, says the Lord." (Jeremiah 29:8-9 AMP)

"Beloved, Do not put faith in every spirit, but prove (test) the spirits to discover whether they proceed from GOD; for many false prophets have gone forth into the world." (1 John 4: 1 AMP)

People are practicing in ministry who are anointed, not of GOD, but of the devil. They will only prophesy lies and falsehoods. They are so good in that false anointing that crowds follow and believe in them.

We have to become knowledgeable and aware that there is a HOLY ANOINTING, but there is also a false anointing. 1 John 2:27 AMP, talks about the existence of this false anointing. "As for you, the anointing [the special gift, the preparation] which you received from HIM remains [permanently] in you, and you have no need for anyone to teach you. But just as HIS ANOINTING teaches you [giving you insight through the presence of the HOLY SPIRIT] about all things, and is true and is not a lie, and just as HIS ANOINTING has taught you, you must remain in HIM [being rooted in HIM, knit to HIM]."

In 1 Corinthians 3, KJV Paul spoke about building the church upon the foundation of the apostles and prophets. People of GOD we need to develop our intellect. We must listen carefully and understand what we hear to be able to recognize false teaching. When GOD truly comes into our lives, we can recognize a holy anointing.

When an individual is preaching, teaching and prophesizing what the Scripture declares we can verify it personally. Study the scriptures, fast and pray. Seek GOD for guidance and conformation. Than we can be comfortable in knowing it is the anointed Spirit of the living GOD."

How do we learn GOD's anointing? The word of GOD tells us to, "Study to shew thyself approved unto GOD, a workman that needeth not to be ashamed, rightly dividing the word of truth. ...This know also, that in the last days perilous times shall come. For men shall be lovers of their own selves, covetous, boasters, proud, blasphemers, disobedient to parents, unthankful, unholy, Without natural affection, truce breakers, false accusers, incontinent, fierce, despisers of those that are good, traitors, heady, high-minded, lovers of pleasures more than lovers of GOD; having a form of GODliness, but denying the power thereof: from such turn away." (2 Timothy 2: 3-5 KJV)

CAN WE RECEIVE AN INCORRUPTIBLE CROWN?

"Know ye not that they which run in a race run all, but one receiveth the prize? So run, that ye may obtain.

And every man that striveth for the mastery is temperate in all things. Now they do it to obtain a corruptible crown; but we an incorruptible. I therefore so run, not as uncertainly; so fight I, not as one that beateth the air: But I keep under my body, and bring it into subjection: lest that by any means, when I have preached to others, I myself should be a castaway." 1st Corinthians 9:24-27 KJV speaks about an incorruptible crown.

How do we obtain this incorruptible crown? We can only achieve this incorruptible crown by receiving the LORD JESUS CHRIST as our SAVIOR and allowing HIM to perfect our personality.

Personality is the total of what a person is physically, emotionally, spiritually, and mentally. Personality is that which makes an individual a distinct person. There are some things that we need to examine in our lives to understand who we are and our reactions to the diversity of experiences we encounter.

1. Self-identity -We should take time periodically to examine what we are doing, why, and whether or not our life patterns are nourishing our spiritual growth or draining it. We must begin our search by

finding out who we are and who we want to be. We need to learn a sense of responsibility for our development and self expression.

What may be frustration for one person in life is an often opportunity for another. What is a need for one can be undesired by another. What provides satisfaction and fulfillment for one may prove to be a burden for another. When we dwell on the positives in our lives and learn to accept the things we cannot change, we will be one step closer to obtaining that perfected personality.

2. Rid ourselves of unhealthy fear- This is a fear that is unacknowledged; whose presence is known only by its effects upon us. Those things that we do and feel which we don't want to do or feel because they drain and limit us, yet we keep on doing them in spite of ourselves. What rescues us from this unhealthy fear is faith. Our society tends to rate us regarding measurable achievements, i.e., income, social position and public recognition. Most of us are anonymous, average and ordinary, just regular people. Consequently, many of us limp around with wounded egos, hiding our self-doubt, secretly wondering if we are worth anything to anybody. Don't be misled by what society says, our value doesn't depend upon real worth or social achievement but upon the gracious will of GOD.

Trials and temptations can sometimes lead to unhealthy fears. When we face negative and troubling situations, we must turn to the word of GOD. "Blessed is the man that endureth temptation: for when he is tried, he shall receive the crown of life, which the LORD hath promised to them that love HIM." (James 1:12 KJV) "There hath no temptation taken you but such as is common to man: but GOD is faithful, who will not suffer you to be tempted above that ye are able; but will with the temptation also make a way to escape, that ye may be able to bear it." (1 Cor. 10:13 KJV)

We can all obtain that incorruptible crown. We have to make every effort, use all are our resources and strive for it.

PROVOKED TO PRAY

1 Samuel 1:5,6,7 (AMP)

"But to Hannah, he gave a double portion, for he loved Hannah, but the LORD had given her no children. This embarrassed and grieved Hannah, and her rival provoked her greatly to vex her because the LORD had left her childless. So it was year after year; Whenever Hannah went up to the LORD's house, Peninnah provoked her, so she wept and did not eat."

I researched synonyms for the word provoke ("call forth emotions, feelings, and responses"; "arouse pity"; "raise a smile"; "evoke sympathy") I was grateful to see that the definition did not only include negative responses.

I received a clearer understanding of the scripture in 1 Thessalonians 5:16-18 AMP

"Be happy [in your faith] and rejoice and be glad-hearted continually (always); Be unceasing in prayer [praying perseveringly]; Thank [GOD] in everything [no matter what the circumstances may be, be thankful and give thanks], for this is the will of GOD for you [who are] in CHRIST JESUS [the REVEALER and MEDIATOR of that will]."

As we go through the day if we are honest with ourselves, we all experience feelings and thoughts of worry, fear discouragement and anger.

The Bible admonishes us. "Do not be anxious or worried about anything, but in everything [every circumstance and situation] by prayer and petition with thanksgiving, continue to make your [specific] requests known to GOD. And the peace of GOD [that peace which reassures the heart, that peace] which transcends all understanding, [that peace which] stands guard over your hearts and your minds in CHRIST JESUS [is yours]." (Philippians 4:6 AMP)

Prayer is our weapon to use in fighting spiritual battles.

"With all prayer and petition pray [with specific requests] at all times [on every occasion and in every season] in the Spirit, and with this in view, stay alert with all perseverance and petition [interceding in prayer] for all [a]GOD's people." (Ephesians 6:18 AMP).

As we go through the day, prayer should be our first response to every fearful encounter, every anxious thought, every undesired circumstance and every successful triumph.

When we are aware that GOD is in control of every situation we face in life, prayer becomes our primary source for survival.

For years Hannah had yearned and longed for a son, but she was barren. Hannah had to watch her rival have children and taunt her about what she desired desperately to have. I know what it feels like to work for something for years and watch others seem to pass me and easily achieve what I was struggling to get? I am not talking about coveting someone else's achievement but wanting to accomplish your goal for yourself.

While we are trying to hold it together, swallow the discouragement and disappoint of the delays and impediments blocking our progress, someone comes along who has for the moment, and I repeat for the moment surpassed us. That rival and often a former friend will sometimes confront us with a condescending attitude and say, "you mean to tell me you're still trying to reach that position, that goal, that vision? You need to face the fact it's never going to happen for you. Look at me I started when you did, and I've been successful for years. Give up! You're wasting your time."

If we have ever experienced those types of setbacks and faced those comments from others, then we can relate to Hannah. We will find ourselves provoked to pray.

SUMMONED TO A FEAST OF LOVE

"HE has brought me to his banqueting place, And HIS banner over me is love [waving overhead to protect and comfort me]." (Song of Solomon 2:4 AMP)

In the Song of Solomon 2:4 it talks about a feast of love. What is love? The word love is used in Hollywood, the newspapers, on the stage, the radio, in the pulpit and the Bible.

Lovers repeat the word to one another; parents to children, children to parents and it means something different in each case.

Love expresses itself not so much in what it says, but in what it is and does. Love is a language all its own. It's a universal language which everyone thinks they understand.

The best songs, the most familiar songs, the songs we all love to sing and hear are love songs. Love is something to sing about. It fills the mind with images dreams and visions.

Love is a recurring theme in the Scripture. The Bible begins with the love story of Adam and Eve in the Garden of Eden. They were one flesh made for each other and GOD. How familiar are the words that Jacob served fourteen years for Rachel, "So Jacob served [Laban] for seven years for [the right to marry years for Rachel, and they seemed unto him but a few days for the love he had for her." (Genesis 29:20 AMP)

GOD loves us, and HE invites us to come and dine with HIM. HE prepares a feast of love for us.

No one can take GOD's love from us unless we allow them to. GOD'S love is a possession within us. It is a part of our being, and we are a different person because of this possession.

When CHRIST lives in us, it's easy to write a love letter when people turn their back and walk away from us. It is easy for us to embrace and hug others when we know that they have talked about us and tried to bring us down. It's easy to cast into the sea of forgetfulness those evil and nasty things the enemy allowed others to say about us. We need to affirm and let it be known that we love GOD too much and want to be in HIS presence too badly to allow anyone to separate us from that love.

When we have GOD'S love, we can recognize that people who cause confusion and hurt have never had the privilege of dining at the MASTER'S table. They have never been summoned to the feast of love. When invited to GOD's feast of love, they did not take up the plate filled with love. They left the table as empty as they came.

Without the love of GOD, it is hard to smile in difficult circumstances. Without the love of GOD, we often find ourselves cynical, bitter and keep a history book of memories about the wrong things that have been done to us.

We need to be aware that people aren't thinking about the sleepless nights we have and the frustration that we are experiencing because of things our minds won't allow us to forgive or forget.

When we answer the invitation to the feast of love, one taste of GOD'S love will cause us to put those obstacles the enemy is using to destroy us in their place. They are just little things to take away our appetite for the feast of love that GOD has prepared for us.

Take two sips of GOD'S love, and we will be able to love our enemy and do good to them. GOD'S love potion is powerful. Money can't buy it. GOD's love is free, all we have to do is accept the invitation to come and dine.

For peace of mind, we need to endeavor to release from our thoughts hate, illness, tension, frustration, financial trouble, heartache, adversarial relationships and accept GOD'S invitation to come and dine with HIM. GOD is calling for each one of us to come to HIS Feast of Love.

The feast of love in the Song of Solomon 2:4 is a place where special favors are given out, and confidential communications can take place. It is a place where GOD shares special privileges and gives blessings to those who obey HIS summons.

When a Prince, Governor or Ruler opens his banner over a fortress or area, he is declaring his determination to protect that place.

As the flag waves in the breeze, it is a warning to anyone who would try to harm or bring danger to that area that it is protected by all the power and resources the ruler must use to keep it safe.

GOD does this for us when HE opens HIS banner of love. When HE summons us to a feast of love, HE opens his umbrella of protection, peace, joy, and happiness over our souls.

GOD covers us with HIS blood while the storms are raging in our lives. HE covers us from the dangers that surround us.

HE covers our unsaved loved ones who have not yet seen the value of coming to the feast of love.

GOD'S thoughts towards HIS people are thoughts of peace, love, and unspeakable joy. Our love for GOD will make HIM real to us. When we have been summoned to a feast of love we won't have any problems giving GOD high praise when we feel overwhelmed and despondent.

To eat together is an act of friendship, to share the same meal together is a beautiful bond of attachment. When GOD invites us to HIS feast it means HE finds pleasure in our company.

HE wishes to draw us closer to HIM.

Natural friendships have a tendency to die out. One gets jealous of the success of the other; one breaks a confidence or becomes too involved in the other's personal life. They begin to cause interference or confusion in each others marriages or family relationships.

Friendships may weaken according to circumstances. Friendship with GOD is eternal. Nothing can separate us from HIS love.

The enemy is shrewd; he will use a little thing to make us miss the feast of love. he is not going to come, at some of us, with drugs, alcohol or sex. he will start with something like, "No one understands me", "I need to be held", "the way you said what you said hurt me". We can't allow anything to keep us from answering a summons to the feast of love.

To be called to come and dine with the SAVIOR is a special privilege. All of our actions in and out of the church, no matter how good they may appear are worthless if they don't flow from the principle of love.

It doesn't matter how much time we put into a beautiful message, if the message does not come from love, it is worthless.

The love of GOD unites us to one another. How can we say we love GOD whom we have not seen and not love our brother whom we see every day? (1 John 4:20 KJV).

If a brother or sister looked at us the wrong way or says something we don't like; we are ready to lower them back into the muck and miry clay of which GOD has already brought them out.

GOD will not allow us at HIS feast of love with a lack of love in our heart, all we will be doing is standing outside looking in.

GOD never leaves or forsakes us; we walk out on HIM. We refuse HIS invitation. GOD gives us the privilege to make choices.

We can't blame GOD when we make a decision to allow feelings and the cares of life to come in between our love for HIM.

A man's worst enemy is usually himself. Sometimes GOD has to use affliction to bring some of us to HIS feast of love. David said, "Before I was afflicted I went astray." (Psalm 119:67 AMP)

Saul's blindness on the road to Damascus made him aware of GODs nearness (Acts 9:1-18 AMP). Jonah's peril in the wale's belly taught him to say "but I will sacrifice unto THEE with the with the voice of thanksgiving; I shall pay that I have vowed. Salvation is of the LORD" (Jonah 2:9 AMP).

GOD has furnished an elegant banquet table and summoned us to dine with HIM. We put off HIS invitation again and again with the promise that we will come someday. We say things like; "when I get myself together" "when I straighten out the sin in my life." We need to understand that all those obstacles can only be resolved when we accept the invitation to GOD'S feast of love.

We can't do it ourselves.

Have you ever come to Church and the anointing and power of GOD was falling, people were shouting and praising GOD, and there you sat wondering what happened and when it happened?

That happens when you have been summoned to the feast of love but fail to pull up a chair and dine at the master's table. Love was on the menu, and your system won't let you digest it.

When that happens, we need to take a hate release enema and clean ourselves out of unforgiveness, iniquity, envy, jealousy, and rebellion so that we can sit down and enjoy the meal.

The feast of love is to gather and keep people together. GOD'S love is displayed in the preaching of the gospel. HE summons us to HIS feast though the word of GOD that is ministered to us in the house of GOD. He summons us when we read and study HIS word in the Bible.

When a city or town is taken, the winning side displays its banner as a sign of victory. GOD has gotten the victory over all HIS and our enemies.

Moses built an altar and called it JEHOVAH NISSI; The LORD is my banner. The LORD had been on his side and defended him and the people of Israel from the Amalekites. We need to learn how to rise a spiritual banner showing the world that GOD is the reason for the victories in our lives.

It was GOD that brought us out of that bad situation. It was GOD that allowed Hurricane Sandy not to destroy our home and families irreparably. It was GOD that gave us the job. It was GOD that gave us the house. It was GOD that gave us the car. It was GOD who protected our children from the hurt, harm or danger that could have befallen them.

After dining at the Master's table, we can proclaim that we are under GOD's Banner of Protection and Victory and it is from GOD that we receive our blessings.

The love of GOD will lift us up and make us healthy.

The LORD continues to love us even though we often fail to measure up to the beautiful Christian life HE suffered and died for us to have.

The love of GOD is that which distinguishes the soul of a believer from other souls. GOD's love must be so rooted in our heart that it won't allow anything to distract us from that love.

GOD is summoning us all to HIS feast of love. When we dine with the SAVIOR, it is like sitting under the shadow of a great tree that protects us from the over penetrating rays of the sun. It's like being under the shelter of a great rock in a wind or sand storm.

GOD will cover us as he did Elijah as he sat under the juniper tree (1 Kings 19:4 KJV). We find that in CHRIST, in HIS name, by HIS grace, HE undertakes for us. HE revives us and keeps us from fainting.

Those that are weary can find rest in CHRIST. It is not enough to be summoned to the feast of love, but we must sit down, at the table and dine with the SAVIOR. Not only does the food at that table provide shelter from the storms that the enemy sends into our lives but it is for the healing of our natural and spiritual body.

At GOD'S table is pleasing nourishing food and for those who accept the invitation, we will taste the sweetness of GOD. Those of us who have been to the feast have tasted that the LORD is gracious, compassionate, merciful and just.

GOD summons us to a feast of love where HE entertains HIS special friends. GOD will help us over our discouragement, take us by the hand and lead and guide us.

At the feast of love, we have access and the privilege to be one on one with GOD himself. GOD'S feast strengthens us and upholds us; it encourages us as we go through. David experienced GOD'S hand supporting him when he said: "yea though I walk through the valley of the shadow of death, I will fear no evil; for THOU art with me; THY rod and thy staff they comfort me." (Psalm 23:4 KJV). Job in a state of desertion and desolation yet found that GOD put strength into him. He was able to say in Job 14:14 KJV "...all the days of my appointed time will I wait, till my change come" and in Job 13:15 KJV, he says "though HE slay me yet will I trust HIM...".

We have been summoned to a feast of love by our SAVIOR. Let us all make haste to come and dine with HIM.

PRAYER OF THANKSGIVING

"HANNAH PRAYED, and said, My heart exults and triumphs in the LORD; my horn (my strength) is lifted up in the LORD. My mouth is no longer silent, for it is opened wide over my enemies, because I rejoice in YOUR salvation." 1 Samuel 2:1 AMP

Hannah looked beyond the gift GOD had given her. She had prayed for a child and GOD had given her Samuel. Her prayer praised the GIVER of the gift. Her heart rejoiced, not in Samuel, but in the LORD.

She acknowledged GOD'S goodness in answer to her prayer.

Thanking GOD for giving us what we desired is expected but before we do that we need to thank GOD every time we pray just for who GOD is.

Hannah first acknowledges GOD's absolute holiness; second HIS perfect existence. She expressed that outside of GOD there is no existence. In calling GOD a rock, she assigns to HIM strength, calm, immovable, enduring security which HE provides. GOD wants to hear us give an introduction to our prayer. That introduction should be about HIM. Like Hannah, I begin my prayer by saying "oh adorable LORD and SAVIOR, JESUS CHRIST." We need to make it clear who we are praying to from the beginning of our prayer.

Hannah had prayed before, but that was mental, this prayer was vocal. When we petition GOD for something, it should be mental, silent. The enemy and those around us don't need to hear our requests. When we praise GOD for answered prayer, it should be loud, let the world hear our praise. Let the world hear us rejoice in the goodness of the LORD.

Hannah had prayed, and her prayer was answered. She had what she prayed for, and she gave thanks for it. Thanksgiving is one kind of prayer. Sometimes we need to take a break from the usual give me; I need prayer. Give GOD praise and chase the enemy with a prayer of total Thanksgiving.

Hannah rejoiced in the LORD, not in her son, not in her husband, not in the wealth and riches they possessed but in the LORD.

She rejoiced in the giver of the gift, not the gift that was given.

"Mine horn is exalted in the LORD..." Hannah's countenance was sad when GOD had shut up her womb, and her adversary provoked her. She had been so full of grief, she could not eat her food, and prayed in the bitterness of her soul. Now she could lift up her head; now she could look pleasant be cheerful, and even triumph because GOD had, greatly favored her.

"My mouth is enlarged over mine enemies.." When Hannah was being provoked by Peninnah and ridiculed for her barrenness by others, she was not able to make a reply. When GOD turned her situation around, she could speak openly in prayer, praise, and thanksgiving for the great thing GOD had done for her.

ATTITUDE OF GRATITUDE

"So Sarai, Abram's wife, took Hagar her Egyptian maid, after Abram had dwelt ten years in the land of Canaan, and gave her to her husband Abram to be his [secondary] wife. And he had intercourse with Hagar, and she became pregnant; and when she saw that she was with child, she looked with contempt upon her mistress and despised her." (Genesis 16:3-4 AMP)

Hagar, who was she? I guess most people, especially during that period of time in the bible, would consider her a nobody. Hagar was a young, Egyptian, slave girl; Sarah's personal hand maid. She became the victim of another woman's jealousy and a man who neglected to stand up for what was right.

Involuntarily Hagar was pulled into the relationship with Sarah and Abraham. She was not given a choice to be made Abraham's secondary wife and bear a son. She was doing her little slave job and minding her own business when Sarah decided to raise her to the position of Abraham's wife. We have to be careful when man elevates us and not GOD. When that happens, our egos won't be able to handle it, and we will begin to think more highly of ourselves than we ought to.

Hagar who was formerly considered a nobody got elevated and thought she was Miss Somebody. She forgot to show gratitude for where she had come from. Arrogance and pride took over her spirit. She had the audacity to disrespect Sarah, the woman responsible for her new position.

Hagar provoked Sarah into putting her back in her place. Pride, contempt and insubordination caused Hagar to lose her new position and she couldn't handle it.

".... And when Sarai dealt severely with her, humbling and afflicting her, she [Hagar] fled from her. "(Genesis 16:6 AMP)

Hagar ran away. She was angry. Her self-esteem was deflated, and she ran.

When GOD has not called and positioned us it is easy to run away from responsibility. Without God's anointing and call on our lives when trouble comes, things get tough, we have to go through suffering and humiliation we don't have a problem walking away from an elevation we didn't earn.

Hagar didn't have an attitude of gratitude. She couldn't face the reality and humiliation that she was not as valuable and important as she thought she had become.

When we allow man to elevate us, we also give them the power to bring us down.

We must make sure that our call is from GOD. When GOD is in control of our lives, our calling will become a reality.

"We are assured and know that [GOD being a partner in their labor] all things work together and are [fitting into a plan] for good to and for those who love GOD and are called according to [HIS] design and purpose."(Romans 8:28 AMP)

Sarah resented Hagar's attitude and treated her harshly. Hagar fled into the wilderness. An angel found her. Even when we have mistaken our calling and had to suffer the repercussions for making wrong decisions and choices, GOD does not forsake us and leave us broken and in despair.

HE will find us when we try to flee from disappointment, humiliation and unrealistic goals. HE will correct us and advise us on how to proceed in our situation.

"But the Angel of the LORD found her by a spring of water in the wilderness on the road to Shur." (Genesis 16:7 AMP)

The angel prophesied to Hagar regarding the character and future of her son, Ishmael. The angel directs Hagar to go back to Sarai. Let her continue oppressing, afflicting and humiliating you. SUBMIT!!! Oh how hard that is for us to do. Do you mean go back and let everybody witness my failure, my loss of status? Sarai placed her in the situation, but it was Hagar's attitude that caused her present distress. There is no evidence that Sarai was ever rebuked or corrected for her abuse to Hagar. Sarai does not appear to have been instructed to change her abusive behavior towards her. Hagar has to return to the same situation from which she had run away.

In her spiritual immaturity, Hagar made the mistake of thinking that she could replace Sarah in bringing forth the promised son. Hagar was not called by GOD to bring forth the promised son. She was mistaken in her assumption. Many have brought a good word when asked to speak at a service; this however does not indicate that GOD has called them to be a minister, evangelist, elder or pastor.

While it is true that Hagar had wronged her mistress by treating her with "contempt", Sarai holds all the power in the relationship. Hagar is utterly vulnerable. Her situation is hopeless. She is trapped between almost certain death in the wilderness and obedience to a messenger of GOD which meant returning to submit to abuse at the hands of her mistress.

Hagar is about to bear a child. She has no visible means of support. She is utterly alone. She is an outcast, cut off from her own people and rejected by her owner. Hagar's only realistic choice is to return to the painful situation she had fled from. She had to return and refuse to operate with the same attitude which caused the abuse?

She had to let the people see that GOD had not called her to her assumed position. She had to be willing to stay and suffer personal humiliation until GOD said differently.

Hagar needed to display an attitude of gratitude for being allowed to move up to her position in life. Had she done that, perhaps her future outcome would have turned out differently?

Let us not forget to display an attitude of gratitude in our present circumstances.

When we show appreciation for where we are, GOD will elevate us to greater positions in life.

YOU CAN'T GO TO HEAVEN
WITHOUT A BATH

"JESUS answered and said unto him. Verily, verily, I say unto thee, Except a man be born of water and of the Spirit, he cannot] enter into the kingdom of GOD." (John 3:5 KJV)

"Thus says the LORD GOD: In the day that I cleanse you from all your iniquities I will [also] cause [Israel's] cities to be inhabited, and the waste places shall be rebuilt." (Ezekiel 36:33 AMP)

"And Peter answered them, Repent (change your views and purpose to accept the will of GOD in your inner selves instead of rejecting it) and be baptized, every one of you, in the name of JESUS CHRIST for the forgiveness of and release from your sins; and you shall receive the gift of the HOLY SPIRIT." (Acts 2:38 AMP)

My text is coming from the book of John where Nicodemus a Pharisee and lawyer encounters JESUS at night. The baptism of John had caught the attention of all Jerusalem. JESUS had also been baptized. Baptism with water required a public profession in the presence of witnesses, and open loyalty to JESUS. Nicodemus was concerned about his public image. He came secretly by night. Even though he came by night, JESUS welcomed Nicodemus and by doing so initiated a new beginning in his life. The message given to Him was to be baptized with water and the HOLY SPIRIT. Nicodemus needed to take a bath. Cowardly Nicodemus came by night, but after the encounter, he owned CHRIST publicly. Nicodemus did not talk with JESUS about state affairs, even though he was a ruler, His concerns were of his soul and its salvation,

We cannot expect any benefit by CHRIST if we don't obey HIS command, which is necessary to our happiness here and hereafter.

We cannot expect any benefit by CHRIST if we don't obey HIS command, which is necessary to our happiness here and hereafter. We don't put clean clothes on a dirty body. We have to bathe first, or the odor of unclearness will be evident.

In the spiritual, if we don't bathe through baptism and receive the gift of the HOLY SPIRIT the stench of sin will seep through and prevent our entrance to heaven.

"Then I will sprinkle clean water on you, and you will be clean; I will cleanse you from all your uncleanness and from all your idols.

26 Moreover, I will give you a new heart and put a new spirit within you, and I will remove the heart of stone from your flesh and give you a heart of flesh. I will put my SPIRIT within you and cause you to walk in My statutes, and you will keep MY ordinances and do them." Ezekiel 36:25-27 AMP

We are born in sin and shaped in iniquity, which makes it necessary that our nature is changed. Unbelief is a sin that needs to be remedied. Sinful works are works of darkness. The wicked world keeps as far from GOD's light as they can. They don't want their sins exposed or have to confess their actions and follow the process necessary to remove them.

To remedy this, we need to take a holy bath. It is written in Mark 16:16, KJV," He that believeth and is baptized shall be saved..."

It is also emphasized in other scriptures in the Bible.

(Acts 2:38, Acts 2:41; Acts 8:12-13, Acts 8:36, Acts 8:38; Acts 9:18; Acts 10:47-48; Acts 16:15, Acts 16:33; Acts 18:8; Acts 22:16; Galatians 3:27).

We must make sure that the will of GOD is in control of our works and the glory of GOD is revealed in what we do.

Working in our strength, and for our selfish desires excludes GOD from perfecting what we do.

JESUS affirmed that baptism was to be the regular and uniform way of entering into HIS kingdom. It was a clear command of GOD. Nicodemus had to take that spiritual cleansing bath.

JESUS also added that he should "be born of the SPIRIT" also.

It was predicted of the SAVIOR, that HE would also baptize with the HOLY GHOST and with fire," (Matthew 3:11 KJV)

Our hearts must be changed; sin must be abandoned, and we must repent of past indiscretions.

We all need to take a spiritual bath, wash away any and everything that will hinder us from turning our life over completely to GOD. We must renounce all evil thoughts and actions and give ourselves to a life of prayer, holiness, meekness, purity, and benevolence. The HOLY SPIRIT can only accomplish this great change. (Titus 3:5; 1 Thessalonians 1:6; Romas 5:5 KJV)

Let us not forget and remind others that we cannot go to heaven without the spiritual bath of baptism and the gift of the HOLY SPIRIT.

LOCKED IN THE ARK BY THE ROCK

Noah was a preacher of righteousness; not of his righteousness, not growing out of his character but given to him by GOD. GOD puts HIS noble spirit in those who trust in HIM.

"The LORD saw that the wickedness of man was great in the earth and that every imagination and intention of all human thinking was only evil continually.

6 And the LORD regretted that He had made man on the earth, and He was grieved at heart.

7 So the LORD said, I will destroy, blot out, and wipe away mankind, whom I have created from the face of the ground–not only man, [but] the beasts and the creeping things and the birds of the air–for it grieves Me and makes Me regretful that I have made them.

8 But Noah found grace (favor) in the eyes of the LORD." (Genesis 6: 5-8 AMPC)

The Bible says Noah found favor in the eyes of GOD. He lived a righteous life when no one else was.

Noah was not a hypocrite or a phony. He did not say he was sorry for sin and that that he had repented but continued to indulge in it. The Earth was full of violence and injustice.

It was no particular nation or city that was wicked but the whole world of humankind. GOD was speaking through the unmistakable signs of the times to everybody, but Noah was the only one who paid attention and listened because he had an honest, right relationship with GOD. It is true today the signs of the end of time is evident, but only a few are paying attention, only a few are listening.

Noah wasn't just righteous in church but living all the rest of the time sinfully. He had a real relationship with GOD. Noah not only foresaw the crisis but did something about it.

GOD said a flood was coming and by faith, he began to build an ark. He began to builds the ark before there was any visible evidence that it would be needed.

According to the story in the book of Genesis, Noah, and his family were given the privilege to continue life on Earth; everyone else perished in the flood.

GOD gave Noah instructions on how to build the ark. In constructing the ark, there was no room left for Noah to add his creativity.

Like the Tabernacle in the wilderness, the ark was fashioned according to a GOD given pattern. Building the ark was a job that involved great labor, patient endurance, heroic self-sacrifice, total cooperation, complete obedience and merciless ridicule. Noah accepted his task in a spirit of meekness and unquestioning faith. Noah is the role model we need to follow when GOD gives us an assignment. "So Noah did this; according to all that GOD commanded him, that is what he did."(Genesis 6:22 AMP)

When obedience is absent faith is not present also. The prediction of a flood and the way to survive in an ark were great trials of Noah's faith. It was beyond man's comprehension. The people couldn't visualize the possibility of what Noah was predicting. When things don't seem possible, we are quick to believe that it will not happen.

GOD told Noah to build an ark. He believed and obeyed what GOD told him to do.

Noah entered into the ark of the safety and deliverance which only CHRIST the solid ROCK can provide. The ark was a symbol of the SAVIOR. The ark was a refuge. The LORD is our refuge and our strength.

The ark was a temple. Noah and his family worshiped there. We have to be in CHRIST if we want to be acceptable worshippers.

The ark was a conveyance, a vehicle for transportation. It took Noah from the wicked old world to a new world that he would be responsible for beginning. It took Noah from the valley of his labors and sorrows to the mountain of rest and plenty.

The ark was a preserver of life. When we are obedient and enter into the will of GOD, we have the opportunity to receive eternal life.

The ark was built using man made instruments and human hands, but the design, as well as the materials of which it was made, were divinely appointed.

For one hundred and twenty years Noah preached and warned the people of GOD's wrath and the judgment to come. No one other than his family listened to him. They heard him and made fun of him but they didn't listen. When we listen to GOD's word as opposed to just hearing it, we take corrective actions.

In his public life, Noah was a preacher. Noah not only spoke the word but acted upon it. He was an example of what he preached. Considering the small number of people that were saved by his preaching, Noah would be regarded as an unsuccessful preacher. GOD doesn't reward us for what appears to be an outward display of success. GOD rewards us for our honesty, integrity, faithfulness, and obedience to HIM.

Noah was dealing with men whose actions were grievous to GOD. Their actions were contrary to GOD's will. GOD's will cannot be changed to please man. Man's will must be changed to please GOD. Noah was sincere and not a hypocrite. He didn't preach one thing to the people and live the opposite in his home. The fact that his family supported him and worked with him is a witness to that. Noah was already locked in the ark of CHRIST THE ROCK's protection.

Noah's purpose was to warn the people of his generation of GOD's impending judgment. He showed by his example the need to prepare for the future that was going to change all of the mankind and every living creature on Earth.

Can you imagine how people must have joked, taunted and even threatened him with bodily harm?

For one hundred and twenty years he worked on GOD's purpose. He had to have gotten discouraged and even questioned GOD at times. No one was listening, not one person outside of his family encouraged or supported him. I am sure there had to be times when he was tempted to give up. There had to be times when he was so weary and discouraged that he wanted to stop GOD's work and surrender to just living in the present.

When we are locked into the ark of the purpose and promise of GOD we can't quit. Galatians 6:9 KJV: "And let us not be weary in well doing: for in due season we shall reap, if we faint not."

We must prepare for the unseen future. Noah's visible sign was the wooden ark he was building. Our physical sign of GOD's return today is all the signs prophesied in GOD's word taking place. Each of us that have been called by GOD has a responsibility to warn people of GOD's soon return and the judgment that is coming upon the Earth.

GOD could have saved Noah by sending angels to remove Noah and his family from the impending destruction.

GOD chose to make Noah work on His means of preservation.

GOD tried Noah's faith and obedience. GOD taught Noah that interdependence is how our relationship with HIM should be. We cannot do our works without GOD and GOD wants us to put our efforts into what we want to accomplish. "Even so faith, if it hath not works, is dead, being alone." (James 2:14 KJV)

The animals entered the ark of their own free will and were divinely guided to it. We must come to GOD of our own accord. No one can force us or intimidate us to serve GOD.

Those of us who work for GOD must follow HIS directions exactly. GOD told Noah to pitch the ark within and without. It was pitched within to take away the bad smells of the animals confined so closely and without to prevent the rain water from seeping in. GOD covers the people of GOD within to keep us holy and without to avoid demonic spirits and witchcraft from entering into us. The benefits we receive from serving GOD outweigh any obstacles we may encounter.

Noah and his sons were not shipbuilders. They did not live in a seaport town where the people were familiar with building ships. He lived in the country far from the sea. Noah could have made the excuse that he did not know anything about building ships.

GOD often calls us to duties that we have no prior knowledge. It is easy to work in areas that we are familiar with and have the knowledge to perform a task. We are rewarded when we step out on faith and follow GOD's direction.

GOD wants to lock us in the ark of HIS anointing and prosperity. For this to occur, we have to be like Noah and be persevering workers, not slothful but fervent in business.

Today people are willing to obey GOD as long as HE tells them to do what they like to do. People today are quick to walk away from difficult tasks.

A sincerely obedient child of GOD will not pick and choose what commands to obey and what to reject when GOD calls them. Noah's call was a personal call, "Come thou." Noah had a call to action; he had to do something. Noah had to go into the ark. He couldn't stand next to it and wait for the raindrops to fall.

When everything was prepared, he had to enter the ark himself. Noah didn't hesitate or delay; he went right into the ark. The ark was for his preservation. There was safety in the ark. CHRIST is the ark, and HE saves us, so we must get inside HIM. To be in CHRIST, we must repent, be baptized and receive HIS HOLY SPIRIT. We can't just come to church on Sunday and sit and enjoy the service that others are rendering for GOD.

GOD is calling for all of us to participate in some form of personal worship and actively work for HIM.

Noah did not personally have to gather the animals into the ark. They came on their own accord because GOD had called them. The unclean animals came by two a male and a female.

The clean animals came by sevens. Clean animals were used for sacrifice so more had to be preserved.

GOD's divine power allowed the animals to enter orderly into the ark.

The lion, tiger, rhinoceros, buffalo, elephant, bear, antelope, wolf, fox, lamb, lizard, rattlesnake, Nightingale, butterfly, eagle, and the hawk, just to name a few, all moving together towards one common goal. Surely watching this orderly procession of all GOD's creatures in harmony entering into the ark must have caused awe and amazement to the people that were observing this supernatural phenomenon. At least some of the people should have been convinced that GOD was orchestrating this entire event, but none other than Noah's family accepted the call. The people's hearts were so hardened that even the sight of such a miracle did not move them.

Today people are planning for the future, enjoying the present and ignoring all the signs that GOD is soon to return. We are careful to make sure our homes and cars are locked, some have additional alarm systems in place, but our true safety for our souls is to be locked in the ark by the ROCK. "For who is GOD save the LORD? Or who is a rock save our GOD?" (Psalms 18:31, KJV) "The LORD is my rock, and my fortress, and my deliverer; my GOD, my strength, in whom I will trust; my buckler, and the horn of my salvation, and my high tower." Psalms 18:2 KJV

"And a stone of stumbling, and a rock of offense, even to them which stumble at the word, being disobedient: whereunto also they were appointed." (1 Peter 2:8 KJV)

One of the amazing things that occurred while Noah and his family were locked in the ark was the change in the disposition of the animals. All hostilities between the creatures ceased. The wolf and the lamb got along. The lion and the bear had fellowship with each other. When the flood was over, they returned to their original temperaments. The wild beast went back to being wild.

The gentle animals maintained their gentle spirit. What a mighty GOD we serve. GOD can change personalities and dispositions, but we have to be willing vessels for HIM to do that.

The LORD shut the door of the ark. GOD locked Noah in to keep him safe and prevent him from allowing undeserving individuals from entering. The door had to be strong and secure to keep the rain out and those left outside from breaking it down. If Noah had been allowed to open and shut the door, his humanness might have caused him to go against the will of GOD.

To lock the door on a perishing world would have been too much responsibility for Noah.

If Noah had been allowed to close the door, he might have let everybody in, and GOD's purpose would have been unfulfilled. GOD shut out the haters, the liars, the deceivers, the discouragers, the thieves, the doubters, the hypocrites and all the unrighteous sinners that HE wanted to be destroyed.

GOD shut Noah in the ark, and GOD shut all HIS enemies out. When we don't obey the word of GOD we become HIS enemy, and GOD will shut the door on our desires, our happiness, and our prosperity. We need to move self out of the way and let GOD shut the door on any and everything in our lives that will keep us bound and delay the tremendous blessing HE has in store for us.

Once we have entered into the safety of GOD's ark, we must be determined to stay there. When we accept GOD's call to come unto HIM, the enemy will try to entice, tempt, deceive and provoke us to leave. David had some issues in Psalms 27 KJV, he wrote, "I had fainted, unless I had believed to see the goodness of the LORD in the land of the living. Wait on the LORD: be of good courage, and HE shall strengthen thine heart: wait, I say, on the LORD."

For twelve months Noah drifted across a trackless sea. Can you imagine the strain on Noah's soul and his faith?

It appears that Noah was shut up in the ark for twelve months without any direct communication from GOD. We do not find that GOD told Noah how long he should be confined and when he should be released.

When our afflictions and struggles have been unusually long and grievous, we are often tempted to fear that GOD has forgotten us. We can become so troubled sometimes that we cannot speak to anyone. We cannot pray. We begin to wonder if GOD's mercy has left us. The word of GOD encourages us by letting us know that GOD shall certainly remember those that remember HIM.

GOD will appoint a set time, and HIS purpose for our lives will not fail.

Not until GOD spoke did Noah dare to do more than lifting the covering and look out. Noah did not exhibit haste to get out of the circumstances in which GOD had placed him. When GOD puts us in uncomfortable positions, we should not try to remove ourselves from those posts. GOD usually works deliverance for us gradually so that victory over the days of small things that happen to us will not be despised.

If we believe in GOD we should not try to run before HIM but wait on the LORD and while waiting to be of good courage and HE shall strengthen our hearts.

GOD finally gave Noah permission to leave the ark. "For the vision is yet for an appointed time, but at the end it shall speak, and not lie: though it tarry, wait for it; because it will surely come, it will not tarry." (Habakkuk 2:3 KJV).

We have to learn how to stay locked in the ARK by the ROCK. Our safety is in the ARK. Our deliverance is in the ARK. Our victory will only come if we stay in the situation that GOD has placed us until HE says move.

After the flood had begun to dry up, Noah had to continue to be patient and the last days of waiting must have been the hardest. "GOD how much longer do I have to endure this?"

Has anyone ever felt that way?

We are tempted to think sometimes that GOD has left us to face impossible conditions and HE no longer seems to care.

1 Corinthians 10:13 (KJV) "There hath no temptation taken you but such as is common to man: but GOD is faithful, who will not suffer you to be tempted above that ye are able; but will with the temptation also make a way to escape, that ye may be able to bear it."

Somebody has gone through what we are going through and made it.

Moses cried, "Wherefore hast thou afflicted thy servant" I am not able to bear all these people alone because it is too heavy for me." (Numbers 11:14 KJV)

Habakkuk exclaimed, "O LORD, how long shall I cry, and THOU wilt not hear! Even cry out unto THEE of violence, and THOU wilt not save!" (Habakkuk 1:2 KJV)

GOD always comes through on time and triumphantly.

When the flood of danger, delay and disappointment seems to be overwhelming, we need to stay locked in the ARK by the ROCK.

BREAK THE CHAIN

"Therefore if anyone is in CHRIST [that is, grafted in, joined to HIM by faith in HIM as SAVIOR], he is a new creature [reborn and renewed by the HOLY SPIRIT]; the old things [the previous moral and spiritual condition] have passed away. Behold, new things have come [because spiritual awakening brings a new life]." 2 Corinthians 5:17 (AMP)

The chain of sinfulness in the family began in the Garden of Eden. GOD asked Adam about his sin of disobedience when he ate the the forbidden fruit. Adam blamed Eve. Eve blamed the serpent.

It is a sin when we don't take responsibility for our wrong actions and blame someone else.

Cain killed Abel because of jealousy when GOD accepted Abel's sacrificial offering and not his. Disobedience led to lying, which led to jealousy and then murder.

A relationship that GOD wanted to nourish was destroyed. Sins we pass to our children multiply. We can Break The Chain.

Lemech, Adam's sixth generation had two wives. He was the first to break GOD's one husband, one wife design. Jacob continued by having more than one wife. David increased his number of wives and Solomon followed. Solomon had seven hundred wives and three hundred concubines.

Daddy had women on the side and granddaddy and great granddaddy, but it is against the will of GOD. It's time to Break The Chain.

Rebekah played favorites among her children. Rebekah was a deceiver. She orchestrated the plan to deceive her husband Isaac so her son Jacob could receive a blessing.

Deception was in her family background. Rebekah's brother Laban tricked Jacob into working seven years for the wrong woman.

Favoritism caused strive between, Isaac and Rebekah.

Jacob became a trickster and Esau a rebel.

Everyone suffers when family members play favorites.

Rebekah got what she wanted, but she also caused Esau to want to kill his brother. Her favorite son, Jacob, had to flee for his life.

Jacob followed his mother's example and played favorites.

He made his son Joseph a coat of many colors which caused his brothers to hate him and want to kill him. They eventually sold him to the Egyptians.

Ruben slept with his father's concubine. Jacob took what was not his by stealing his brother's birthright, and Ruben took it to another level.

Judah deceived his daughter in law into believing she would marry his younger son. She had to use deception, play a harlot, and became pregnant by her father in law.

Levi and Simeon tricked a whole nation of people into circumcising themselves and then killed all the men because their sister Dinah had been raped.

Break The Chain of showing favoritism, lying, and deceit that causes destruction in our families.

David, a man after GOD's own heart, had a dysfunctional family. David committed adultery with Bathsheba. He had her husband killed to cover his sin. The child Bathsheba conceived by David died. David's son Amon raped his sister. Tamar's brother Absalom killed Amon, and started a rebellion. David slept with Bathsheba in secret but his son Absalom slept with his father's concubines openly. He increased his father's sin.

David's poor example as a father produced a rapist, murderer, traitor and a womanizer. Break The Chain that escalates a life style that is displeasing to GOD in the family.

We need to Break The Chains that have bound many of us to the past mistakes of our Parents, GrandParents and Great Grandparents. Many have and will continue to pass curses on to the next generation. We can Break The Chain.

Break The Chain of adultery, abuse, depression, suicide, cancer, poverty, deceit, and murder that has been passed from generation to generation.

The Bible gives us instructions on how to do it.

"Therefore if anyone is in CHRIST [that is, grafted in, joined to HIM by faith in HIM as SAVIOR], he is a new creature [reborn and renewed by the HOLY SPIRIT]; the old things [the previous moral and spiritual condition] have passed away. Behold, new things have come [because spiritual awakening brings a new life]." (2 Corinthians 5:17 AMP)

"And it shall come to pass, if thou shalt hearken diligently unto the voice of the LORD thy GOD, to observe and to do all HIS commandments which I command thee this day, that the LORD thy GOD will set thee on high above all nations of the earth: And all these blessings shall come on thee, and overtake thee, if thou shalt hearken unto the voice of the LORD thy GOD. Blessed shalt thou be in the city, and blessed shalt thou be in the field. Blessed shall be the fruit of thy body, and the fruit of thy ground, and the fruit of thy cattle, the increase of thy kine, and the flocks of thy sheep." (Deuteronomy 28:1-5 KJV)

When we give our lives over completely to GOD, HE will Break The Chain of sin that is plaguing our family.

THERE IS A BALM IN GILEAD

"Is there no BALM in Gilead is there no physician there? why then is not the health of the daughter of my people recovered?" Jeremiah 8:22 (KJV)

Gilead, a district of Palestine, East of the Jordan River, is celebrated for its aromatic balm of great virtue for wounds, and sores. Gilead possessed the formula for making a healing balam but needed spiritual healing. The social, political and religious evils were to such a degree that the sources of saving strength were exhausted.

Many professing that GOD is in their life often fail to exhibit the fruit of the spirit when troubled with earthly cares.

"But the fruit of the Spirit is love, joy, peace, forbearance, kindness, goodness, faithfulness, gentleness, and self-control. Against such things, there is no law." (Galatians 5:22-23 NIV)

When Christians appear as downcast as those who don't know CHRIST it causes others to doubt the strength and power of the GOD we proclaim.

"We are troubled on every side, yet not distressed; we are perplexed, but not in despair; Persecuted, but not forsaken; cast down, but not destroyed;" (2 Corinthians 4:8-9 (KJV)

Gilead had among it GOD's prophets and priests to bring the people to repentance and prevent their ruin. They had princes and laws to reform the Nation and help solve their grievances.

Why was their health not restored?

It was not because they lacked physicians but because they would not submit to the methods of the cure. The physician was ready, but the patient was willful and would not follow the rules.

Jeremiah the prophet served as GOD's messenger. He warned Israel of coming judgment. He assured the people of their restoration after seventy years of Babylonian captivity. GOD was threatening the destruction of the sinful people. HE had tolerated their actions for a long time. The people became more and more provoking.

"Why then is this people of Jerusalem slidden back by a perpetual backsliding? they hold fast deceit, they refuse to return.

Therefore will I give their wives unto others, and their fields to them that shall inherit them: for every one from the least even unto the greatest is given to covetousness, from the prophet even unto the priest every one dealeth falsely.

For they have healed the hurt of the daughter of my people slightly, saying, Peace, peace; when there is no peace.

Were they ashamed when they had committed abomination? nay, they were not at all ashamed, neither could they blush: therefore shall they fall among them that fall: in the time of their visitation they shall be cast down, saith the LORD.

I will surely consume them, saith the LORD: there shall be no grapes on the vine, nor figs on the fig tree, and the leaf shall fade, and the things that I have given them shall pass away from them." (Jeremiah 8:5-13)

The people were told that they would be stripped of their comforts.

The people began to sink into despair under the pressures of the calamities they faced.

Is there no BALM in Gilead, no medicine for the sick and dying, no skillful, faithful hand to apply the ointment to cure the disease of sin?

Have the saints of GOD any means for curing the evils of humanity, the miseries of life, the wickedness increasing in the land?

Yes, certainly there is.
GOD can help and heal our every infirmity.
GOD is the balm that heals all our grievances.
We have the WORD OF GOD, and HE has placed men and women among us to lead us to repentance and prevent our destruction.

The blood of CHRIST is the Balm. HIS SPIRIT in us is the physician when we are overwhelmed.

Isaiah tells us, "But HE was wounded for our transgressions, HE was bruised for our iniquities: the chastisement of our peace was upon HIM, and with HIS stripes, we are healed." (Isaiah 53:5 KJV)

"For I reckon that the sufferings of this present time are not worthy to be compared with the glory which shall be revealed in us." (Romans 8:18 KJV)

When serving GOD is our passion and pleasing HIM is our aim, HIS favor becomes our balm.

We forfeit GOD's Balm through disobedience and unbelief.

We can refill the healing BALM through Prayer, worship and Praising GOD. "Be careful for nothing; but in every thing by prayer and supplication with thanksgiving let your requests be made known unto GOD. And the peace of GOD, which passeth all understanding, shall keep your hearts and minds through CHRIST JESUS." (Philippians 4:6-7 KJV)

A proper diet on the WORD OF GOD is a Healing Balm.

When we turn to GOD in our darkest hour, HE will direct our attention to just the scripture we need to heal in any situation we face.

When we survive and overcome our adversities, we can lead others to the BALM in Gilead through our testimonies.

"Set your affection on things above, not on things on the earth." (Colossians 3:2 KJV)

When we place our love and affection on GOD, we have that BALM in Gilead.

WHICH LITTLE PIG ARE YOU?

"And the disciples came, and said unto him, Why speakest thou unto them in parables? HE answered and said unto them, Because it is give unto you to know the mysteries of the kingdom of heaven, but to them, it is not given.

For whosoever hath, to him shall be given, and he shall have more abundance: but whosoever hath not, from him shall be taken away even that he hath. Therefore speak I to them in parables: because they seeing see not; and hearing they hear not, neither do they understand." (Matthew 13:10-13 KJV)

JESUS spoke to people in parables as a teaching method. Parables are, "usually short fictitious story that illustrates a moral attitude or a religious principle e.g. the parable of the Good Samaritan." Merriam-Webster

I would like to relate my version of the Three Little Pigs.

The oldest pig had a messy spiritual life. He liked to roll around in the mud. He liked gossiping and getting into other peoples business. He was a busy body and constantly giving wrong advice. He chose this lifestyle for his spiritual career. His mother found fault with his religious behavior and said, "One day you will be sorry that you did not obey your mom and stay out of other peoples business." But no words of advice or warning could cure the first Little Pig of his bad habits.

The second little pig was a smart pig, but she was greedy. She was always seeking self-satisfaction. She wanted recognition, and a title. She was always striving for the biggest and best positions so people could look up to her. Her mother admonished her for her selfishness and told her, "Someday you will suffer for being so greedy and self-serving."

The third little pig was pleasant, GOD fearing and eager to be of service. He was much cleverer than his brother and sister. The third little pig could always find time to do more work. He understood that studying to be silent and mind minding his own business would allow him to hear from GOD. He was aware that natural and spiritual success didn't happen over night. He had to work for it, suffer for it, and sacrifice for it. Neighbors and family members said to each other, "Someday that little pig will be a prize winning pig, he's going to achieve something great." They recognized the potential that GOD had given the third little pig.

There came a time when the mother pig sent her three little pigs out to seek their future careers and spiritual gifts.

The oldest pig met a saint with straw faith. The pig asked, "May I have some of your straw faith to build my spiritual house? Can I rely on your prayers to get me through hard times? The saint with straw faith said, "of course."

The little oldest pig needed a strong prayer life to move forward in GOD but was willing to build a temporary relationship with GOD by sharing straw faith, praise, and worship with a weak gossiping member like himself. The oldest pig built his house with straw faith. When the enemy began to taunt and tempt him, he didn't realize how powerful the enemy was. He had a shallow prayer life that was limited by his need to involve himself in other peoples affairs. The enemy blew the oldest pig's spiritual house down and would have destroyed him immediately. But somebody was praying for him. The enemy took him to his house to feast on later.

The second pig met a saint with stick faith. That saint was also seeking self-recognition. The second pig inquired, "Do have extra stick faith so I can build my spiritual house? Can I rely on you to fast and pray with me that GOD will give me the position that I seek?" The saint with stick faith said, "I certainly will," knowing that he would not be willing to share his glory with anyone else. The second little pig was a little stronger in the LORD than the oldest pig because she fasted and prayed. But the second little pig only attended service when she was in charge, so she was no threat to the saint with straw faith. The second little pig built her house of straw. When the enemy showed up, he had a little difficulty because sticks are sturdier than straw. Part time fasting and praying can hold you for a while, but we owe GOD selfless service. The enemy blew the second little pig's house down and carried her off to his feast.

The third little pig pleaded the BLOOD of JESUS. He rebuked the enemy and demanded him to leave his life. He anointed himself and cried aloud unto GOD to deliver him. He began to sing praises unto GOD and quote the WORD OF GOD. The enemy can't stand to hear us praise GOD, so he has to flee.

When the third little pig knew he was safe, he didn't
forget about his brother and sister. He went out to look for them. He found them and restored them.

"Brethren, if a man is overtaken in a fault, ye which are spiritual, restore such an one in the spirit of meekness; considering thyself, lest thou also be tempted." (Galatians 6:1 KJV)

Considering the spiritual life of the three little pigs, which little pig are you?

Now, the third little pig was looking out for his future. He didn't want a temporary fix. He wanted a solid foundation.

He found an active, seasoned saint with brick faith. One who had been through something and survived. A saint who knew the power of prayer and worshiped GOD with all his heart. A humble saint who was willing to work anywhere in the house of GOD, cleaning the bathroom, the church grounds and wherever he was needed. He found a saint who attended prayer service, Sunday School, Bible School, and worship service regularly. He found a saint that sincerely fasted and prayed for others in need and witnessed to lost souls. The third little pig asked for some brick faith.

He built his house on a solid foundation in CHRIST JESUS. When the enemy showed up, he couldn't blow down that house. GOD empowered the third little pig with the strength and knowledge to recognize that he was just being tested.

GOD wanted the third little pig to know that he was able to withstand the temptation of the enemy.

When the enemy could not blow the third little pig's house down, he taunted him about his unsaved family. He threatened his marriage and career. The third little pig was strong in the LORD and the POWER of HIS might. He did not succumb to wiles of the enemy.

"Finally, my brethren, be strong in the Lord, and in the power of his might. Put on the whole armor of God, that ye may be able to stand against the wiles of the devil. For we wrestle not against flesh and blood, but against principalities, against powers, against the rulers of the darkness of this

world, against spiritual wickedness in high places." (Ephesians 6:10-12KJV)

The third little pig pleaded the BLOOD of JESUS. He rebuked the enemy and demanded him to leave his life. He anointed himself and cried aloud unto GOD to deliver him. He began to sing praises unto GOD and quote the WORD OF GOD. The enemy can't stand to hear us praise GOD, so he has to flee.

When the third little pig knew he was safe, he didn't

forget about his brother and sister. He went out to look for them. He found them and restored them.

"Brethren, if a man is overtaken in a fault, ye which are spiritual, restore such an one in the spirit of meekness; considering thyself, lest thou also be tempted." (Galatians 6:1 KJV)

Considering the spiritual life of the three little pigs, which little pig are you?

DROP THE BAGGAGE AND PUSH

"Then JESUS went thence, and departed into the coasts of Tyre and Sidon.

And, behold, a woman of Canaan came out of the same coasts, and cried unto HIM, saying, Have mercy on me, O LORD, thou Son of David; my daughter is grievously vexed with a devil. But HE answered her not a word. And his disciples came and besought HIM, saying, Send her away; for she crieth after us. But he answered and said, I am not sent but unto the lost sheep of the house of Israel.

Then came she and worshipped HIM, saying, LORD, help me.

But HE answered and said, It is not meet to take the children's bread and to cast it to dogs.

And she said, Truth, LORD yet the dogs eat of the crumbs which fall from their masters' table.

Then JESUS answered and said unto her, O woman, great is thy faith: be it unto thee even as thou wilt. And her daughter was made whole from that very hour." (Matthew 15:21-28 KJV)

In this story, we find a woman who put pride aside and got the victory. Desperation had wiped away any sinful pride in this mother. She broke through cultural barriers seeking help from JESUS. She was ready to take whatever left overs in attention JESUS could give her.

In the eyes of the Jews, she belonged to the most hated race of all, the Gentile race. She showed meekness and perseverance rarely equaled by others.

The woman appears to have come from some distance. She was by culture and language a Greek and by religion a pagan.

She was simply a mother who loved her child.

Most parents desire that their children survive them. A mother's love was the motivator. The woman was on a mission to save the life of her child. The woman's daughter was said to be demon possessed.

The greatest blessing we can ask for our children is that GOD would break the power of satan so that their soul may be temples of the HOLY SPIRIT.

JESUS left Galilee because it was no longer safe for HIM to remain. He retires from the Holy Land to the heathen countries of the north. HIS purpose may have been for rest, safety, to prepare HIS disciples to carry on HIS work or perhaps to encounter this woman as another example of HIS mission on Earth.

The woman had obviously heard of the miracles Jesus performed. Trouble, anguish, and desperation brought her to JESUS.

Pain, anxiety, and frustration are blessed things if they bring us to GOD.

The woman called JESUS, "LORD, son of David" acknowledging HIM as King and Savior.

The disciples were annoyed and wanted to be free of her presence. They desired that JESUS send her away.

She's annoying us. She's a problem. She's not fit to be among us.

The disciples were inconsiderate and unsympathetic.

They still had not fully realized that JESUS was sent to minister to the lost and unfit.

The woman faced a greater trial. As she cried and poured her heart out in prayer, JESUS was strangely silent. HIS silence had to be distressing to the woman and perplexing to the disciples.

JESUS had never before refused a person in need.

We do not read in the gospels that JESUS turned away from anyone seeking his help, as it appeared HE did to this woman.

She tells her urgent request, but there is no response.

The LORD is silent. It is a silence of love. Jesus acted as though HE did not hear to reveal the woman's perseverance and faith.

Her love for her daughter and her faith in JESUS overcame any external baggage she was facing.

Too often we give up on what we want GOD to do for us because we think HE does not hear us.

When GOD doesn't answer us right away many of us find other solutions to our problems that are not in GOD's will.

Someone with weaker faith would have been discouraged by the cold and selfish reception she received. The woman continued to push forward and not become distracted by the selfish and ungracious attitude the disciples were displaying. She continued to push for a solution in the midst of GOD's silence.

She refused to be deterred by the negative baggage surrounding her.

The bible says then she came and worshipped HIM. She was determined to get GOD's attention. She continued to push for GOD to recognize her need. JESUS gave the impression that HE was unconcerned and judgmental.

"But he answered and said, It is not meet to take the children's bread, and to cast it to dogs."

JESUS knew what HE intended to do.

First, the woman had to acknowledge her unworthiness.

If the woman did not have great faith, she would have given up.

JESUS saw a woman of courage, confidence, and persistence in getting what she wanted.

JESUS was aware of the good qualities the woman possessed, and they allowed GOD to test her faith.

We must drop the baggage of insecurity, pride, dismay, disappointment, and despair. Despite the negative baggage we face for the moment, we must push for the blessing we seek.

GOD tried her faith and perfected her patience.

She believed GOD could work a miracle for her daughter.

JESUS speaks of her in such a manner as to almost quench all hope. HE calls her a dog, and she confesses it.

Among the Jews dogs, were scavengers, of the streets with no masters and no homes.

The Greeks had affection for their dogs. They tamed and trained their dogs. The dogs to which JESUS compared this woman were not excluded from the house. As a gentile, the woman's perception of a dog was a pet living in the house.

The woman at once turned the argument in her favor.

To take the remark of JESUS in verse 27 as sincerely meant would be contrary to HIS SPIRIT. GOD tests our faith and determination to see had badly, we want what we are requesting.

The woman replies, Yes LORD I accept the position of a dog for the little "dogs under the table eat of the Master's crumbs."

She didn't deny that the Jews were the first object of JESUS' care. The fact that crumbs are left over from bread gave her the courage to push forward.

The woman acknowledges herself to be a little dog and becomes more earnest in prayer. She would not take no for an answer. She was not discouraged by all the negative baggage being placed upon her.

The truth hurts. JESUS called her a dog, and she said,

"Truth LORD." Faith doesn't dispute the LORD. Faith agrees with all the LORD says. "Truth LORD."

The woman was willing to accept a crumb. A small mercy compared with GOD's greater mercies.

The woman skillfully turned our LORD's reason for refusing her request into a reason for granting it.

Her firmness of purpose, her strength of will, her great humility, her earnestness and above all her outstanding faith, allowed her to obtain the blessing she sought.

We all have baggage we need to drop. Drop negativism, rejection, inconsiderateness, prejudice pride, fear, doubt, selfishness, impatience anger, unforgiveness, iniquity and a rebellious spirit. Push determination, humility, worship, praise, perseverance, courage, contentment, compassion, forgiveness, tolerance, patience joy, love for GOD, others and ourselves, and above all push faith.

STRUGGLING WITH PRIVATE ISSUES BEFORE A PUBLIC BLESSING

"And he rose up that night, and took his two wives, and his two womenservants, and his eleven sons, and passed over the ford Jabbok. And he took them, and sent them over the brook, and sent over that he had. And Jacob was left alone; and there wrestled a man with him until the breaking of the day. And when he saw that he prevailed not against him, he touched the hollow of his thigh; and the hollow of Jacob's thigh was out of joint, as he wrestled with him. And he said, Let me go, for the day breaketh. And he said, I will not let thee go, except thou bless me."(Genesis 32:22-31 KJV)

Jacob was returning to the Land of Canaan a man of mature age. In his early life, he had twice taken what belonged to his brother, Esau by deception. He deprived his brother of his birthright and his blessing.

Jacob was about to meet Esau whom he had angered.
He was so afraid that it drove him to pray.
Isn't it amazing how we can find time to pray when we get in trouble?
Jacob in the past had been a man who used self-reliance and personal effort to accomplish what he wanted. He had to learn that his advancement as the heir of the covenant could not be brought about by what he could master on his own but by earnest reliance upon GOD.

Twenty years earlier when Jacob fled from Esau, he had a vision at Bethel. He dreamed of a ladder that reached to heaven. There GOD promised to give him, and his seed the land where he lay and his descendants would be as the dust and be blessed. GOD promised not to leave him and bring him back to the land.

After the vision at Bethel Jacob was a religious man.

Religious saints make a friend of GOD for the good that GOD gives.

Upon Jacob's second encounter with GOD at Jabbok, he desired to know more of GOD not to get more from GOD.

He became a spiritually minded man.

The need we all should seek is to become spiritually minded and learn more about GOD.

"And Jacob was left alone, and there wrestled a man with him until the breaking of the day." (Genesis 32:24 KJV)

Jacob wrestled with GOD. He received a wound and a blessing. It is by wrestling, struggling, that we win the divine blessing. We often struggle with doubt, temptation, feelings of inadequacy and fear. To gain the victory over our struggles we have to fight to hold on to our faith in GOD.

The crime Which Jacob committed against his brother, banished him. He found twenty years of safety, but he had to face his old wrong. Jacob faced a crisis. There was mental and bodily wrestling. It was a struggle lasting all night. Jacob wanted to get right with his brother.

In his struggling, he was taught that he must first get right with GOD.

Jacob was a grabber. He grabbed his brother Esau's heel at birth. He grabbed his brothers birthright and blessing. At Jabbok, Jacob grabbed on to GOD and would not let go. All the things we acquire in life become liabilities if we have not gained the greatest thing and that is a relationship with GOD.

In Jacob's encounter, he learned how to cling to GOD. GOD changed Jacob's name from Jacob, the supplanter, "And he said, Is not he rightly named Jacob? for he hath supplanted me these two times:..." (Genesis 27:36 KJV) the conniver, the manipulator to Israel, one who clings to GOD. He becomes one for whom GOD HIMSELF would strive.

Jacob finally understood that the ultimate power was in GOD's hands not in his strength or cunning.

Many fall short of GOD's blessing because they don't like the struggle.

Jacob halted on his thigh and probably limped through the rest of his life.

He carried from that place of struggle and triumph a reminder of his dependence upon GOD.

Until we yield to GOD we can receive little from HIM.

Clinging to GOD does not mean that we persuade HIM to give us what we want. It means we learn what GOD really intends for us to have.

Esau came with four hundred men and ran to meet Jacob and embraced him. GOD's blessing turned Jacob's enemy to a friend.

We must resolve within ourselves never to give up until we get the blessing GOD has in store for us.

Making it through the struggle is the way to the blessing. There is a breaking of self-will and pride before the blessing. Jacob was broken physically and emotionally to reveal the character GOD wanted to use.

Jacob was alone when he struggled with GOD.

Nobody sees that private struggle. They don't see the anguish, the disappointment, the discouragement, the fasting and praying we go through when GOD is preparing us for greater things.

The struggle is done in private, but everyone sees and desires the public blessing.

PASS THE GRAPES

Numbers 13 and 14 KJV

Moses was told by GOD to send a leader from each tribe to spy out the land of Canaan.

Everybody can't be a leader. I noticed that the leaders were listed in a certain order or position. The tribe of Reuben and Simeon the two oldest brothers were listed first. Caleb from the tribe of Judah the fourth brother was next followed by Issachar the nineth brother. Next came Joshua from the tribe of Ephraim (Joseph's son), the eleventh brother. Every tribe had a chosen leader, but not all were listed in line according to the order of their birth. That was significant to me. It doesn't matter how long we have been in the church when GOD chooses to place us in position for a particular work.

Moses warned the leaders to be strong, and not to get discouraged. He let them know that completing the task would not be easy or look like the outcome would be positive, but don't give up.

GOD has a gift for each of us. It is up to us to see the potential and have the courage to hold on despite the fact that we encounter obstacles.

Moses told the leaders to bring back some fruit of the land. The Bible says it was the time of first ripe grapes.

The leaders were obedient. They cut down a branch with one cluster of grape that had to be carried between two leaders.

One blessing that was so heavy that it was it was too much for one leader to take alone.

The grapes were a sign that GOD had given the people the land. The grapes should have given the leaders the faith and determination to accomplish GOD's purpose and plan.

The leaders returned forty days later. It was not an overnight assignment. It took some time to prepare to receive the promised blessing.

The Leaders were obedient and went where they were told. They acknowledged that the land flowed with milk and honey and that they saw the potential and the blessing. They returned with the fruit. The real test began when those of faith and determination to obey GOD were separated from the cowards and unbelievers. The self-sacrificers from the selfish. Those working for the Glory of GOD from those working for self-preservation.

Ten leaders came back with excuses.

1. The people are strong that dwell in the city. All leaders have to deal with bad attitude, rebellious, confusion causing people.

2. The cities are walled and very great. The task is monumental. Some things will temporarily block our progress. GOD is aware of all that we will encounter and never leaves us without HIS guidance and support.

3. There were giants in the land. We will encounter people who appear more powerful, knowledgeable with better skills and creativity than we possess. If GOD chose us, "Greater is HE that is within us, than he that is in the world."

4. They were surrounded by powerful outside forces. We can't allow people who are not part of GOD's program to intimidate us. The people began to panic. When leaders show weakness and doubt, it causes the people to get discouraged and become frantic.

The bible says Caleb quieted the people. I believe he looked at Reuben and Simeon, and said, "Pass The Grapes. You can't see the vision. You are carrying the proof of GOD's blessing, and you can't handle it so Pass The Grapes.

Behind Caleb was Issachar but he must have gotten out of line. We can be the next individual GOD chooses to use but lose our position because of the opinions and influence of others. Behind Issacar was Joshua and he picked up the other end of the grapes, the vision, with Caleb. I believe Joshua said, "Caleb Pass The Grapes, I'll help you carry the vision and the blessing that comes with seeing GOD's program go forward.

GOD knows where we stand in our sincerity and determination to work in HIS kingdom. GOD's promotion, HIS favor, doesn't come by how old we are or how long we have been in the church. GOD blesses us for how obedient, committed and faithful we are. Caleb said, "Let's go up at once and take possession for we are well able to overcome it."

Moses had warned the leaders before they started out not to get discouraged. He let them know that they would encounter things that would make them afraid and want to give up.

He admonished them to be vigorous and courageous and don't Drop the grapes, the blessing. Don't let go of the blessing.

Leaders must hold onto the fruit of patience, tolerance, unity and one accord. Where there is unity, there is strength; divided we fail. Together we can block the influence of the enemy.

Ten leaders were discouraged and quickly dropped the grapes, the blessing.

Leaders should be a part of the solution, not the problem.

Ten leaders looked at the situation, the problems they would face and forgot the problem solver chose them.

They let their natural vision overwhelm their spiritual potential. Negative people, complainers, fault finding, critical people pass the blame instead of the grapes, the blessing.

I can hear Caleb saying, "I realize that anything worth having is worth the struggle. I'm not going to throw away what GOD has told me was mine. Please, Pass The Grapes, I know we can handle it, we can make it work and be successful."

Ten leaders got together and decided to drop the grapes, the blessing. They had the majority in numbers but were in the minority in spiritual insight.

They saw themselves as grasshoppers, without the talent, skills, and the power to accomplish GOD's purpose.

They developed a rebellious spirit. They became cowards ready to run from the challenge and responsibility instead of standing still and relying on the power and promise of GOD.

The cynical leaders influenced the congregation.

The congregation lifted up their voices, cried and began to look back to Egypt.

Moses and Aaron fell on their faces. Joshua and Caleb tore their clothes. It is a grievous thing to watch the enemy divide and destroy the people of GOD. Carrying the responsibility of spiritual grapes can become cumbersome.

Weak saints drop what GOD has promised them because they lack the stamina and faith to persevere.

Ten leaders caused themselves and a whole generation not to see the promised land. A whole generation wandered around in the wilderness for forty years. They were not able to progress or receive their blessing.

Joshua and Caleb were the only two leaders who were able to go forward and get the promised reward.

When saints of GOD are disobedient, rebellious, and cause division it brings the wrath of GOD.

We need to separate from negative fault finding individuals who don't want to be part of GOD's plan and purpose.

Tell those who refuse to handle the commitment GOD has given them to Pass The Grapes.

SERMONETTE 92

OUT OF THE WRECK I RISE

"Who Shall Separate us from the love of CHRIST? Shall tribulation, or distress or persecution or famine or nakedness or peril or sword?"(Romans 8:35 KJV)

"We are troubled on every side yet not distressed; We are perplexed but not in Despair. Persecuted but not forsaken. Cast Down but not destroyed." (II Corinthians 4:8 KJV)

The sin of self-pity can be devastating. Self-pity blocks GOD out and puts self-interest above everything else.

Peter said, "Beloved, think it not strange concerning the fiery trial which is to try you, as though some strange thing happened unto you." 1 Peter 4:12 (KJV).

Trials have a purpose in our spiritual development.

Discouragement, fear, depression, and doubt are obstacles that can interfere when we seek to live a productive life for GOD. We have to be determined to rise out of the overwhelming personal wrecks we encounter.

GOD doesn't keep us immune from trouble. HE said HE would be with us in trouble. It doesn't matter what the pain or the problem is, it cannot separate us from the love of GOD unless we allow it to.

The word of GOD tells us that we are more than conquerors in all difficult situations we face.

We are often responsible for creating our wrecks.

We experience a wreck when we allow the cares of this world to take precedence over the service we should be doing for GOD. We become careless about GOD's business.

Some of us are careless about what we eat and how much we eat. As a result, we become over weight and experience health issues. We find ourselves begging GOD to help us to lose the weight and heal our bodies.

We have control over what we choose to eat.

We can discipline our selves to eat healthier and exercise regularly.

Some people put GOD last in HIS tithes and offering.

They are careless about paying bills. Some individuals use the rent money, phone money, car insurance money to get a new out fit, expensive hair weaves and manicures. There are some who regularly over extend their credit cards and find themselves crying out to GOD when the electricity is turned off, the car is repossessed, and they receive an eviction notice. Then there are the saints that borrow from the church get angry and leave the church when they are required to pay back. I shake my head at the ones who neglect cleaning their homes; substitute fast foods for proper meals for their families, their husband or wive's needs are ignored and fail to supervise their children's activities. The marriage falls apart; the children become unruly, and they question GOD, "Why me?" We can rise from the wrecks we make for ourselves.

Before Lazarus, whom JESUS raised from the dead, could come forth GOD had to release the grave clothes that bound him.

Before GOD can help us rise, from our self-made wrecks, we have to admit to ourselves that we are personally responsible for what we have done. GOD has given us free will. We often make negative choices. We choose to neglect responsibility both natural and spiritual. We cannot blame the church, or other people for the wrecks we create.

Some of us rely on the prayers and strength of others.

I called Bishop Richardson and my mother when I faced a crisis and asked them to pray. Then I would relax depending upon their prayer.

When GOD took them away, I began to sink into despair. I became a wreck because my support team was gone. GOD moved them to allow me to have my own relationship with HIM in prayer. I had to learn how to rise personally from life's wrecks. GOD showed me my capabilities, and my strength. HE took away my self-doubt and low esteem, and out of the wreck of dependency on others, I began to rise.

GOD wants us to seek HIM and keep an attitude of complete trust in HIM. We don't need affirmation from others. We become a wreck when people don't fulfill that need.

GOD wants to lift some of us out of bad relationships with negative people before we become a total wreck.

When we rise above one wreck, another might follow.

I thought I had mastered rising above wrecks. I had learned to trust GOD in so many areas, my finances, my health, my secular career and my ministry but I faced a situation regarding someone I dearly loved that threw me completely. I begged, pleaded, bargained with GOD, and turned in all my stored up prayer and fasting. I agonized over it. I cried, I became depressed and desperate for GOD to answer.

I became a natural and spiritual wreck. I was drowning both naturally and spiritually because I didn't hear GOD. I didn't hear GOD because I wanted HIM to answer my way. GOD didn't answer me. GOD in HIS silence said, "No, I am not going to let it happen for you."

I Finally got it right. I prayed, "LORD raise me up from this wreck I am placing myself in, give me peace. Quiet my mind, my spirit, my soul." Then I heard GOD. HE said, "Listen to yourself. You don't want my will. You want your way. You spent all your energy and time asking for a natural thing in this individuals' life, but you haven't exercised that same urgency for their spiritual life." GOD told me to rise from that feeling of despair, relinquish my desire and submit to HIS will and praise HIM for not getting my way.

I obeyed, and the peace of GOD that surpasses all understanding began to flood my soul. The love I had for GOD began to overflow in my spirit.

I thanked GOD for not answering and believed that what HE had in store for my loved one was better than my desire. I told GOD that I believed HIS WORD when HE said, "...no good thing will HE withhold from them that walk uprightly." (Psalms 84:11 KJV)

If I had gotten my way, it might have turned out tragically later on. I made up in my mind that I would no longer let this particular circumstance hold me down. I refused to let it take away my joy and destroy my relationship with GOD.

So out of the Wreck, I Did Rise.

WILLFUL DECEPTION BRINGS PUBLIC SHAME

"But he went in, and stood before his master. And Elisha said unto him, Whence comest thou, Gehazi? And he said,

Thy servant went no whither.

And he said unto him, Went not mine heart with thee, when the man turned again from his chariot to meet thee?

Is it a time to receive money, and to receive garments, and olive yards, and vineyards, and sheep, and oxen, and menservants, and maidservants?

The leprosy therefore of Naaman shall cleave unto thee, and unto thy seed for ever. And he went out from his presence a leper as white as snow." (11 Kings 5: 25-27 KJV)

Naaman was the commander in chief of the Syrian army. He was a mighty man in a position of power, with military honors. He was prosperous, a family man with servants but he was a leper. The disadvantage of leprosy did not prevent him from his accomplishments.

He had an Israelite servant girl, captured in a raid, who told Naaman's wife about the prophet Elisha who was a healer.

The Prophet Elisha instructed Naaman to bathe seven times in the muddy Jourdan river. The healing was not in the water but the power of GOD, Naaman's faith, and obedience.

It was a humbling experience. Naaman was looking for something great, but the solution was simple obedience to what he didn't want to do.

Naman's servants persuade him to obey the prophet, and Naaman is healed.

As a token of thanks, Naaman brings a gift to the Prophet Elisha of expensive clothing and about $80,000.00.

Elisha refused the gifts, there was no charge for the healing. The glory belonged to GOD. Naaman had to learn the true and living GOD. Elisha was concerned about Naaman's soul.

To show his gratitude for the healing he received after witnessing the power of GOD, Naaman said "...for thy servant will henceforth offer neither burnt offering nor sacrifice unto other gods, but unto the LORD. In this thing the LORD pardon thy servant. that when my master goeth into the house of Rimmon to worship there, and he leaneth on my hand, and I bow myself in the house of Rimmon: when I bow down myself in the house of Rimmon, the LORD pardon thy servant in this thing. And he said unto him, Go in peace. So he departed from him a little way. (II Kings 5:17-19 KJV) He who wins a soul is wise.

Gehazi, a man of GOD, Elisha's armor bearer, ate, slept, and traveled with Elisha. He watched the miracles, Elisha performed. He was aware of Elisha's character and connection with GOD, but Gehazi did not have the spirit of Elisha. Just being connected to someone serving GOD does not make us a servant of GOD. We have to develop, a relationship personally with GOD.

Elisha refused Naaman's gift, but the desire for wealth stirs up Gehazi's greed. It blinded his eyes, and stifled his conscience. Gehazi runs after Naaman and says his master sent him. "Behold, even now there be come to me from mount Ephraim two young men of the sons of the prophets: give them, I pray thee, a talent of silver, and two changes of garments." (II Kings 5:22 KJV)

Gehazi runs after Naaman; he couldn't pursue Naaman right away, that would have been questionable. He couldn't stay away too long, Elisha might call for him. The devil will have you running to sin and destruction. Gehazi proceeds to lie on his master.

Sin starts as a thought, usually a selfish one. It grows to covetousness, deception, and lying. Much is expected of those us who profess GODLINESS. GOD holds us accountable when we cast a stumbling block in the way of new believers.

Gehazi is successful and obtains more than he required.

Naaman had to send two servants to help Gehazi because the wealth was more than he could carry. When we play the enemy's game, he rewards us well, but there's a hefty price to pay.

Gehazi stops the servants a little distance before the gates of the city. He didn't want Elisha to find out what he had done. He hid what he has gotten and went casually into Elisha's room.

Elisha asks Gehazi where he had been? That should have been a clue for Gehazi. Deceit and dishonesty never bring blessings from GOD. Gehazi's willful deception began with a desire for wealth. He coveted what was not his. He plotted how he could obtain it. He lied on his master. Then he had to sneak and hide what he had gotten. Finally, he had to lie to the man of GOD to protect himself. Gehazi calmly stands before Elisha and says, he didn't go anywhere. Gehazi's actions were not hidden from Elisha; the LORD had shown them to him.

"And he said unto him, Went not mine heart with thee, when the man turned again from his chariot to meet thee? Is it a time to receive money, and to receive garments, and olive yards, and vineyards, and sheep, and oxen, and menservants, and maidservants?

The leprosy therefore of Naaman shall cleave unto thee, and unto thy seed for ever. And he went out from his presence a leper as white as snow" (II kings 5:26-27 KJV)

Gehazi's punishment, his shame, was that the leprosy of Naaman should cleave to him. Not only was the disease to be upon Gehazi but his seed forever. His children would be cursed.

Gehazi's leprosy was extreme. He could not hide it. He went out white as snow. Everyone could see his shame.

How much delight and pleasure could Gehazi have with his ill gotten wealth when he had to suffer a public, loathsome disease.

We can't willfully deceive and make unholy bargains for fame and money without losing our peace, purity, and integrity with GOD. "For what shall it profit a man, if he shall gain the whole world, and lose his own soul?" (Mark 8:36 KJV)

When Christians practice willful, planned deception, it will surely bring public shame.

I'M DOING A GREAT WORK; I CANT COME DOWN

"And I sent messengers unto them, saying, I am doing a great work, so that I cannot come down: why should the work cease, whilst I leave it, and come down to you?"
Nehemiah 6:3 (KJV)

Nehemiah was a Jew; a child of the Babylonian captivity. He did not return to Jerusalem after liberty was proclaimed. He had achieved an influential position in the palace of the Persian King.

Nehemiah was the King's cup bearer. GOD had designed that place for him. GOD never makes a mistake when HE places HIS anointed in any position. Nehemiah was a man of prayer. He was a visionary who inspired others and worked humbly beside them.

Nehemiah lived in contentment but could not forget his brethren in distress.

The Jews had recently returned out of Babylonian captivity to their land. Nehemiah was informed about the ruins of the city.

The walls of Jerusalem were broken down leaving the people in danger.

Nehemiah fasted and prayed for mercy for his people Israel. He asked GOD to prosper him in his undertakings and give him favor with the king. We need to ask GOD to help us find favor in the sight of our employers, landlords and anyone else who can make a difference in our lives.

Nehemiah prevailed in prayer. He prevailed with the king who sent him to Jerusalem with a commission to build a wall and granted him what he needed to accomplish it.

Nehemiah appeared sad before the king. The king questioned Nehemiah's disposition because he had never looked sad before. Nehemiah immediately prayed to GOD to give him the wisdom to ask properly and find favor. Before we get involved in any project, we need to seek GOD's wisdom and support.

The king granted Nehemiah's petition and appointed the captain of the guard and horsemen to go with Nehemiah.

Nehemiah was in Jerusalem three days unknown to anyone.

He got up at night and viewed the ruins of the walls. He had to see for himself the devastation and what could be salvaged.

Nehemiah didn't tell the people at first why he was there. We can't be too quick to share information with people before GOD has given us the format for what needs to be done.

Nehemiah did not try to start the work without the people. He did not demand that the people help even though he had the king's permission. He was able to excite the people and make them eager to assist.

The people saw a need, but no one had initiated the work. We all need competent leadership to inspire and encourage us. When we decide to accomplish GOD's vision, we have to be steadfast, unmovable always abounding in the work.

The children of Israel started the work immediately.

The people all took a share of the work, some more, and some less according to their ability.

The people did not make excuses that they could not leave their jobs or had personal family matters. They did not use age; I'm too old or too young. The people understood that whatever they had to sacrifice for the work of GOD would indeed be rewarded.

GOD's work cannot be achieved without opposition.

The enemy reproached and ridiculed the work. The people responded with prayer and a mind to work harder. The people progressed rapidly for the people had a mind to work.

The enemy tried to hinder the people by force.

Nehemiah positioned the people according to families.

He supplied them with swords and encouraged them to fight.

With one hand the people held weapons and with the other hand they worked. We can't stop GOD's work to concentrate on the enemy. The enemy tries to discourage us with words and scare tactics but we can't stop working.

When we begin to build up GOD's work, the enemy will try to tear it down. The enemy will send individuals to seek to stop and block our progress. Tobiah and Sanballat, two Samaritans, attempted to hinder the work.

Tobiah and Sanballat despised the work and ridiculed it. They solicited assistance from neighboring people, but their efforts were in vain.

The people became discouraged. They got tired. Nehemiah had to face the threats of the enemy and the fears of his people. Nehemiah looked to GOD. He put himself and his cause under divine protection. He shared all his cares, all his fears with GOD. The enemy plotted four times to gain Nehemiah's confidence and destroy him, but he refused to stop GOD's work.

"And I sent messengers unto them, saying, I am doing a great work so that I cannot come down: why should the work cease, while I leave it, and come down to you?" "Nehemiah 6:3 (KJV)

In our Christian work when we face conflict, have struggles, get discouraged we need to pray as Nehemiah did,

"... Now, therefore, O GOD, strengthen my hands (Nehemiah 6:9 KJV)

The enemy hired a false prophet to persuade Nehemiah to hide in the temple for his safety. Had Nehemiah listened to the false prophet the people would have left their work and run for safety also.

The enemy doesn't give up. He uses sickness, temptation, fear, false prophets, gossip any thing he can to interrupt GOD's program.

Nehemiah did not yield to temptation and was a victorious winner.

When we are doing a great work for GOD, we can not stop to defend ourselves, to please people, or succumb to the tricks of the enemy. We cannot come down from our divine assignment until GOD's work is completed.

LOOKING FOR A MIRACLE?

"And he stretched himself upon the child three times, and cried unto the LORD, and said, O LORD my GOD, I pray thee, let this child's soul come into him again. And the LORD heard the voice of Elijah, and the soul of the child came into him again, and he revived." (I Kings 17:21-22 KJV)

A miracle is "an effect or extraordinary event in the physical world that surpasses all known human or natural powers and is ascribed to a supernatural cause."
www.dictionary.com/browse/miracle

Elijah GOD's ambassador boldly confronts wicked King Ahab and told Ahab unless he repented and reformed, there would be no rain and a grievous famine would come upon Israel.

GOD gave Elijah explicit instructions to get away, turn east, and hide by the brook Cherith which flows from Jordan, drink from the brook and ravens would feed him.

Whatever GOD told Elijah to do, he did. He waited patiently for further instructions. We must be taught the value of the hidden life. When GOD sends us into temporary retirements or inactivity, GOD wants us alone. HE wants us away from all distractions so we can depend solely on HIM.

Shielded from Ahab's anger, GOD provided for Elijah's needs.

Elijah was cut off from all human aid.

The miracle while Elijah was in seclusion was the unlikely caters. Ravens brought Elijah bread and meat twice a day. Ravens are birds of prey; they were more likely to have taken Elijah's food.

When we are obedient to GOD, our relief will come from the most unexpected sources. GOD who furnished a table in the wilderness and made ravens cooks and servers for the prophet Elijah, can supply all our needs according to HIS riches in glory.

The brook dried up. GOD could have prolonged the amount of water. Elijah had to risk detection to seek nourishment elsewhere. In the famine, GOD had other miraculous plans. GOD causes one thing to fail to show us how tremendous HIS resources are.

The brook drying up led Elijah to new opportunities.

The prophet was guided from the problem of saving his own life to the privilege of saving a widow's faith and her son's life.

Jezebel was Elijah's greatest enemy, so GOD found a place of hiding for him in her country. Elijah was sent to a widow of the land of Baal. He was sent to the land of Jezebel's father, not to a widow of Israel to whom were the promises of GOD.

Elijah encounters the widow gathering stick. That was not an encouraging sign. She had no food for herself. She who was to sustain Elijah's life is herself ready to die.

The widow was given an opportunity. She entertained a prophet and received a prophet's reward.

Elijah asks for water and a morsel of bread. To deny herself and give a stranger a little cake from the handful of meal that was left before the cravings of hunger in herself and her son was a miracle itself.

The widow gave and got; she gave unselfishly.

There was a miracle of abundance.

How calmly she spoken of her child's death and her own when she expected to die for lack of food, when Elijah first approached her. Now that her son dies and not so miserably as by famine, she is extremely disturbed.

It is hard to stay calm and faithful when troubles come suddenly, unexpectantly, and in the midst of our peace and prosperity.

Sometime later the widow's son dies. Elijah had been a year in her home. He had developed a relationship with the child. Elijah entreats GOD to restore the child's life. GOD restored the child's life.

"And the woman said to Elijah, Now by this, I know that thou art a man of GOD, and that the word of the Lord in thy mouth is truth" I Kings 17:24 KJV)

The widow received a material miracle as well as a spiritual one.

In this chapter, there were several miracles.

The heavens responded to Elijah and there was no rain or dew for three years resulting in a famine. The ravens fed Elijah twice a day. A widow's meal and oil remained undiminished, and her son was brought back to life.

Are you looking for a miracle?

"Trust in the LORD with all thine heart; and lean not unto thine own understanding. In all thy ways acknowledge HIM, and HE shall direct paths." (Proverbs 3:5-6 (KJV)

"...for verily I say unto you, If ye have faith as a grain of mustard seed, ye shall say unto this mountain, Remove hence to yonder place; and it shall remove; and nothing shall be impossible unto you." (Matthew 17:20 KJV)

GOD works miraculously for those who are in constant communion with HIM and serve HIM diligently according to HIS will.

"And we know that all things work together for good to them that love GOD, to them who are the called according to HIS purpose." (Romans 8:28 KJV)

SERMONETTE 96

IN ALL THINGS GIVE THANKS

The Bible says, "Thank [GOD] in everything [no matter what the circumstances may be, be thankful and give thanks], for this is the will of GOD for you [who are] in CHRIST JESUS [the REVEALER and MEDIATOR of that will]." (1 Thessalonians 5:18 AMP)

Since my illness, which I now know, was for a particular purpose, I am striving to give GOD thanks continually. I did not have the physical strength to function in my former capacity in ministry, so GOD gave me the opportunity to minister in new areas. I refused to lie idle in bed and have an ongoing pity party.

"Idle hands are the devil's workshop; idle lips are his mouthpiece." Proverbs 16:27-29 Living Bible (TLB)

I was inspired by GOD to write a Sunday morning message. At Bishop Harris' suggestion, I have published them as SERMONETTES FOR A SUNDAY MORNING.

I continue to have input in Sure Foundation Child Care Inc. and oversee church functions.

I thank GOD for technology. I also thank GOD for sending competent and understanding individuals to support me in both of those areas.

I have never backed out on anything GOD has purposed for me to do so I persevere and continue moving forward.

I implemented a new bookkeeping and accounting system for Grace

Cathedral International that I could maintain at home. I began the daunting task of recording the income and expenses of Grace Cathedral International. I had no idea the magnitude of responsibility that Bishop Harris was facing in those areas. The new format was a check and balance on what would be submitted to an accountant. Bishop and I are firm believers in seeing that GOD's, as well as our personal finances, are handled impeccability. It was a challenge and consumed an exorbitant amount of time. I have always welcomed a challenge, and with the time my illness afforded me I delved wholeheartedly into the project.

One thing GOD requires is that we work diligently and wholeheartedly at any task we undertake to HIS glory.

As Pastor, I want to instill that type of work ethic into the people of GOD.

When we accept a commitment for GOD, the journey will not be easy. We often want rewards and continued praise for everything we do. No one likes criticism, but the only way to perfect our craft is to face the areas that need improvement.

Spiritual boot camp is tough. It will either make us stronger in GOD's service or cause us to give up. If we give up, GOD didn't appoint us. If it makes us stronger and more determined GOD will provide us with favor in HIM and reward us.

We cannot expect people to appreciate and praise us all the time. In spiritual boot camp, we will sometimes be pushed beyond what we think we can endure. The Bible says, "Thou, therefore, endure hardness, as a good soldier of JESUS CHRIST."

(2 Timothy 2:3 KJV)

I now understand why I had to be subjected to illness. I had to know what it felt like to have been vigorous and independent then suddenly find myself weak and dependent on others. I can minister to others who are experiencing devastating illness with empathy, not just sympathy because I have experienced it.

In her book "On Death and Dying", "Elisabeth Kübler-Ross described a type of emotional journey among people who are facing death. Since she wrote that book, similar terms have been used to describe people's reactions to other major losses. (Shock or Disbelief, Denial, Anger, Bargaining, Guilt, Depression, Acceptance, and Hope. Sometimes, people speak of five stages of grieving, putting together: Shock/Disbelief and Denial Bargaining and Guilt...the stages do not occur the same way for all individuals; they can last very little time or a longer period, and they can be interrelated."

(http://lifesherpa.com/stress/grief-stages.htm)

I have gone through the stages as mentioned above over the past four years. Have I mastered the acceptance stage? Not completely, I am a work in progress in that area.

I have been able to comfort the caregivers for those who are ill. When we respond in anger to those who have tried to care for us, it is not that we are unappreciative. We are frustrated, confused and despondent about the situation we are facing. We often take those emotions out on the ones closest to us. I encourage caregivers to be patient and understanding and allow your loved one to vent. We are grateful for every sacrifice and expression of love that we receive.

The days that my illness forces me to remain in bed, GOD has given me new visions for the MINISTRY and ideas to improve things that are already in place. I can counsel individuals privately, without rushing and in a relaxed atmosphere from home.

GOD has given me a new area to minister praise and worship. I need your prayers that I will have the boldness and master the skill needed to implement it.

I thank GOD for allowing me to continue ministering in my spiritual gift in spite of my physical limitations, my thorn in the flesh.

"Paul speaks of a "thorn in the flesh" in 2 Corinthians 12:7 KJV. No one likes affliction in any form.

"Paul sought the LORD three times to remove this source of pain from him" (2 Corinthians 12:8KJV).

I now realize the LORD had other plans for me.

GOD was concerned about strengthening my character and preventing pride.

GOD did not remove the thorn from Paul. Paul learned that GOD's "power is made perfect in weakness" (2 Corinthians 12:9 KJV).

"All has been heard; the end of the matter is: Fear GOD [revere and worship HIM, knowing that HE is] and keep HIS commandments, for this is the whole of man [the full, original purpose of HIS creation, the object of GOD's providence, the root of character, the foundation of all happiness the adjustment to all inharmonious circumstances and conditions under the sun] and the whole [duty] for every man. For GOD shall bring every work into judgment, with every secret thing, whether it is good or evil." (Matt. 12:36; Acts 17:30, 31; Rom. 2:16; I Cor. 4:5.]" Ecclesiastes 12:2, 13-14 AMPC)

"Consider it wholly joyful, my brethren, whenever you are enveloped in or encounter trials of any sort or fall into various temptations. Be assured and understand that the trial and proving of your faith bring out endurance and steadfastness and patience.

But let endurance and steadfastness and patience have full play and do a thorough work, so that you may be [people] perfectly and fully developed [with no defects], lacking in nothing." (James 1:2-4, AMPC)

I encourage each of you to grow in GOD. Walk in the purpose GOD has chosen for you. Work diligently and wholeheartedly in your endeavors to become effective and not just efficient in your service to GOD. Seek the favor of GOD more than the praises of men.

I will end with some words that I heard from Bishop Harris that have inspired me.
"When life hands you lemons, make lemonade."
"There Is Purpose In Pain" (Philippians 3:10, Psalms 121:1, 2)
Five Truths About Suffering
Suffering is multifaceted.
Suffering is bearable
Suffering equips you for ministry.

Suffering becomes a battleground
Suffering prepares us for glory.
Learn to suffer well.
Above all, In All things Give Thanks.

PRAYER # 4

Dear GOD:

I love YOU deep down in the depths of my soul.

Thank YOU for choosing me to work for YOU.

YOU created me for YOUR purpose. Please help me to learn how to accept YOUR will and not my own. Give me a greater desire to apply YOUR WORD in my life. YOU told me in Your Word to lean on, trust in, and be confident in YOU with all my heart and mind and do not rely on my insight or understanding. In all my ways to know, recognize, and acknowledge YOU and YOU will direct and make straight and plain my paths.

I need YOUR help to make YOUR WORD come alive in me. LORD give me what YOU desire for me to have and let it come from YOUR hand and not my hand. I know that YOU love me. I know that YOU will provide for me.

Help me to continuously realize that if I freely choose to love YOU, YOUR love can be perfected in me. Help me to place selfish desires aside and seek GODly wisdom. I need to get understanding and draw positive energy from YOUR WORD and my life experiences. I realize that I was created to do good works. LORD, mold me and shape my life according to YOUR design. Give me the strength to let YOU decide what YOU want me to do. Help me to remember that YOU died on the cross for my sins and that we all have a cross to bear. It is painful, and it is not desirable, but if I suffer because of my love and obedience to YOU, I will gain eternal life. I thank YOU for all the experiences I have encountered because they have drawn me closer to YOU. "Not that I speak in respect of want: for I have learned, in whatsoever state I am, therewith to be content." (Philippians 4:11 KJV)

Dear GOD as I pray for others help us all to find out how to "Trust in the YOU with all our heart, And lean not on our understanding; In all our ways acknowledge YOU and YOU shall direct our paths." (Proverbs 3:5-6 KJV)

Help us to stop trying to work life out our way. Please help us to be grateful for YOU giving us according to our needs.

LORD help us to stop focusing so much on giving ourselves a prosperous life and trying to find comfort in this present life.

We need to know beyond a shadow of a doubt that we have prepared ourselves to meet YOU one day and live peacefully and luxuriously in eternity.

Help us to choose to live for YOU.

When we have needs may it point us back to a SAVIOR who can supply all our needs.

Give us the desire to work hard to win souls to YOUR Kingdom by witnessing and drawing others to YOU.

This life we are living here on Earth is a temporary one; help us to strive for eternal life with YOU.

Dear GOD let YOUR Spirit lead us. Help us to seek first the kingdom of GOD, trusting that YOU will provide for all the other needful things. For our lives are no longer ours, but it belongs to YOU.

LORD help us to lay down our excessive desires in this life to pick up a greater relationship with YOU. We believe that YOU intend to provide us with everything we need.

LORD help us to humble ourselves under YOUR mighty hand knowing that YOU may exalt us in due time. Help us to cast all our cares upon YOU for YOU care for us.

LORD make our thoughts agreeable to THY will.

Let our desire today be to please YOU in our thoughts, in our actions and interactions with others.

Help us to become more intimately acquainted with YOUR will. LORD help us to have the mind of CHRIST JESUS who came not to be served but to serve.

Help us to understand that as we serve YOU in a manner that is pleasing to YOU, we obtain YOUR favor.

When we tear down each other, YOU are not pleased, and we put the favor of GOD in jeopardy. LORD, we don't want to miss one single blessing YOU have for us because we allowed people to interfere with our focus on pleasing YOU.

Thank YOU for the determination to serve YOU with all our hearts, minds, souls and bodies.

LORD cause our thoughts to become agreeable to THY will and so shall our plans be established and succeed. LORD, give us faith to let YOU make choices for us. Create in us a desire for a greater knowledge of who YOU are.

We do many things to satisfy our own goals that are contrary to YOUR will.

Help us all to keep in mind that the negative things we experience are temporary. They are light afflictions preparing us for greater things to come.

LORD cause our thoughts to become agreeable to THY will and so shall our plans be established and succeed.

LORD, give us faith to let YOU make choices for us. Create in us a desire for a greater knowledge of who YOU are. Amen.

PASTOR NOVELLA HARRIS, AAS, BA, BRE, TH. B, MSE

Pastor Novella Harris is married to Bishop R.W. Harris for 52 years.

They have four (4) children, four (4) grandchildren, and three (3) great-grandchildren.

On March 31, 1996, Novella Harris was consecrated Pastor.

She pastors under Bishop R.W. Harris Sr. Prelate, of Grace Cathedral International, Uniondale N.Y. Her desire for a school was accomplished in May 1995 when Sure Foundation Child Care Inc., (a newly constructed $600,000.00 structure, and playground) was completed.

Pastor Harris retired from a successful career in the teaching profession, in Malverne, N.Y.

She has taught Art Education, Environmental Studies, Nursery, Kindergarten through Twelfth Grades, and Inclusion. She served as a member of the Literacy Standards Committee.

Pastor Harris has her Masters of Science Degree in Education from Hofstra University.

She is pursuing a second Masters in English and Language Arts. She has her Bachelors of Religious Education and her Bachelors of Theology From United Christian College. She has training in Assertive Discipline and Teacher Effectiveness (College of St. Rose). She studied The Adlerian Approach To Parent/ Child Counseling (Hofstra University), Caring and Crisis Counseling (LI Council Of Churches) and Stress Management.

Pastor Harris has Certificates in Program Design And Implementation For Children with Autism, Introduction to Applied Verbal Behavior and Principles of Applied Behavior Analysis (Kidz Therapy Services, LLC), Differentiated Learning Styles and Supportive Supervision.

She received a certificate of membership from the Association for Supervision and Curriculum Development (Developing Leadership for Quality in Education).

Pastor Harris became a VIP member of the National Association of Professional Women (August 2011) and was selected by the VIP Division as the 2011/2012 "Professional Woman of the Year." Pastor Harris received the Sojourner Truth Award from the National Association of Negro Business & Professional Women's Club. (August 2011)

She is a lifetime member of the NAACP. She is a past PTA President, Girl Scout Leader, and former member of 100 Black Women. Pastor Harris received a NAACP award for "Changing The Lives of Children in 2008. She became a member of Who's Who Among America's Teachers 2004-2005. She received the NAACP "Educational" Award in 2004. She was honored by The Woman Substance, as The Woman of The Year in 2003. She received the 2002-2003 Teacher Of The Year Award for her "Outstanding Commitment And Dedication To The Children Of The Malverne School District." She became a member of Who's Who Among America Executives for her successful work in organizing a Nationally Accredited Child Care Center, servicing over 80 children. (1998)

GOD has given Pastor Harris a personal ministry to wounded and abused souls. It is Pastor Harris' desire to serve GOD with all her heart, mind and soul. Her goal is to be an example of womanhood that GOD is calling for in these last and evil days.

Printed in the United States
By Bookmasters